CATALOGING NONBOOK MATERIALS

Problems in Theory and Practice

By
CAROLYN O. FROST

Edited by
Arlene Taylor Dowell

1983
LIBRARIES UNLIMITED, INC.
Littleton, Colorado

LIBRARIES UNLIMITED, INC.
P.O. Box 263
Littleton, Colorado 80160-0263

Library of Congress Cataloging in Publication Data

Frost, Carolyn O., 1940-
    Cataloging nonbook materials.

    Bibliography: p. 377.
    Includes index.
    1. Cataloging of non-book materials. 2. Descriptive
cataloging--Rules. 3. Anglo-American cataloguing--
Problems, exercises, etc. 4. Weihs, Jean Riddle.
I. Dowell, Arlene Taylor, 1941-   . II. Title.
Z695.66.F76   1983   025.3'4   82-18711
ISBN 0-87287-329-3

Libraries Unlimited books are bound with Type II nonwoven material that meets
and exceeds National Association of State Textbook Administrators' Type II
nonwoven material specifications Class A through E.

To
MAMA OLIVIA
DAD
EMMA
and
FRANCES

TABLE OF
CONTENTS

FOREWORD

Seldom does an editor have a chance to learn as much about her "area of expertise" as I have learned in the process of editing this manuscript. Carolyn Frost has brought together here a historical and theoretical discussion of nonbook cataloging that is as interesting as it is informative. Cataloging rule books and manuals of practice for using those rule books typically give instruction for what is currently done or for what the rule makers are advocating should be done. Seldom do they explain earlier practice that did not work entirely satisfactorily and thus led to the evolution of the currently recommended rules. Yet such an explanation, in my experience, enables the cataloger to understand more fully the intentions of the current rules. With such an understanding, use and interpretation of the rules become much easier.

Frost has drawn her material from a number of scattered sources and has organized it to give a new perspective to the cataloging of nonbook materials. We learn how nonbook materials have progressed from being virtually ignored to becoming cataloging's stepchild to finally being integrated (although not yet quite *completely* integrated) into cataloging practice. We learn the difficulties encountered as catalogers have attempted to apply "book" concepts to nonbook materials.

Frost does not stop with a theoretical framework, however. The final chapters give us full examples that help us to understand how to choose chief sources of information, describe items, and choose access points. The author's detailed explanations provide a wealth of interpretive information, including definitions and other such data, that cannot be obtained from any one set of rules. These chapters will be of value to anyone who catalogs nonbook materials, whether such cataloging is done infrequently or on a more regular basis.

As our society moves into a time of increasing use of nonbook materials as sources of information, knowledge, and entertainment, it becomes of greater importance to provide bibliographic control of and access to these materials in libraries. This book will be of great assistance in this endeavor.

Arlene Taylor Dowell

PREFACE

This book is intended for students as well as for practicing professionals interested in the organization of nonbook materials. Its purpose is to provide a background of the development of cataloging standards for nonbook materials, to discuss some of the theoretical and practical issues which make nonbook cataloging both challenging and interesting, and to illustrate, through detailed examples, the application of two major codes for cataloging nonbook materials, the *Anglo-American Cataloguing Rules*, Second Edition (AACR 2), and Jean Weihs' *Nonbook Materials: The Organization of Integrated Collections*.

For many years, the development of codes for cataloging nonbook materials was marked by diversity and the absence of a nationally accepted standard. With the appearance of AACR 2 in late 1978, librarians now have access to comprehensive and carefully planned standards which are compatible with those developed for books and other print materials.

While there are a number of manuals and texts which show the application of AACR 2 to nonbook materials, it is hoped that this book will make its contribution by:

1) presenting questions and issues which have been addressed by various cataloging codes, and through these questions and issues, examining and comparing the basic theoretical principles of the codes

2) providing an extensive set of examples which illustrate and compare the application of the two major codes

3) assisting the cataloger in the use of the combination of chapters which must be consulted to provide a complete bibliographic description of an item. (Examples give a wide range of main entry problems, including corporate body main entry. Included also are complex descriptions requiring the use of several categories of chapters, for example, serial sound recordings, or serials and maps reproduced on microforms.)

4) placing the current codes for cataloging nonbook materials into a historical perspective.

Many librarians, when dealing with the cataloging of nonbook materials, have come to recognize that the standards used for nonbook materials were originally designed with books in mind. How appropriate is it to treat nonbook materials as if they were books? When are special rules needed? Questions of this sort have come to the fore with AACR 2's objective of providing a standard pattern of description for all materials. Already, controversy has arisen as the claim is made that certain kinds of materials—microforms, maps, and sound recordings, for example—should be excluded from some of the general rules for all materials. Thus emerge both practical and theoretical problems for which there are many possible answers. With this in mind, a principal theme of this book looks at the way in which bibliographic models developed originally for books have been extended to nonbook materials, and at how bibliographic concepts such as *author* and *edition* have been applied to materials other than books.

The types of media discussed in this book are: cartographic materials, sound recordings, motion pictures and videorecordings, graphic materials, three-dimensional artefacts and realia, microforms and kits. Serials, manuscripts, and music scores reproduced in audiovisual formats are also included. There are of course obvious difficulties with a term such as *nonbook* because of its negative orientation, and because of its implicit lack of specificity, encompassing as it does anything not a book. Other terms, such as *audiovisual media*, or simply *media*, were considered, but for lack of a better term, *nonbook* will be used here, and the focus of the discussion will be on defining the scope and nature of the category, rather than on the selection of the most appropriate terminology.

I would like to acknowledge the invaluable assistance and support of many friends and colleagues. Those who have read through and commented on the narrative portions of the manuscript include my husband, Robin Downes, professional colleagues Julie Todaro, Joan Repp, and friend Kenneth Northcott. Arlene Taylor Dowell read through the manuscript in its entirety. The advice and assistance of many practicing catalogers is also very much appreciated. Colleen Bednar and Jim Minton read through and provided suggestions for the chapters on microforms and cartographic materials, respectively. Ben Tucker and Paul Winkler of the Library of Congress have answered numerous questions on LC rule interpretations. Several classes of students have struggled through most of the cataloging examples and offered suggestions and corrections. In particular I would like to acknowledge the contributions of two dedicated and talented students who served as editorial assistants, Karen Novak and Karen Sinkule. Thanks are also due to typists Shirley Culliton, Elaine Schmitz, Karen Williams, Mary Spirito, and to Richard Suiter for his proofreading.

Material from *Anglo-American Cataloguing Rules*, second edition, is reprinted by permission of the publishers, copyright © 1978 by the American Library Association, Canadian Library Association, and the Library Association. I would also like to acknowledge the permission granted by Jean Weihs and the Canadian Library Association to cite from the rules in *Nonbook Materials*, second edition, and the permission granted by the Association for Educational Communications and Technology to cite excerpts from *Standards for Cataloging Nonprint Materials*, fourth edition.

1

THE DEVELOPMENT OF BIBLIOGRAPHIC STANDARDS FOR NONBOOK MATERIALS:
A Historical Survey

EARLY GUIDELINES

The term *library* has for centuries evoked in the minds of most people a collection of books, and the term *cataloging* has brought to mind the description and organization of these collections. Although codes for the cataloging of books were becoming well established as early as the mid-nineteenth century, the need for the codification of cataloging for nonbook materials did not become recognized until significant collections of such materials began to evolve a century later. Thus the cataloging of nonbook materials is an idea relatively new to librarianship, and the beginning of the development of nonbook cataloging codes can be dated within the lifetime of most librarians today. Two distinct kinds of responses to the need for cataloging guidelines for nonbook materials made their appearance in the 1950s, and with these responses, two divergent directions were established which were to shape developments in the decades which followed. These directions were determined by the needs of two different kinds of libraries: school and academic.

A response to the needs of school libraries was the first to appear, provided by Eunice Keen in her *Manual for Use in the Cataloging and Classification of Audiovisual Materials for a High School Library.* The manual was issued in a preliminary mimeographed edition in 1949 and was later revised and published in 1955. During this period it was a key source of guidance for the organization of nonbook collections. Its popularity was widespread in the United States and some foreign countries. It is primarily significant today as one of the first systematic attempts to deal with the cataloging of nonbook media, and, more importantly, as an indicator of the types of cataloging codes which were to gain a foothold in the decade to come.

The manual was the work of a school librarian whose collection included films, filmstrips, phonorecords, and slides, and who had sought guidance in the cataloging of these materials. Finding no guidelines which she considered appropriate to the needs of school librarians, Keen decided to develop her own manual, which she began as a student at the University of Chicago under the direction of Jesse Shera.

Keen felt that audiovisual materials "should have a common code just as there is for books," and thus her book brings together in one volume a set of guidelines for diverse materials which would be included in the collection of a typical high school library. The work drew upon ideas from various practices of the time, supplemented "with a few original additions and modifications" and illustrated with sample catalog cards. Not only was Keen's book well received, but it led to her appointment in 1955 as chair of the Special Committee on the Bibliographic Control of Audiovisual Materials within the American Library Association.[1]

While relatively successful, Keen's book was nevertheless the independent effort of an individual acting without the official endorsement of a national professional organization. The book thus stood little chance of being acknowledged as a national standard. In contrast to Keen's manual were the officially recognized standards developed by the two bodies serving as national arbiters of cataloging practice, the American Library Association and the Library of Congress. Rules for the choice of entry and the form of heading for books and a few types of nonbook materials were contained in the *A.L.A. Cataloging Rules for Author and Title Entries* (ALACR) prepared by the ALA Division of Cataloging and Classification and published in 1949.[2] The *Rules for Descriptive Cataloging in the Library of Congress* (RDC), also published in 1949, was issued by the Descriptive Cataloging Division of the Library of Congress and adopted by ALA for use in conjunction with its own rules for entry.[3] In many respects, these codes and the supplements that followed them were typical of the kinds of rules drawn up to prescribe official standards sanctioned by national professional organizations, and thus were an influential force, but not the only force, in the development of nonbook cataloging codes.

Rules, issued jointly by the Library of Congress and ALA, for entry and description of additional types of materials were included in three authoritative supplements to the RDC and ALACR. The supplement *Phonorecords* appeared in 1952,[4] *Motion Pictures and Filmstrips* in 1953,[5] and *Pictures, Designs, and Other Two-Dimensional Representations* in 1959.[6] The *Phonorecords* supplement drew upon a code published in 1942 by the Music Library Association, but took into account technological changes in the field of sound recordings as well as the growing presence of nonmusical recordings. The supplement contained rules for entry as well as for description, and was intended to be compatible with ALACR and RDC.

As with the rules for phonorecords, work on the rules for the cataloging of motion pictures and filmstrips had begun at least as far back as the 1940s. In 1951, these two types of media were treated in a preliminary set of rules drafted by the Library of Congress Film Cataloging Committee and based on guidelines developed by the U.S. Copyright Office in 1946 for motion pictures and filmstrips being registered for copyright. The guidelines from the Copyright Office had emerged in part from responses to a questionnaire sent out to libraries with film collections. In 1953, the Library of Congress issued the rules for motion pictures and filmstrips in a second preliminary edition.[7]

Pictures, Designs, and Other Two-Dimensional Representations was published in 1959, seven years after the Library of Congress established an interdepartmental Committee on Rules for Cataloging Prints and Photographs. Libraries, museums, and art publishers were asked for input, just as specialists in the fields of motion pictures and sound recordings had been invited to comment on the drafts of the rules for those media. After its approval by the Descriptive

Cataloging Committee of the American Library Association, the supplement was published as the official rules of the Library of Congress and the American Library Association.

Thus, in the 1950s, codes for nonbook materials emerged which represented the official position of the ALA and the Library of Congress. Characteristics of these codes were to leave their mark upon the development of their officially approved successor in the 1960s, the *Anglo-American Cataloging Rules* (AACR). However, certain shortcomings of the codes themselves and of their method of development made them unacceptable to large numbers of libraries contending with the problem of nonbook materials. These shortcomings eventually led to the emergence and popularity of several nonbook cataloging codes which lacked the official backing of the ALA and the Library of Congress.

The codes which were published from 1949 to 1959 were designed and developed by cataloging specialists working in the committee structure of ALA and at the Library of Congress. Thus, these codes represented the interests of only part of the constituency of libraries with media collections. Input was sought from varied authorities, but those consulted tended to be experts in specialized collections of materials most likely to be found in academic libraries. Little or no attention was paid to the kinds of problems dealt with in school or public libraries. The rules were designed to be used by cataloging specialists, and the formal language of the code, its detail, and the paucity of examples did not encourage use by the novice cataloger. The organization of the rules was also a hindrance to the nonspecialist. The reader was required to make use of five separate volumes: one giving rules for the entry and heading of print materials, maps, and microforms; a second for descriptive cataloging in general; and three supplementary volumes for description and entry of certain special types of materials.

These cataloging rules could also be criticized for placing nonbook materials in separate portions and chapters of the codes, and thus emphasizing their "special" character and setting them apart from the rules for books. It must be noted, however, that the rules themselves attempted to a large degree to apply principles of entry and description which had been developed for books; the separate supplements for nonbook materials were intended to achieve catalog entries which could be integrated into a catalog for a collection of books.

One indication of the response to the "official" codes was discovered in a survey conducted in the mid-1950s. The survey was created in 1955 by a Special Committee on the Bibliographic Control of Audiovisual Materials, appointed by ALA and chaired by Eunice Keen. The Special Committee's charge was to "survey needs and existing practices" and to "make recommendations for future action."[8] The committee prepared a questionnaire to elicit information on cataloging and classification procedures used for motion pictures, filmstrips, and phonorecords. The findings of the survey, issued in 1957, revealed that only 17% of the record libraries and 27% of the film libraries surveyed made use of catalog cards prepared by the Library of Congress based on the "official" rules for film materials and recordings. It was felt by many that Library of Congress cards were not suited to the needs of school and public libraries. The limited scope of cataloging coverage was also cited; too few of those titles found in typical school and public library collections were acquired and cataloged by the Library of Congress.

A need for "standardization of the essential elements in cataloging audio-visual materials" was listed first among the recommendations made by the committee.[9] The committee report also expressed the hope that the Library of Congress would play a greater role in achieving the desired standardization. In its recommendations, the committee called for "a standardized manual or procedure for the handling of audio-visual materials." It was urged that such a manual include: "a simplified but easily expandable system for small collections," as well as "directions for cataloging with adequate examples and sample cards."[10]

The findings of the survey foretold a need for further guidance in the cataloging of nonbook media and indicated the beginning of a growing demand for attention to the cataloging needs of school and public libraries, a demand which was eventually to be met not by the efforts of organizations such as ALA and the Library of Congress, but by individuals and organizations in the school library field who had sought guidance in the cataloging of nonbook media and had found the nationally sanctioned guidelines wanting.

ANGLO-AMERICAN CATALOGING RULES

The year 1967 marked a major event in the field of cataloging, with the appearance of the *Anglo-American Cataloging Rules* (AACR).[11] As seen earlier, cataloging rules for nonbook materials were gaining rapidly in importance among catalogers at this time, and the need for standardization of rules for these materials had long been recognized by the time of the code's publication in 1967. However, inadequate attention to the preparation of the rules for nonbook materials in the new code was to lead to further diversification of standards and thus leave the library community even farther away from the goal of standardization.

On the one hand, AACR represented a significant step forward by bringing together into one volume rules which dealt with both entry and description and which covered books as well as the different types of specialized materials. A substantial revision was recognizable in the rules for entry and heading, whose underlying principles were based on the "Statement of Principles" adopted by the International Conference on Cataloguing Principles held in 1961. It is all too apparent, however, that in the case of rules for nonbook materials, little more had been done than to incorporate the former Library of Congress supplements for special materials into a single code.

The obvious result of this failure to revise and update the coverage of nonbook materials was to render AACR outdated at the time of its publication. Many of the newer instructional media were given scant attention in AACR, and some were omitted altogether.

The types of nonbook media covered in AACR were those which would typically form part of the collection of a research library. The emphasis of the code was made clear in the introduction, which pronounced that the rules "have been drawn up primarily to respond to the needs of general research libraries" (p. 1) and "are as comprehensive as they could be made in their coverage of types of materials that are acquired in research libraries."

Although provision was made, at least in theory, for some of the newer forms of "instructional" media more likely to appear in public, school, and junior college libraries, the emphasis in any particular category or chapter was on scholarly materials. For example, the chapter on graphic media devoted much of its attention to problems in the cataloging of art works. Three-dimensional materials, such as games, models, and dioramas, were excluded. Media which had not yet come into prominence at the time of the preparation of AACR, notably, videorecordings and machine-readable data files, were also excluded.

The new code also continued the traditional assumption that each individual type of medium required its own distinct set of rules. This was seen by some critics of AACR as compromising the idea of an integrated catalog, in that it encouraged librarians to regard nonprint media as an offshoot from the mainstream of library collections and bibliographic control.

Intense criticism of AACR emerged almost immediately upon its publication. Critics focused principally upon the failure to provide adequate rules for many of the materials commonly found in school and public library collections. The intensity and breadth of the criticism made it obvious immediately that some action was needed by a responsible agency. The Library of Congress promptly accepted this charge, and proposed a revision of chapter 12 (motion pictures and filmstrips), as announced in the Library of Congress *Information Bulletin* in mid-1968.[12] The proposal for a revision of chapter 12 was submitted to the code revision committee of ALA in September 1968. The promptness of this action attests to the immediate disfavor with which part 3 was met. The revision proposed by the Library of Congress suggested that chapter 12 be expanded from motion pictures and filmstrips to include slide sets and other audiovisual materials.

The proposal was withdrawn in 1969, however, after it became evident that a more thorough revision would be required than had been contemplated by the Library of Congress. One of the principal architects of the code, C. Sumner Spaulding, himself later acknowledged that "the *Rules* do not provide instructions for description of many of the newer media which have been produced in great numbers by commercial firms serving the interests of our educational community," and that "there are certain inconsistencies between rules for one media and another which are presently being re-examined."[13]

STANDARDS FOR CATALOGING, CODING, AND SCHEDULING EDUCATIONAL MEDIA

While plans for revisions of chapter 12 of AACR were being made, the first of the major contenders to part 3 of the code made its appearance with the publication in 1968 of *Standards for Cataloging, Coding, and Scheduling Educational Media*.[14] This set of standards subsequently appeared in revised editions in 1971, 1972, and 1976, and enjoyed wide popularity among school media centers. It is significant that one of the major codes for the cataloging of nonbook media thus originated not from a library-related organization, but from a division of the National Education Association. In 1966 the Department of Audiovisual Instruction (DAVI) of the National Education Association organized a Task Force on Computerized Cataloging and Booking of Educational Media. Among the responsibilities of the Task Force was the development of standards for the cataloging and for the computer coding of educational media. The resulting standards were intended to be provisional, and when they were published in 1968 it was hoped that their distribution would lead to suggestions for revision and to the eventual development of a national standard. The DAVI code did not regard itself as an adjunct to AACR, but was developed independently of those principles and practices which had evolved in libraries and had been codified by library associations. The most significant indication of this departure from AACR was the prescription of title main entry for all materials, in straightforward disregard of the conventions of authorship and the concept of an integrated catalog of all forms of media.

NON-BOOK MATERIALS:
The Organization of Integrated Collections,
Preliminary Edition

A second major response to the inadequacies of part 3 of AACR was introduced in 1970 by a Canadian publication. *Non-book Materials: The Organization of Integrated Collections*, Preliminary Edition (NBM/PE), was written by Jean Riddle (Weihs), Shirley Lewis, and Janet Macdonald in consultation with the Technical Services Committee of the Canadian School Library Association.[15] This work was in part the culmination of the efforts of a small group of Toronto librarians with a common interest in creating a uniform system for cataloging nonbook materials. Their shared concerns led first to a series of discussions beginning in 1968 and later to the formation of the Technical Services Committee of the Canadian School Library Association. Earlier drafts of NBM/PE appeared under the title *The Organization of Non-book Materials in School Libraries*. As the drafts evolved under the aegis of the committee, the ideas developed in the work were tested in selected school libraries. Thus the impetus for a second major alternative to AACR was once again provided by concerned media specialists in the school library area.

Since the coverage of materials was one of the principal grounds for the immediate criticism of AACR, the codes which followed included a much broader range of materials. The preliminary edition of NBM, like the DAVI code, was one of the first major codes to include many of the newer instructional media lacking in AACR, such as charts, dioramas, flash cards, games, kits, videorecordings, microscope slides, models, realia, and machine-readable data files. The NBM/PE and DAVI codes were also alike in that the rules were presented in a language and style more suited to those who are not cataloging specialists. While similar in format, organization, and level of presentation, however, the two codes differed substantially in their view of a multimedia catalog. DAVI's standards defined a catalog for nonbook media which was relatively independent of standards for the cataloging of books. This point of view was not unique to the framers of the DAVI standards; indeed, many cataloging specialists at the time were of the opinion that nonbook materials were so unlike books in their bibliographic characteristics that there was little purpose in attempting to create a consistent pattern of description for all publication formats.

The authors of NBM/PE, however, started out with the objective of providing an integrated catalog for all media, and suggested that the rules used for the cataloging of books—rules which have stood the test of time and have been adequately treated in codes—be applied to other media "as far as is consistent with good sense." Thus, the authors agreed in principle with the idea of an integrated catalog suggested in AACR, but felt that AACR had not been consistent enough in applying its own precepts. NBM/PE's contribution was to apply rules consistently to all materials, with adaptations provided "only when the nature of the material demands them." This concept eventually was to shape the direction of the major forthcoming nonbook codes.

Careful attention to the opinions of catalogers from a broad spectrum of libraries helped to make NBM/PE and its successive editions widely popular. The efforts of the code makers to seek input from users continued after the publication of the code. Letters of comment were solicited in the introduction to the code and were considered in the preparation of the following edition. One of the code's objectives was to standardize terminology, and to this end a poll was constructed to seek the opinions of over 250 media specialists in North America and Great Britain as to the most authoritative terminology used in the description of nonbook materials.

Recognition of the acceptance of the code was evidenced by its endorsement in 1970 as an interim guide by the Cataloging and Classification Section of the Resources and Technical Services Division of ALA, as well as by the Council of the Canadian Library Association. The endorsement by ALA contained a proviso that "a permanent ALA/CLA committee be established to work on any necessary revision for the final edition and its supplements."[16]

The introduction to NBM/PE states that it was written specifically for school libraries, but that its principle can be applied to "any library system which houses books and other media together and has a single, unified list of its holdings." In giving a qualified approval of the code, ALA stipulated that the next edition be designed with a wider range of libraries in mind.

As these differing codes emerged, attention began to be focused on the need for standardization of cataloging rules for nonbook materials. Within ALA, one indication of concern was to be seen in the establishment of an ad hoc Committee for the Use of Audiovisual Materials in Libraries. The committee was charged with an investigation of "the feasibility of developing a national standard or standards which would guide libraries in the organization of nonbook materials." At an open meeting called by the committee in 1969, it was recommended that a nationally acceptable manual for the cataloging and classification of nonbook materials be identified, a recommendation which had been foreshadowed by the Keen committee a decade earlier.[17]

The committee's response to the task at hand began with the collection and analysis of nonbook cataloging manuals and guides in use at the time. These manuals included those developed by individual libraries, school systems, state departments of education, state associations, private publishers, and associations such as DAVI and the Canadian School Library Association. If nothing else, the variety of materials examined served to emphasize the diversification to be found among nonbook cataloging manuals. This scrutiny of diverse sources was expected to provide a basis for recommendation of a representative national standard for cataloging. Among other points, the committee recommended that any new standard should use AACR as the basis for selecting main entry for all media. Also advocated was a full and explicit treatment of each media format, with sample cards to illustrate the rules. An outline for a code or manual for the organization of media in libraries and media centers was prepared by the members of the committee, but it was only a preliminary step toward a national standard.[18] Responses to the needs cited by the committee in its recommendations were forthcoming in the next several years, but leadership in this area was not to come from ALA.

The need for a cataloging guide suited to the requirements of school libraries had already been apparent at the time of Keen's manual, but the problem became recognizably acute in the 1960s. The decade was marked by the development of many forms of instructional media, and by the acquisition of these media on a large scale by school libraries, often with the assistance of generous federal grants. For large research libraries whose collections remained predominantly book-centered, the problem was not nearly as severe, and at the Library of Congress those audiovisual materials acquired for the permanent collection were limited both in variety and quantity. The research libraries and the Library of Congress typically generated much of the demand for cataloging rules which were both standardized and fully elaborated. However, neither of these was compelled by its own internal needs to supply the leadership required to develop standards for nonbook materials.

Since no acceptable national standard had yet been established, school librarians began to produce their own manuals for the cataloging and processing of media. The later 1960s and early 1970s were marked by the proliferation of diverse cataloging codes for nonbook materials, and many, if not most, of these codes or manuals were drawn up in school library environments. Independent codes sprang up as a codification of the practice of a particular school, district, or state, and thus represented a considerable degree of duplication of what was being done by others. Typical of these was a code published in 1966, *Cataloging Manual for Non-Book Materials in Learning Centers and School Libraries*,[19] which reflected the local practice of school systems in Michigan. Another example was a manual first published in California in 1967, *Organization of Non-Book Materials in School Libraries*, by Warren B. Hicks and Alma M. Tillin.[20] These two manuals contained features typical of many of the locally developed codes. Both included instructions for the physical processing as well as the cataloging of media, and gave scanty attention to cataloging rules. Among the rules in a later edition of the Hicks-Tillin volume is the instruction that title main entry is to be used for all nonbook materials, with the rationalization that "the busy librarian who devotes the major portion of her time to working with individuals and groups cannot find the hours necessary for searching out various rules for main entry which differ for each type of material."[21] The position argued on behalf of the "busy librarian" is indicative of the perceived requirements of the users of the local and school codes. JoAnn Rogers, a specialist in the organization of nonbook materials in school media centers, has pointed out the lack of communication between school media specialists and shapers of cataloging policy at the national level, evidence of which has already been presented.[22] Cataloging specialists in academic or research libraries were well represented in national councils. Those responsible for the organization of nonbook materials in school media centers usually lacked a background in technical services, and had little opportunity to develop the skills needed to use the complex set of cataloging rules contained in the Anglo-American rules. The problem became even more acute in view of the fact that in school libraries, the cataloging of media was often assigned to non-professional staff members. Thus, a "simplified" approach to cataloging as well as information on the processing and storage of media were felt to be desirable.

Although many of the individual "local" codes differed greatly from AACR in the scope of their coverage of media and in their style and format, their most basic differences lay in a departure from historical precedent in cataloging principles. In contrast, the significance of the NBM/PE code lay in its attempt to build as far as possible on principles established for books and to apply these principles consistently. Such an approach had the practical advantage of helping to bridge the gap between book collections and nonbook materials, between school and academic libraries, and between local and national standards. This unifying theme was to assume increasing importance as the economics of shared cataloging were given extraordinary impetus by the emergence of bibliographic utilities.

NONBOOK MATERIALS:
The Organization of Integrated Collections,
First Edition

The next edition of *Nonbook Materials* (NBM 1)[23] provided further encouraging signs that a nonbook cataloging manual designed to meet the needs of school librarians could be consistent with standards used by the library community at large. As noted earlier, the preliminary edition of NBM had been accepted as an interim guide by the American Library Association, with the proviso that work on the next edition be undertaken in concert with a permanent committee comprised of representatives from the American Library Association and the Canadian Library Association. In the writing of the 1973 ("first edition") of *Nonbook Materials*, the three authors were assisted by a Joint Advisory Committee on Nonbook Materials, with members from the American Library Association, the Canadian Library Association, the Association for Educational Communications and Technology, and the Educational Media Association of Canada. Drafts of the code were reviewed by the committee, whose members also lent their assistance by acting as resource persons and liaisons for the organizations they represented. Whereas the preliminary edition had been written primarily with school librarians in mind, an effort was made in the first edition to serve the needs of a broad range of libraries and media centers. The principal author, Jean Weihs, concluded, "We became aware of the fact that you cannot write for schools without writing for all kinds of libraries, and the new work will try to show cataloging in a wide variety of styles."

There was also some indication that the Joint Advisory Committee intended the new edition of NBM to resolve differences between the preliminary edition of *Nonbook Materials* and the other leading code for school libraries, *Standards for Cataloging Nonprint Materials*, published by the Association for Educational Communications and Technology (AECT) in 1971 as a successor to the DAVI code. AECT, for its part, was interested in coming to some agreement with the *Nonbook Materials* code, as well as with standards being developed by the British.[24] Although an accord was not to come about until much later in the 1970s, the work of the Joint Advisory Committee was an early sign of interest in a national standard at a time when such a standard was sorely needed.

NBM 1 was first endorsed by the Canadian Library Association. At the 1973 Annual Conference of the American Library Association, a recommendation was made by the Cataloging of Children's Material Committee that the code be designated as an interim guideline. This proposal was submitted to the Executive Committee of the Resources and Technical Services Division's Cataloging and Classification Section. Such endorsement, however, was not granted by the Executive Committee, which preferred that efforts be concentrated on the completion of the upcoming revision of the *Anglo-American Cataloging Rules* rather than on the provision of an interim standard. NBM 1 was, however, accepted as a source document to be used in the revision of AACR.[25] Since the revision of AACR was still years from completion, many libraries adopted

NBM 1 as their own unofficial "interim guide," and a year after its publication the work had sold 16,000 copies.[26]

NON-BOOK MATERIALS CATALOGUING RULES

Another code which was destined to be used as a source document for the revision of AACR was the *Non-Book Materials Cataloguing Rules* (NBMCR).[27] Prepared and published under the auspices of the (British) Library Association and the (British) National Council for Educational Technology (NCET), this code represented a combination of both "library" and "media" interests.

Since the British had not had an opportunity to make a substantial contribution to the section on nonbook materials in AACR, the Library Association was eager to develop in the revision of AACR a set of guidelines consistent with standards of its own making. Soon after the publication of AACR, the Cataloguing Rules Committee of the Library Association had decided that a piecemeal revision of the rules would not be the best approach.[28] At the same time, the NCET was at work on the development of a centrally held machine-readable file of records giving data on media resources available on exchange from commercial producers and educational institutions. It was recognized that a file of this kind would require a standard form of description for the materials to be listed.

Thus the objectives of this educational technology organization were similar to those of the NEA's DAVI, at the time that the latter educational organization developed its standards for the coding and description of audiovisual materials. Fortunately, however, in this case the NCET was able to work in concert with a national library association. Communication between the NCET and the Library Association was assigned to a Media Cataloguing Rules Committee, which was set up by the Library Association and given financial support from the NCET. The committee established contacts with North American colleagues who also were involved in the development of nonbook cataloging standards, and was represented at annual conferences of ALA in 1971 and 1972, at which time an opportunity was afforded for an examination of preliminary drafts of the NBMCR code.

The NBMCR was regarded by its creators both as a draft standard for the revision of AACR and as "a self-contained code of practice in its own right." One objective of NBMCR was "to establish, as far as possible from first principles and the evidence of current needs and practices in Great Britain, a comprehensive set of rules having the widest practical utility in those institutions in which the documentation of nonbook materials is a substantial and significant activity."[29] In format and layout, the British code bore little resemblance to other codes exclusively devoted to nonbook materials. Examples were relatively few, and no model catalog records were provided. The language was, in general, more formal and thus similar to AACR in style.

Designed with the objective of achieving a single national bibliographic standard for nonbook media, the NBMCR was intended for collections of nonbook materials in all types of libraries. Specialized film and record libraries were considered within the province of the code, and an appreciable percentage of the membership of the Media Cataloguing Rules Committee was made up of representatives from film and archival libraries.

While NBMCR contained rules covering the range of instructional materials found in many of the post-AACR codes, a notable feature of this code was its coverage of film materials. Included were unedited film, stock shots, and trailers—material eventually to be made a part of AACR 2. This may be attributable to the sizeable representation of archival specialists among the code drafters.

REVISED CHAPTER 12 OF AACR

The third of the four primary sources which came to be used in the development of rules for nonbook materials in AACR 2 was the revised chapter 12 of AACR, North American text.[30] After the Library of Congress retracted its first proposed revision of chapter 12 in 1969, five years passed before another draft was submitted to the library community. Published in 1975, the revised chapter was officially adopted as part of the North American text of AACR.

The revision was prepared jointly by the American Library Association, the Canadian Library Association, and the Library of Congress, with the drafts written by Ben R. Tucker of the Library of Congress. As in the preparation of NBM 1, there was input from a number of sources, and the principal documents considered included three major nonbook cataloging codes: NBMCR, NBM 1, and the third edition of the AECT rules. In Tucker's opinion, "an examination of the codes made it immediately apparent that there was great similarity both in general philosophy and in many details in description." He found that the codes were generally in agreement in substance, but he also recognized major points of divergence on the issues of medium designators and main entry.[31]

One purpose of the revised chapter 12 was to improve the rules for the two types of material included in the original chapter: motion pictures and filmstrips. Eventually, the decision was made to write an entirely new chapter with a considerably broadened scope, one which would allow the addition of rules for materials previously included in other chapters in AACR as well as rules for media which had not been included at all.

The revised chapter 12 of AACR greatly expanded the scope of the original chapter. In some ways, this expansion was accomplished by incorporating media previously contained in other chapters in AACR. Slides and transparencies, for example, were transferred from AACR's chapter on pictures and two-dimensional objects. For the most part, however, the scope of coverage of revised chapter 12 was expanded through the introduction of new categories—three-dimensional media, kits, and videorecordings.

With its inclusion of "the principal audiovisual-media" as well as a wide range of "certain materials intended mainly as instructional aids," the revised chapter 12 was in fact more ambitious in its coverage than any other "chapter" in AACR. It may indeed be regarded as comprising a relatively self-contained set of rules dealing with nonbook materials.

As a cataloging standard officially sanctioned by the Library of Congress and ALA, the revised chapter 12 was in the best position of all of the newly developed codes for nonbook materials to be adopted by national cataloging agencies and disseminators of cataloging information. In 1975, the Library of Congress expanded the coverage of its MARC format for films to accommodate the audiovisual media included in the revised chapter 12. In the following year, the revised chapter 12 was implemented by the Library of Congress for nonprint materials within the scope of its cataloging program. Provision for entering audiovisual media into the data base of the Ohio College Library Center (now known as "Online Computer Library Center") was made possible in 1976 with the issuance of a films format derived from the MARC standard.

REVISED CHAPTER 14 OF AACR

A revised version of AACR's chapter on sound recordings (chapter 14) was published in 1976 in order to bring together in a single text a number of revisions announced in the Library of Congress *Cataloging Service Bulletin*.[32] This chapter, like the revised chapter 12, was seen as an interim standard, subject to further revisions in the second edition of the *Anglo-American Cataloguing Rules*. However, the changes in the revised chapter 14 were not as systematic or as substantial as in the revised chapter 12. The revised rules for sound recordings remained the same as the original in terms of scope of coverage and rules for main entry.

STANDARDS FOR CATALOGING NONPRINT MATERIALS, FOURTH EDITION

The fourth document to serve as a foundation for the revision of rules for nonbook materials in AACR 2 was the fourth edition of *Standards for Cataloging Nonprint Materials* (AECT 4), written by Alma Tillin and William J. Quinly, and published by the Association for Educational Communications and Technology in 1976.[33] The AECT manual had come a long way since its first edition published in 1968 under the title *Standards for Cataloging, Coding and Scheduling Educational Media*. The rules were first revised in 1971, at which time the title was changed to *Standards for Cataloging Nonprint Materials*. This change reflected the revised code's exclusive concern with cataloging standards. Subsequent revisions were issued in 1971 and 1972. The second revision incorporated rules for newer media, additional sample catalog cards, and ideas gained from discussion with other groups sharing similar concerns. Consistently through its first three revisions, the code continued to adhere to the point of view that principles developed for printed materials should not be applied to nonbook materials.

There were many features which served to differentiate rather sharply the fourth edition from its preceding editions. The volume of the code was increased almost fourfold as the number of examples was expanded, and an extensive narrative was provided to explain and justify the rules. Flexibility was another distinguishing feature of the code, with numerous options provided and many decisions left to the cataloger. One of the most significant changes was in the code's reversal of its position on main entry. Title main entry was still preferred for most audiovisual materials, but author or "creator" main entry was allowed when primary intellectual responsibility could be clearly established and when the name was significant in identifying the work.

THE INTERNATIONAL STANDARD
BIBLIOGRAPHIC DESCRIPTION*

In the 1970s, the thrust for the creation of bibliographic standards assumed an international dimension. A major impetus for these developments was the International Federation of Library Associations (IFLA), which through its program of Universal Bibliographical Control helped bring about the International Standard Bibliographic Description (ISBD), designed as a set of requirements to delimit elements of description, their order of presentation, and punctuation. An international bibliographic standard of this kind was seen as a way of making it possible for 1) bibliographic data for publications of one country to be readily understood by other countries, 2) records produced to be integrated more easily into files, and 3) conversion into machine-readable form to be accomplished with a minimum of editing.

For nonbook materials, the exchange of publications on an international level bears a special significance, since many forms of nonbook materials transcend barriers of language. At the Grenoble conference of IFLA in 1973, the concept emerged of a worldwide information system to facilitate exchange of bibliographic data for publications of all formats. As one expression of this goal, the General Council of IFLA recommended establishing a working group for an ISBD for nonbook materials [ISBD(NBM)]. To lay the foundation for this international standard, IFLA contracted with UNESCO for a survey which would examine "existing systems and current proposals for the cataloguing and description of non-book materials collected by libraries, with preliminary proposals for their international co-ordination."[34] The survey, which was concluded in 1974, included a thorough examination and evaluation of codes and standards in 24 countries, a systematic articulation of the problems encountered in the description of nonbook materials, and a comparison and analysis of both familiar and lesser-known codes. Christopher Ravilious, the author of the survey, believed that it would be possible to devise an ISBD applicable to a wide range of nonbook materials and basically compatible in all major respects with the ISBD which had been developed for books. With this in mind, Ravilious' analysis of codes proceeds systematically through the structure provided by the ISBD for monographs [ISBD (M)]. This consideration of the component parts of bibliographic description and the ways in which different nonbook codes have dealt with media calls to attention those characteristics of nonbook materials which are hardest to accommodate within a single bibliographic standard. Ravilious' excellent analysis was published in 1975, but regrettably in an edition with limited distribution, under the title *A Survey of Existing Systems and Current Proposals for the Cataloguing and Description of Non-Book Materials Collected by Libraries, with Preliminary Suggestions for Their International Co-ordination.* A final working draft for the ISBD (NBM) was distributed in 1976 at the IFLA General Council at Lausanne, and the work was published in 1977.[35]

Any standard for international description tacitly assumes that there is a similarity among items within one medium sufficient to allow a single mode of description. In the case of nonbook materials, however, the wide range of materials raises the question of whether there is a similarity among *several* media which could justify a single standard description. In addition, if compatibility

---

*See also the discussion of ISBD in chapter 2.

with the existing ISBD (M) and with cataloging codes for print media is to be effected, the various nonbook materials must also share characteristics in common with books. Ravilious considered the possibility of devising a "medium-neutral" ISBD that would be capable of accommodating all types of media within a single structure, but concluded that such an idea would not be feasible "since it would appear that individual categories of material impose their own conditions on the structures evolved for their control" and that "intrinsic characteristics of discrete categories of material" made it appropriate to develop different ISBDs for serials, nonbook materials, maps, and music.[36] The later development of an "umbrella" ISBD for all materials — the General International Standard Bibliographic Description [ISBD (G)] — was to retain in part the idea of a "medium-neutral" ISBD while at the same time allowing the development of separate ISBDs.

The need for a framework such as the ISBD (G) was recognized during the preparation of the second edition of the *Anglo-American Cataloguing Rules.* In 1975, the Joint Steering Committee for Revision of AACR was concerned that drafts then being developed for specialized ISBDs showed signs of divergence from the ISBD for monographs and from each other. The Joint Steering Committee's proposal for consideration of a general international standard bibliographic description suitable for all types of materials found in library collections was welcomed by IFLA. Representatives from the Joint Steering Committee and the IFLA Committee on Cataloguing met in Paris in October 1975. At this meeting, the Joint Steering Committee's proposal was discussed and agreement was reached on the basic details of what was to be known as the ISBD (G) — a framework which would serve to provide a basis for the description of all types of media, and would also be used as the basis for all specialized ISBDs.[37]

ANGLO-AMERICAN CATALOGUING RULES, SECOND EDITION (AACR 2)

An interval of only 11 years separated the publication of AACR in 1967 from AACR 2 in 1978, a period which, as Michael Gorman notes, "may seem indecently short in relation to the usually glacial rate of change of cataloguing practice."[38] During this time, as has been seen, significant steps had been undertaken to improve bibliographic standards for nonbook materials, and two of AACR's chapters on nonbook materials had been issued in revised versions. Still, these and other important changes made to the 1967 text had been brought about on a piecemeal basis, and it became apparent that a more systematic and comprehensive revision was needed.

In 1974, a meeting was held to discuss the preparation of a new edition of AACR which would reconcile the British and North American texts and incorporate revisions already adopted. It was at this time that the Joint Steering Committee for Revision of AACR was formed to coordinate the revision efforts. The Joint Steering Committee was comprised of representatives from ALA, the British Library, the Canadian Committee on Cataloguing, the Library Association, and the Library of Congress. As stated in the preface of AACR 2, "[the Joint Steering Committee's] function has been to appoint the editors, to assess for final approval the rules framed by the editors, and to present the final text for publication; and thus to be the ultimate authority for the content and presentation of this second edition." Two of the four guidelines which helped to shape the direction of the committee's work are directly relevant to nonbook materials:

> Continuance of conformity with the ISBD(M) as a basis for the bibliographic description of monographs, and commitment to the principle of standardization in the bibliographic description of all types of materials.
>
> Determination of the treatment of non-book materials primarily from a consideration of the published cataloging rules of the Canadian Library Association, the Library Association, and the Association for Educational Communications and Technology, and of the ALA revision of chapter 12 of the 1967 text.[39]

These two guidelines bear a special significance when the development of nonbook cataloging codes is considered. Promotion of the idea of a standard framework for the systematic description of all library materials pays formal tribute to the premise that there are basic principles for description which are applicable to all media. Secondly, recognition is made of the need for compatibility among the cataloging codes of different nations, and thus for standardization on an international basis. To this end, the Joint Steering Committee initiated the creation of the ISBD (G) to ensure uniformity of description within AACR (i.e., AACR 2) and between AACR and ISBDs for special materials. The use of AECT 4, the Canadian NBM 1, the British NBMCR, and AACR's revised chapter 12 as source materials reveals the respect paid to differing perspectives. In general, the code's attempts to solicit input from a wide variety of audiences is evidenced by its efforts to include representatives from many library constituencies in the revision process.

The changes from AACR to AACR 2 as Carol Kelm has observed, are "less revolutionary than evolutionary" and represent a continuum of development.[40] Certainly the changes that took place in the area of nonbook cataloging constitute some of the more substantive shifts away from AACR, but many of these changes were already present in the revisions made in the interval between the publication of the two editions.

NONBOOK MATERIALS:
The Organization of Integrated Collections,
Second Edition (NBM 2)

While the first edition of *Nonbook Materials* had arisen largely out of a need to address deficiencies in AACR's treatment of nonbook materials, it might be said that the second edition is designed less as an alternative to AACR and more as a complement. As the introduction suggests, it serves as "a companion volume" to AACR 2.[41] Since many of the principles present in the first edition had served as a basis for the development of AACR 2, the transition to a second edition involved relatively few changes.

NBM 2 regards its audience as "all types of libraries and media centres which wish to have an all-media catalogue"; thus it has selected from AACR 2 those rules which would be used most frequently with nonbook materials. The rules selected have been paraphrased for simpler reading and restructured into a format consisting of a brief set of rules followed by rules for the entry and description of individual media formats. As in NBM 1, there are sections on subject analysis and guidelines for the care, handling, and storage of different kinds of media.

Rules are illustrated by sample catalog records. Thus NBM 2, while conceptually consistent with AACR 2, also includes features which make it appropriate for use as a manual of practice to assist in the understanding of AACR 2.

While NBM 2 was expressly designed to be consistent with AACR 2, there are occasional points of difference between the two codes. These differences are not as far-reaching as those found in NBM 1, which had advocated a more integrated approach to rules for entry. Instead, NBM 2 offers a number of rules which are slight modifications of AACR 2 or provides rules for new types of media not included in AACR 2.

Users of AACR 2 will thus find NBM 2 helpful for its suggestions in areas not treated extensively or consistently in AACR 2. Of particular note is the section on technical drawings, which has been expanded from AACR 2 with a view toward satisfying the requirements of engineering libraries. This is also illustrative of the way in which NBM 2 has evolved from a code primarily directed toward school libraries to a code appropriate for academic and special libraries as well. The examples used to illustrate the rules are drawn from a variety of subject areas and audience levels.

CURRENT TRENDS TOWARD A NATIONAL STANDARD

Recent surveys show that standards for the cataloging of nonbook materials have yet to gain the degree of acceptance that standards for the cataloging of books have achieved. However, there are promising signs that AACR 2 may serve as a national standard, especially in view of the increased use of shared cataloging in computer-based bibliographic data bases.

"Project Media Base," sponsored by the National Commission on Libraries and Information Science and the Association for Educational Communications and Technology, explored the prospects for developing a national bibliographic system for audiovisual informational resources. As part of these efforts, the project conducted an inventory in late 1976 of automated systems providing bibliographic control of and access to audiovisual resources. The findings revealed that no single standard for cataloging audiovisual materials was used by all systems. Only 38% of the respondents reported using AACR, while 18% used AECT, and 44% used standards other than AACR or AECT.[42]

JoAnn Rogers' 1977 survey of the use of nonbook cataloging standards in school libraries revealed that "school librarians in relatively few responding states used codes emanating from national professional organizations." Rogers found that AECT was more widely used than any other code, and that approximately a fifth of the respondents reported using AACR.[43]

In a 1980 survey of practices concerning audiovisual materials in academic libraries, Nancy Olson found that only 35% of the responding libraries used AACR.[44] However, a survey conducted after the implementation of AACR 2 suggests the increasing acceptance of a national standard. Sheila Intner's survey of the use of cataloging rules for nonprint materials in public libraries revealed that while 22% of the respondents were still using AACR, 46% were using AACR 2. About 32% were using codes other than AACR or AACR 2, but many libraries reported plans to implement AACR 2 in the near future for nonprint materials.[45]

NOTES

1. Eunice Keen, "Cataloging and Classification of Audiovisual Materials," in *Bibliographic Control of Nonprint Media*, ed. Pearce S. Grove (Chicago: American Library Association, 1972), pp. 333, 334, 336, 337.

2. *A.L.A. Cataloging Rules for Author and Title Entries* (Chicago: American Library Association, 1949).

3. Library of Congress, Descriptive Cataloging Division, *Rules for Descriptive Cataloging in the Library of Congress* (Washington, DC: The Library, 1949).

4. Library of Congress, Descriptive Cataloging Division, *Rules for Descriptive Cataloging in the Library of Congress: Phonorecords* (Washington, DC: The Library, 1952).

5. Library of Congress, Descriptive Cataloging Division, *Rules for Descriptive Cataloging in the Library of Congress: Motion Pictures and Filmstrips* (Washington, DC: The Library, 1953).

6. Library of Congress, Descriptive Cataloging Division, *Rules for Descriptive Cataloging in the Library of Congress: Pictures, Designs, and Other Two-Dimensional Representations* (Washington, DC: The Library, 1959).

7. Katharine Clugston, "The Library of Congress and Nonprint Media," in *Bibliographic Control of Nonprint Media*, ed. Pearce S. Grove (Chicago: American Library Association, 1972), p. 157.

8. Frances Hamman, "Bibliographic Control of Audio-Visual Materials: Report of a Special Committee," *Library Resources and Technical Services* 1 (Fall 1957): 180-89.

9. Ibid., p. 188.

10. Ibid., p. 189.

11. *Anglo-American Cataloging Rules, North American Text* (Chicago: American Library Association, 1967). (AACR was issued in two editions: the North American text and the British text.)

12. Library of Congress, Processing Department, *Cataloging Service Bulletin*, no. 83 (September 1968), p. 2.

13. C. Sumner Spaulding, "The Anglo-American Cataloging Rules," in *Bibliographic Control of Nonprint Media*, ed. Pearce S. Grove (Chicago: American Library Association, 1972), p. 197.

14. National Education Association, Department of Audiovisual Instruction, *Standards for Cataloging, Coding, and Scheduling Educational Media* (Washington, DC: National Education Association, 1968).

15. Jean Riddle (Weihs), Shirley Lewis, and Janet Macdonald, *Non-book Materials: The Organization of Integrated Collections.* Preliminary edition (Ottawa: Canadian Library Association, 1970).

16. Jean Riddle Weihs, "The Standardization of Cataloging Rules for Nonbook Materials: A Progress Report — April 1972," *Library Resources and Technical Services* 16 (Summer 1972): 306-307; Jean Riddle Weihs, Shirley Lewis, and Janet Macdonald, *Nonbook Materials: The Organization of Integrated Collections.* First edition (Ottawa: Canadian Library Association, 1973), p. vii.

17. Richard L. Darling, "Nonprint-Media Organization in the American Library Association," in *Bibliographic Control of Nonprint Media*, ed. Pearce S. Grove (Chicago: American Library Association, 1972), p. 327.

18. Ibid., pp. 328-30.

19. Judith Loveys Westhuis and Julia M. De Young, *Cataloging Manual for Non-Book Materials in Learning Centers and School Libraries* (Ann Arbor: Michigan Association of School Librarians, 1966).

20. Warren Hicks and Alma M. Tillin, *Organization of Non-Book Materials in School Libraries* (Sacramento: California State Department of Education, 1967).

21. Warren Hicks and Alma M. Tillin, *Developing Multi-media Libraries* (New York: R. R. Bowker, 1970).

22. JoAnn V. Rogers, "Nonprint Cataloging: A Call for Standardization," *American Libraries* 10 (January 1979): 46.

23. Weihs, Lewis, & Macdonald, *Nonbook Materials.* First edition.

24. Evelyn Geller, "A Media Troika and MARC: A Progress Report on A/V Cataloging Standards and Services," *School Library Journal* 97 (January 1972): 25, 26.

25. Lois Mai Chan, "Year's Work in Cataloging and Classification 1973," *Library Resources and Technical Services* 18 (Spring 1974): 109-110.

26. Ronald Hagler, "The Development of Cataloging Rules for Nonbook Materials," *Library Resources and Technical Services* 19 (Summer 1975): 275.

27. *Non-Book Materials Cataloguing Rules.* NCET Working Paper No. 11 (London: National Council for Educational Technology with the Library Association, 1973).

28. Library Association. Cataloguing Rules Committee, "Minutes" 79 (November 27, 1969).

29. *Non-Book Materials Cataloguing Rules*, pp. 2-4.

. 30. *Anglo-American Cataloging Rules, North American Text; Chapter 12 Revised: Audiovisual Media and Special Instructional Materials* (Chicago: American Library Association, 1975).

31. Ben R. Tucker, "A New Version of Chapter 12 of the *Anglo-American Cataloging Rules*," *Library Resources and Technical Services* 19 (Summer 1975): 261-62.

32. *Anglo-American Cataloging Rules, North American Text: Chapter 14 Revised: Sound Recordings* (Chicago: American Library Association, 1976).

33. Alma Tillin and William J. Quinly, *Standards for Cataloging Nonprint Materials: An Interpretation and Practical Application*. Fourth edition (Washington, DC: Association for Educational Communications and Technology, 1976).

34. Christopher Ravilious, *A Survey of Existing Systems and Current Proposals for the Cataloguing and Description of Non-Book Materials Collected by Libraries, with Preliminary Suggestions for Their International Co-ordination* (Paris: UNESCO, 1975), p. 4.

35. *ISBD (NBM): International Standard Bibliographic Description for Non-Book Materials* (London: IFLA International Office for UBC, 1977).

36. Christopher P. Ravilious, "Descriptive Account of a Survey of Existing Systems and Current Proposals for the Cataloguing and Description of Non-Book Materials Collected by Libraries." (Mimeographed document prepared for distribution at the 1975 IFLA Conference, Washington, DC).

37. *Anglo-American Cataloguing Rules*, Second edition, p. viii; "ISBD (G): AACR to Incorporate a New International Standard," *Catalogue & Index*, no. 39 (Winter 1975): 6.

38. Michael Gorman, "*The Anglo-American Cataloguing Rules*, Second Edition," *Library Resources and Technical Services* 22 (Summer 1978): 209.

39. *Anglo-American Cataloguing Rules*. Second edition (Chicago: American Library Association, 1978).

40. Carol R. Kelm, "The Historical Development of the Second Edition of the *Anglo-American Cataloging Rules*," *Library Resources and Technical Services* 22 (Winter 1978): 22.

41. Jean Weihs, Shirley Lewis, and Janet Macdonald, *Nonbook Materials: The Organization of Integrated Collections*. Second edition (Ottawa: Canadian Library Association, 1979).

42. *Problems in Bibliographic Access to Non-Print Materials* (Washington, DC: National Commission on Libraries and Information Science, 1979), p. 25.

43. Rogers, "Nonprint Cataloging," p. 46.

44. Nancy B. Olson, *Cataloging of Audiovisual Materials: A Manual Based on AACR 2* (Mankato: Minnesota Scholarly Press, 1981), p. 2.

45. Sheila S. Intner, "Access to Media: An Investigation of Public Librarians' Bibliographic Practices and Attitudes towards Nonprint Materials" (Ph.D. diss., Columbia University, 1982).

2

BIBLIOGRAPHIC CONCEPTS AND THEIR APPLICATION TO NONBOOK MATERIALS

The terms *title page, author, edition,* and *publisher* are key concepts for the bibliographic description of books. While these terms have a clear meaning in the context of print materials, some modifications are necessary if the terms are applied to materials in general.

This chapter considers the problems that arise in defining these concepts in a way that is appropriate to the description of nonbook materials. Also considered is the one element of bibliographic description—the medium designator—for which there is no precedent in the description of books.

The major portion of this chapter shows that, with some modifications, the same bibliographic concepts can be applied to both books and nonbook materials. It is argued here that the generalization of these bibliographic concepts makes it possible for catalog codes to employ a general set of principles applicable to the description of all materials. The concluding portion of this chapter examines this possibility, and looks at the extent to which cataloging rules for nonbook materials have actually been governed by an underlying set of principles.

THE CONCEPT OF TITLE PAGE

The title page has long been a standard part of books and is an obvious choice as the most appropriate source for the derivation of bibliographic data. The information it contains is readily findable in certain standard locations and provides most of the data needed to describe bibliographic characteristics. For most nonbook media, however, it is seldom the case that bibliographic data are consistently grouped together in one convenient location. As Christopher Ravilious has observed:

> By long established convention the title page has become a magnet at which bibliographical minutiae collect like iron filings: no such convention is found among producers of audio-visual materials, who may select any from a fairly wide range of possible locations as the repository for bibliographical statements.[1]

Compounding the problem is the fact that the term *nonbook materials* embraces a disparate assortment of media and formats. We must thus come to terms with the existence of a wide variety of title page substitutes, each with its own set of characteristics and problems.

In the case of motion pictures and filmstrips, the title page tradition is evident to some degree. Bibliographic information is usually found on the title frames, which, like a title page, can appear at or toward the beginning of the film's sequence, or, as is more common in some modern films, towards the end, like a colophon. Since film is a visual medium, this information can be presented in written form and is contained within the item itself — once again, resembling the convention for books. On the other hand, the bibliographic data are not easily transcribed, since the item must be screened in order to be viewed in eye-readable form. Thus the information found on a container or accompanying textual material may appear more convenient as a bibliographic source.

With certain "non-linear" visual media such as sheet maps, pictures, photographs, and drawings, a different problem emerges. Here the bibliographic sources can be read easily enough without special equipment, but these media often present all of their information — whether graphic message or bibliographic data — on one sheet. Thus the information appears in a simultaneous mode, as compared with the sequential mode in the case of film. In theory, a standard location for bibliographic data could be established for both the simultaneous and the sequential modes of display. Thus, it could be argued: since filmmakers present bibliographic information in one place in a film's sequence, why could not mapmakers or publishers of pictures decide for their part upon a preferred location (such as the upper left-hand corner) for the provision of such information? In the absence of this type of preferred order, there is no single location which can be identified as a definitive source of information. Compounding the problem here is the fact that some of these graphic media — most notably maps — may contain more than one title.

Another set of circumstances is present in the case of sound recordings. Since these are aural communications, it would be theoretically possible for such media to identify themselves in their own mode of communication — with an announcer giving the details of title, creator, etc., at the beginning or end of the recording. This is seldom the case with commercial recordings, and so such information is presented in textual form on a label or container. With sound discs, the label can be attached directly to the item, but with tapes we must rely instead upon a label attached to the container. In some instances, these external labels will serve a marketing or promotional function as well as a descriptive one.

Many types of nonbook materials are likely to appear as a collection of single items issued in sets — maps and pictures, for example. This occurs as well, of course, with books, but on a less frequent basis. In such instances, logic dictates that the bibliographic description be given for the item as a collective unit. Very often, the data appropriate to the item as a unit are found not on the individual components but on their container. The container may also be appropriate as a source of information in the case of three-dimensional objects, where frequently there is no label of any kind on the item itself.

As we have now seen, bibliographic information for nonbook materials can appear on the item itself, as a label affixed to the item, or on the container of the item, among other possibilities. The particular challenge here for cataloging theorists and code makers has been to decide which of these sources comes closest to serving as a title-page substitute. In selecting criteria for such a substitute, it is helpful to keep in mind those properties of the title page which make it so attractive as a chief source of information.

A principal criterion is that of location. The title page of a book is, of course, uniformly located at or near the beginning of the complete sequence of pages. In extending this criterion to nonbook media, code makers have sought to identify equivalent sites with the same quality of consistent location. As we have seen in the case of "sequential" media, the preferred location is at the beginning of a sequence. Such a location has been defined even more specifically by some codes. In AECT 4, for example, the frames closest to the subject content of the item are preferred in the case of microforms, filmstrips, and motion pictures.

Criteria of location usually prescribe that information found on the item itself be preferred to information from an outside source. For Christopher Ravilious, this preference amounts to "a criterion of persistence": the label found on a disc or cassette will typically remain with the item longer than the album cover or accompanying material. This preference for "persistence" can be applied to the case of the container which houses the contents of a kit or game; a container of this kind is likely to be retained and may thus be suitable as a primary source of bibliographic information.

A second major criterion accords precedence to the source providing the most complete or comprehensive information. Often this will be in conflict with the criterion of location; a notable example is the case of microform reproductions. A preference for the first title frame will frequently result in the selection of a frame whose primary purpose is to provide brief "housekeeping" information and which presents its information in abbreviated form, leaving the representation of the original title page to supply fuller bibliographic detail. In other instances, as is the case with sound recording discs, space limitations on the label will not allow bibliographic details to be presented in the degree of fullness possible in sources such as the record jacket or accompanying booklet.

In prescribing sources of information for nonbook materials, cataloging codes have kept the model of the title page clearly in mind, and as we have seen, those attributes of the title page deemed most attractive for this purpose are its location and its comprehensiveness. Of the two, location is clearly the dominant factor in modern cataloging convention.

A survey of the major codes used in the cataloging of nonbook materials reveals that in the overwhelming majority of cases, information derived from the item itself is preferred over labels or other sources. If the item itself does not provide the necessary data, as is the case with most sound recordings and with some motion pictures, the next choice is a substitute which has some permanent association with the item. The International Standard Bibliographic Description for Non-Book Materials — ISBD (NBM) — lists this criterion as its first principle in establishing an order of preference among sources of information, and application of this principle is evident as well throughout AACR 2.

The consistent pattern in AACR 2 of preference for information on the item itself represents a change from the first edition of the code, which allowed the container of a sound recording and the label of a motion picture cassette to serve as principal sources of information even if data were to be found on the disc or in the title frames. In AACR 2, information on the item itself is preferred over information on a label, but if information is lacking on the item, a container permanently associated with it may be used as a chief source. Thus, the labels found on sound discs, tape cassettes, video and motion picture cassettes, and the mounts on stereo reels and slides are preferred over such "fugitive" containers as disc sleeves and boxes. The latter may be used as a chief source, however, when the container alone describes the item as a collective unit. Only in the case of three-dimensional materials, such as games, models, and realia, are containers and accompanying materials regularly regarded as chief sources, and even here, information on the item itself is preferred, if available.

A lesser degree of uniformity is present when the item itself cannot be used as a source of information. In these cases it is necessary to establish an order of preference for alternative sources. For graphic items, cartographic materials, and microforms, AACR 2 prefers the container to accompanying materials; on the other hand, accompanying materials are preferred for motion pictures and videorecordings, three-dimensional materials, and sound recordings.

The assignment of a hierarchy of sources determines not only which source is to be preferred to another, but also how the information for the source is to be recorded. For example, in all of the codes discussed here, titles supplied by the cataloger are indicated in brackets. And AACR 2 prescribes that titles derived from locations other than the chief source must be accounted for in a note, while titles from the chief source can stand without further explanation.

For the most part, NBM 2 closely follows AACR 2's rules for chief source, and frequently adds to these rules its own interpretations and elaborations. One such example can be found in the rules for choosing among conflicting titles given in the same source. In its general rules, NBM 2 states that "if there is more than one title on the material, precedence is given to the one positioned closest to the physical content" (p. 17). Applications of this principle are found in the specific provisions dealing with multiple titles on maps, filmstrips, or technical drawings. Since AACR 2 provides no rule to the contrary, application of the NBM 2 principles would be compatible with AACR 2.

In its general chapter, AACR 2 provides a rule (1.0H) which deals with items having more than one chief source of information. For multipart items, these guidelines accord precedence to the "first part," a term which would appear to apply to items issued in successive parts. NBM 2 offers its own interpretation of the term *first part*, and suggests that for nonbook materials this might be "the part which gives meaning to the various parts," as, for example, a manual or a container which serves as a unifying element.

There are a number of other instances in which NBM 2 has made modest changes from AACR 2. For mounted or framed graphic items, such as transparencies, slides, and pictures, NBM 2 gives precedence to information on the item itself rather than the mount. This interpretation seems to be clearly consistent with, and perhaps even a logical extension of, rules contained in AACR 2. In slight variation from AACR 2, NBM 2 allows the frame of an art original to be regarded as a chief source of information. For globes, which can be regarded as another case of an item which often contains its own integral label, NBM 2 expands on AACR 2 and gives as its own order of precedence the container, cradle, and stand.

In AECT 4, primary emphasis is again given to the item itself as a source of information; and an exception is made for most three-dimensional objects in which the container serves as the principal source of information. The rules differ from AACR 2 and NBM 2 in that an order of preference for alternative sources is at best implied rather than specifically stated—also, in that sources are prescribed only for titles, and not for other elements of bibliographic description. Like NBM 2, AECT 4 provides assistance in choosing among conflicting titles from a single source. The code is guided in general by the principle of physical proximity of the source to the content it describes. Thus, for example, the title closest to the subject content is chosen for microforms, motion pictures, videorecordings, and filmstrips. Titles within the border are preferred for maps. For charts, however, the code prefers the most conspicuous title, or the title in the lower margin.

MAIN ENTRY AND THE CONCEPT OF AUTHOR

In determining access points, and particularly in the selection of a principal access point or *main entry*, some agreement as to the meaning of the term *author* is indispensable. While the term *author* is familiar to most people, the same term as applied to nonbook materials is much less clearly understood. Extending the concept of author to nonbook materials has been one of the principal stumbling blocks in the cataloging of nonbook materials.

This discussion looks at the way in which the term *author* has been understood in major cataloging codes, and how rules for main entry have been influenced, if not determined, by these definitions. Rules for the determination of choice of access points have traditionally given priority to entry under author. A common agreement as to the meaning of the term *author* is essential in formulating a set of rules for main entry which are general enough to apply to all media.

CONCEPTS AND DEFINITIONS OF AUTHORSHIP

The standard concept of an author as the person chiefly responsible for the creation of the intellectual or artistic content of a work is one that has appeared, with slight variations in wording, in established cataloging standards such as the ALA rules, AACR, and AACR 2. For certain categories of materials, it was relatively simple to decide which aspect of the work constituted its principal intellectual or artistic content, and then to identify the person chiefly responsible for this creative function. Photographers, composers, artists, and cartographers were thus recognized as the "authors" of the works they had created.

A more liberal interpretation, found in NBM 1, broadened the term *author* to include a wider variety of creative functions. While this is not explicitly stated, a look at some of the examples provided in the chapters of NBM 1 reveals that the code was prepared to consider as *author* not only those responsible for textual or graphic content as found in microforms, machine-readable data files, and filmstrips, but also those who have contributed to the content of media such as videorecordings and games.

A further broadening of the concept of authorship is evidenced in AACR 2. Here the term *author* includes creators of a wide spectrum of media, and the rules for choice of access points are applicable to all materials regardless of medium. Perhaps the most liberal definition of authorship was found in AECT 4, which was willing to extend the concept of authorship not only to a few selected media with clear author analogues, such as art prints, but to media in general. AECT 4 thus applies the term *creator* not only to an author, artist, photographer, or composer, but also to a "performer, producer, director, scriptwriter, consultant, or any other person who has made a significant contribution to the creation of the work" (p. 6). It is further argued that although many of these creators have "traditionally been excluded from consideration insofar as main entry is concerned, their importance in creating the work should be judged in relation to the nature and purpose of the particular medium. They may perform functions that are different from the accepted ones of author, composer, or artist, but they are, nevertheless, essential in the creation of a work in an audiovisual medium. They should, therefore, be considered for creator main entry" (p. 6).

Antony Croghan, who is included in the acknowledgments for AECT 4, proposed a similar argument, and suggested the term "Creator" for "author" in his *Code of Rules for ... Integrated Cataloguing of Non-Book Media*:

> Who is the Creator of any one medium? This definition must be peculiar to each medium and will arise out of its own nature.... It becomes necessary to look at the functions needed to create a medium and who or what performs these functions. These are the creators of that medium. (p. 17)[2]

With this principle in mind, AECT 4 maintains that creators can be responsible for the primary intellectual content of games, flashcards, machine-readable files, and even realia, where "in a few instances, persons such as scientists, archeologists, artists, inventors, etc., ... are responsible for discovering or collecting natural or historical realia...." (pp. 178, 179).

For certain specific types of materials, some codes have defined authorship by indicating types of persons who can be associated with a creative activity. In the case of maps and atlases, the ALA rules considered the following persons or corporate bodies as those who might be regarded as responsible for the content of a work: cartographers, editors, publishers, government bureaus, societies or institutions, engravers, if known to be mapmakers, and copyright claimants (p. 26, rule 10).[3]

Likewise, AACR provides an extension and modification of the concept of intellectual responsibility for cartographic materials. Among persons and corporate bodies considered as principally responsible for the geographic content of a work are "1) the individual whose survey provided the basis for the cartography, 2) the cartographer, 3) the engraver, if known to be also a cartographer, [and] 4) the corporate body, including a map publisher, that prepared the map" (rule 211B).

For two-dimensional graphic materials, the ALA rules and AACR again indicate specific types of works or categories of creative responsibility. The ALA rules list drawings, engravings, paintings, sculptures, and photographs as types of works for which an artist can be responsible. In AACR, the concept of "artist or other person or body responsible for the content of the work, whether artistic or documentary" (rule 260A) is extended beyond artists to include copyright owners, printers, publishers, studios, or other individuals or corporate bodies recognized as being solely responsible for the content of a work.

The concept of *author* is most accessible when the author is identified as being the person responsible for the single creative activity which forms the basis for the intellectual or artistic content of the work. In cases of authorship involving a single creative function, writers, composers, cartographers, artists, or photographers are considered as authors of the works they create.

More complex are those types of works involving more than one creative activity. Sound recordings and motion pictures are prime examples. Coming to terms with the concept of author in sound recordings is particularly complex. Involved here is the theoretical issue of the effect of transferring an intellectual or artistic idea from one medium to another. Phonograph recordings may document simultaneously the intellectual or artistic idea found in a music score and also the performance of it.

In the *Phonorecords* supplement to the ALA rules, and in AACR, the *author* or person primarily responsible for the intellectual or artistic content of a recording was the composer or author of the work in its printed form. In the case of classical music, this works out reasonably well, but questions can be raised in popular music, where it is generally the performer who is known and less often the composer. What is the primary artistic content of such a work and who is responsible for this content? From a more practical point of view, we can ask, What person will the patron associate with a popular recording?

Some acknowledgment of the role of the performer was given by NBM 1. Its general rules caution that "authorship is not normally attributed to ... performers," and the specific rules for sound recordings prescribe title main entry for the works of more than one composer issued with a collective title. But an alternative rule allows entry under the performer or performing group "primarily responsible for the artistic interpretation of the works performed."

AECT 4 goes much farther than its contemporaries in recognizing the dimension of the performer in the sound recording of a work. This approach is typical of the code's attention to the characteristics of a particular medium and the nature of its artistic or intellectual content. Following the principle that it is the interpretation rather than the composing of the work which constitutes the primary artistic content of popular music, AECT 4 allows entry under performer or performing group. In advancing its argument, AECT 4 uses as a model a statement contained in AACR's revised chapter 12 cautioning that the transfer from one medium to another may involve additional intellectual or artistic responsibility. This principle of the transfer from a visual to an aural medium is applied in AECT 4 to sound recordings.

In AACR 2's rules for the entry of sound recordings, implicit recognition is made of two types of authorship contributions: the creation of the written form of a work — music, text, etc. — and the rendering of that work in a recorded performance. Primacy is accorded to the first type of contribution. A sound recording of one work is entered "under the heading appropriate to that work," that is, under the heading that the work would receive if it appeared in written form. Similar treatment is given to a recording of two or more works all by the same author (or composer) or collaborating authors. Main entry under the performer of a sound recording is prescribed only if: 1) the recording contains works written or composed by different persons, and 2) no more than three persons or groups are represented as principal performer(s). If the sound recording contains works by different persons or groups, and there are either no principal performers or more than three principal performers, the main entry is under title. Thus, as with the basic rules of this code, main entry is given to the author responsible for the composition of the work. In the case of collections by different authors, however, the rules for sound recordings allow for a "substitute" author to be considered as primarily responsible for the collection. Recognition is accordingly made of the unity which a single performer or performing group can impart to the collection.

To define an *author* for motion pictures is at best complex, and many codes would say it is impossible. The ALA rules and AACR presume that in the case of motion pictures the condition of collaborative authorship completely precludes the identification of a principal author. NBM 1 acknowledges that "the difficulty of ascribing authorship in motion picture production mitigates against author entry" but does allow an exception "in adherence to the 'auteur' theory."

AECT 4's rules for motion pictures illustrate the thesis, given in the general rules, that different types of creative functions are present in the making of audiovisual media and that those responsible for these functions should be recognized as authors. While recognizing that, for most motion pictures, it is difficult to "establish a creativity priority among the many functions performed in the production of a film," the code goes on to acknowledge that current technologies make it possible for a motion picture to be the result of a creative endeavor of one person; thus, the problem of collaborative authorship will not likely arise in the case of some 8mm films, which can readily be produced by one or two persons.

The same principle is acknowledged, albeit less explicitly, in the revised chapter 12 of AACR. As in the original version of AACR, the code recognizes that diffuse authorship is likely to occur in the creation of motion pictures, and takes note of the fact that "several persons or bodies contribute to the intellectual or artistic content of the typical motion picture by performing different functions" (p. 4). However, a basic, if somewhat subtle, departure from AACR is introduced in the revised chapter. It is now recognized that diffuse authorship, while no doubt the likely case in films, is not necessarily a condition to be assumed. One of the sample catalog records reflects the principle that authorship can occur in a film if a single person is responsible for its content.

In AACR 2, there is again the implicit acknowledgment that, in certain instances, motion pictures can have authors — assuming, of course, that one recognizes what constitutes authorship for a given medium. This is indeed a crucial recognition. The rules for entry in AACR 2 are applicable to all materials regardless of medium, and for the most part, materials can be assigned to the appropriate authorship category without any special consideration as long as it is understood what is meant by the term *author*. Many of the categories are indeed relatively independent of the definition of authorship. For example, if a work is of unknown authorship, or if it is a collection with a collective title, a definition of authorship is not essential since the main entry will automatically be under title.

Those categories whose application presupposes a definition of authorship are those which allow one to three persons to be identified as chiefly responsible for the intellectual or artistic content of the work. Such categories subsequently prescribe that the main entry for the work be given under the heading for the *author* thus determined. Of these categories, two — works of single authorship, and works of shared authorship — involve situations in which there is a single authorship activity or function. Thus, the *author* of a work can be considered as the person(s) responsible for the single creative activity which generates the intellectual or artistic content of the work. If a single creative activity of this kind can be identified in the case of a motion picture, then the motion picture can be considered as having an *author*.

Thus far, NBM 1 and a lesser-known code by Antony Croghan have been the only codes to suggest that principal intellectual responsibility for films can reside with the director. Croghan defines the creator of a film as follows:

> The creation of the film is shared between the Director, the Cameraman and the Scriptwriter. The Director is taken as having the Principal responsibility; the others are Secondary Creators; should however one person perform more than one of these functions he

should be regarded as the Principal Creator. If two people are listed as sharing the function equally both are considered the Creator.[4]

Thus Croghan's has been the only code to venture, in AECT 4's parlance, to "establish a creativity priority among the many functions performed in the production of a film."

In the absence of a creativity priority, authorship with mixed responsibility (in which different persons perform different kinds of intellectual or artistic activity) can be characterized as "diffuse." The question of how to regard "diffuse authorship" has been a major point of difference among the codes. Probably more than any other single factor, it has stood in the way of agreement on a uniform set of rules for main entry.

THE DEVELOPMENT OF UNIFORM PRINCIPLES FOR MAIN ENTRY

Since the Anglo-American tradition of main entry rests squarely upon the principle of main entry under author, a common agreement on the meaning of authorship is essential if a single set of rules for entry is to be applied to all materials.

This discussion will consider three approaches to general principles for main entry rules. The first point of view, of which the ALA rules and AACR are examples, recognizes essential similarities between nonbook materials and books, and thus sees as valid the general idea of a single set of principles. However, this point of view maintains that some nonbook media are sufficiently different to warrant some exceptions to the general rules. As will be seen, it is usually the medium of motion pictures for which exceptions are considered necessary.

A second approach, exemplified by AACR 2, maintains that a single set of rules can be applied to *all* materials. A third point of view as represented by NBMCR and AECT 3, holds that nonbook materials and books are essentially different, and thus proposes that the main entry rules developed for books are not at all appropriate for nonbook materials.

The ALA rules for entry contained a single set of principles for the choice of main entry. These rules were applied to the cartographic and graphic materials covered by the code. Categorized as "works of special type," these materials were part of a range embracing music, mediumistic writings, ships' logs, and heraldic visitations. The single set of principles for these diverse materials prescribed main entry under the personal or corporate author chiefly responsible for the intellectual content of the work. Thus, maps and atlases could be entered under cartographer, drawings and paintings under artist, and heraldic visitations under the name of the herald or king of arms making the visitation (with added entries for other heralds assisting in or continuing the visitation). Subsequent supplements covering additional graphic materials and phonorecords contained rules for entry which were compatible with the general rules in the main volume. Underlying the supplement for motion pictures and filmstrips, however, was the major premise that "the extent and nature of collaborative authorship of films make author entry inappropriate," and that "films are most commonly identified by title." Thus mandatory entry under title was prescribed. In this respect, as well as in the rules for the descriptive cataloging of films, the supplement saw itself as taking "account of certain attributes of the materials and of the conditions under which they are generally cataloged and used."

In AACR, two basic principles governed the rules for entry:

1) Entry should be under author or principal author when one can be determined.

2) Entry should be under title in the case of ... works whose authorship is diffuse, indeterminate, or unknown (pp. 9-10).

These principles varied in their application to specific categories of media. Microforms, for example, were part of the group called "Photographic and Other Reproductions" and appeared in the section for books and book-like materials. They were thus governed entirely by the main entry rules for those materials. Since the intellectual content of microforms is no different from that of the book materials they reproduce, no special rules for entry were given.

In the case of other media groups, special rules modified or interpreted the basic rules in light of characteristics peculiar to the particular medium, but the basic rule of entry under principal author was applied.

The special rules for entry of motion pictures and filmstrips also had their basis in the general principles outlined above, but here, as in the ALA rules, the principles took into account certain attributes of the medium. The condition of collaborative authorship which the code assumed to be characteristic of films fell under the category of "diffuse" authorship and thus required title main entry under the second of the general principles of the code.

This rule for mandatory title main entry for motion pictures was not so much a departure from the general principles themselves as it was a departure from the application of these principles. The rules for choice of entry, according to the code's introduction (p. 5), were "treated as a problem of determination of authorship responsibility." For the most part, the pattern of authorship responsibility which governs the selection of main entry choice was determined according to an analysis of each work in question. In the case of films, however, an authorship pattern (i.e., "diffuse authorship") was *assumed* and entry was determined according to the medium or format of the work.

This view of the nature of film was understandable for its time but failed to take into account filmmaking accomplished through individual effort, a type of filmmaking which was to become more prevalent after the time of the writing of the code. The rules were presented in a way which precluded any exceptions or modifications for individual cases. Neither was there a recognition of a distinction between the conditions of authorship present in the making of motion pictures and conditions found in the making of filmstrips, the other medium treated in the chapter on motion pictures.

There is certainly nothing about the nature of filmstrips which would require their exemption from general rules for main entry. This recognition was made by NBM 1, which made the point that an integrated catalog is best served if a uniform set of cataloging principles is applied to all media. In specifically advocating a uniform set of entry principles, NBM 1 placed itself in the forefront among cataloging codes. However, in the case of motion pictures, NBM 1 continued to prescribe main entry under title, on the premise that "the difficulty of ascribing authorship in motion picture production mitigates against author entry" (p. 60).

Further progress toward a uniform set of principles was reached in revised chapter 12 of AACR, which presented a single set of rules for all materials. The rules for entry in revised chapter 12 were "general statements intended to supplement rather than replace the basic principles and rules found in Chapter One" of AACR. However, while recognition was again made of the "extent and nature of collaborative authorship of films," significantly, no overall exception to the general rules was made for films. The revised chapter referred to diffuse authorship as characteristic of the *typical* motion picture while acknowledging the fact that such a condition *usually* requires entry under title. This change, coupled with the presentation of a single set of entry rules for all of the many media included in the chapter, thus allowed motion pictures to be treated no differently from any other medium in the determination of main entry.

The move toward a uniform set of rules for all materials was most pronounced in the AECT 4 rules. The third edition of AECT had maintained that "the extent and nature of the collaborative authorship of most audiovisual materials ... makes author entry inappropriate." This statement had been taken almost word for word from AACR, but whereas in the latter code the statement was made in reference to films, in AECT 3 it had been applied to audiovisual media in general. In AECT 4, the appropriateness of title main entry for most audiovisual materials is still emphasized, but author main entry is possible when primary intellectual or artistic responsibility can be clearly established.

Like revised chapter 12 of AACR, AECT 4 recognizes that the condition of collaborative authorship for many types of nonbook materials often results in "difficulty in establishing that the overall responsibility for the whole of the work can be attributed to one person" (p. 5). At the same time, however, the code does not represent that a separate set of rules for main entry should be adopted for nonbook materials.

While liberal in its approach to concepts of authorship, AECT 4 displays a decidedly cautious attitude toward the assignment of author main entry. Whereas other codes use primary intellectual or artistic responsibility as the sole criterion for determining authorship, an additional element is added by AECT 4: identification capability. In every instance in which creator main entry is permitted in AECT 4, the stipulation is made, with underlining and italics, that such an entry is to occur only "*if the name is significant in identifying the work.*" This emphasis on identification represents a departure from the considerations made by AACR and most other "author-oriented" codes in assigning main entry. While it is true that the rules for books have been designed with the idea that authors are the primary mode of identification, one must distinguish between identification as a general underlying principle, and as a criterion to be applied in each specific instance. Certainly, few catalogers would decide against an author main entry for a book because the author was not considered sufficiently well known. The claim is made in AECT 4 that most audiovisual materials are identified by title and are cited as such in trade and reference sources. Even if one assumes that identification of an author plays a more crucial role in the case of nonbook media, the application of the identification criterion can be uneven or subjective when the cataloger tries to determine how well known a particular name will be to a given public.

The precedent set by revised chapter 12 of AACR and by AECT 4 in setting up a uniform set of entry rules is continued in AACR 2. A single set of rules is to be applied, for the most part, to the various media included. Only in three instances — art, music scores, and sound recordings — are special rules given for a particular medium or kind of material. When these special provisions appear, they do not constitute a self-contained body of rules to be set apart from the general principles for choice of access points, but instead are logical extensions of the overall framework which treats the problem of works with mixed responsibility. All other aspects of entry of art works, music scores, and sound recordings are governed by the rules set out for library materials as a whole.

In sharp contrast to the idea of a uniform set of entry rules is the view that nonbook materials as a whole require their own special rules. NBMCR was one such example.

In framing the rules for the NBMCR, the authors decided to work from first principles, and to thus avoid "taking the existing cataloguing codes designed primarily for books and printed materials and bending the needs of non-book documentalists to them." One result of this decision was the code's departure from the tradition established by previous cataloging codes in regard to the question of whether a single set of rules can be applied to all media.

The code made use of the familiar argument that the intellectual or artistic content of nonbook materials is the result of diverse creative activities, and that a priority for the relative importance of these creative activities or functions cannot be established. As a result of this situation, it was felt that the General Principles for the entry of books and book-like materials as presented in AACR were not applicable to nonbook materials. However, this argument was not used to provide a rationale for mandatory title main entry, as in AACR's chapter 12, or in AECT 3. Nor was it employed, as in the revised chapter 12 of AACR or in AECT 4, to predict or encourage a large percentage of title main entries. Rather, the argument was used to play down the importance of determining primary intellectual or artistic responsibility. Although the code contained rules for choice of access points, the importance of this aspect of the bibliographic record was deliberately minimized. Such innovations notwithstanding, the code still managed to address quite traditional issues in that it provided for a "statement of primary intellectual responsibility in respect of a person or body, if any, [who has] overall responsibility for the work," as well as a "primary name heading" for the "person or body (if any) having primary intellectual responsibility for the content of the item...." The primary name heading, if appropriate, then formed an integral part of the "standard catalogue entry" and was included in all added entries, or "secondary headings."

In anticipation of the question as to the difference between "standard catalogue entry" and "main entry," Peter Lewis, who chaired the committee which drafted the rules, explains:

> The familiar "main entry" carries in AACR such an implied emphasis on the determination of authorship as the first consideration of the cataloguer that its use was felt to be positively misleading in a part of the cataloguing field where authorship, in the large majority of cases, is either undeterminable or relatively unimportant for the retrieval of descriptive data.[5]

The viewpoint expressed in NBMCR is that the establishment of a body of descriptive information should receive primary emphasis, and should form the starting point of the process of creating a bibliographic record. Access points to this descriptive information are then derived from the names and titles which have been provided in the body of description. In the sequence of rule notation, the rules for access points (i.e., for "primary name heading" and for "secondary headings") appear twelfth and thirteenth in a list of 16 rules.

AACR 2, while upholding the importance of the main entry concept, was to adopt a similar sequence, with rules for description preceding those for choice of access points. This order was seen to "follow the sequence of cataloguers' operations in most present-day libraries and bibliographic agencies" (rule 0.3).

THE MEDIUM DESIGNATOR

The *medium designator* serves to indicate the class of material to which an item belongs. Although the term can encompass a designator used to indicate a specific class of material (as in the *specific material designation* in AACR 2), the *medium designator* is usually understood to denote a term descriptive of a broad class of material (as in the *general material deseignation* in AACR 2).

Understood in the latter sense, the *medium designator* is the one element of bibliographic description originally devised specifically for nonbook materials. Lacking a bibliographic precedent in the model afforded for the description of books, code framers and theorists in nonbook cataloging found no common ground for agreement in decisions to be made on the location of the medium designator, on the degree of specificity to be used in its terminology, or even on its very justification for existence. Controversy over the medium designator has centered primarily around its function, and this major point of difference has in turn served to determine the direction of opinions on the other factors of location and specificity. Now that the general material designation has been made an optional feature of AACR 2, and can thus be included or omitted at the cataloging agency's discretion, the controversy over the justification for the medium designator takes on new significance.

FUNCTION

The medium designator has been generally recognized as serving three functions:

1) as a statement of the nature or basic format of the item cataloged and thus as a means of informing the user as to the type of material at hand;

2) as a description of the physical characteristics of the medium and as a means of alerting the user to equipment needed to make use of the item;

3) as a device to distinguish different physical formats which share the same title.

The first two functions have received the greatest attention in the medium designator controversy, since they are concerned with the role played by medium designators in determining the user's interest in a given item. The "early warning" camp views the medium designator as a device which reduces the need for reading unwanted information if the user is not interested in the format or has no access to the necessary equipment. Once having spotted the "early warning device," the user moves on to another entry in the catalog.

The opposing view would not accord such urgency to the need for designating the medium of an item. While the character of the item and the indication of the equipment needed for its use are both regarded as important elements of information, it is felt that such information should not serve as a basis for outright selection or rejection. The term "warning device" is an unfortunate one, and its negative connotations have served to obscure some of the issues involved. Peter Lewis saw the argument for an early warning device as an indication of bias or "discrimination" against nonbook media, a signal with the message " 'Look out! This is not a book!' as if the book were a minimum standard below which nonprint media fall." Lewis admonished that "there should, in equity, be no discrimination in respect of medium in a multimedia library, any more than of colour or creed in a multiracial society."[6]

Such an attitude, it would seem, entertains an exaggerated notion of the power of the medium designator in influencing the choices made by users. One can ask, Is the user with no interest in films, microforms, or sound recordings likely to be any more receptive to these formats after having read through a bibliographic record in its entirety? At the same time, one can usually recognize a valid reason underlying a preference for one medium over the other. It is, after all, necessary to take into account the unique qualities of individual media and the capabilities that each type of format brings to bear in communicating its message. A musicologist who wishes to analyze the structural components of a musical composition will probably prefer a printed score to a recording of that work. A student of automotive engineering may prefer a visual representation of a mechanical process to a verbal description. One cannot regard preference as a "bias" against the type of format not selected, or assume that in another context, the recording or the text would not be selected to suit a different purpose. Even in those cases in which a medium is rejected solely because equipment is needed for its use, it is fair to presume that if the item were of sufficient interest its value to the user would outweigh the inconvenience of securing the necessary equipment.

With these considerations in mind, it is possible to regard the medium designator not as an "early warning device" lying in wait to ward off would-be users of nonbook media, but as a primary element of bibliographic description.

LOCATION

Where should the medium designator be located? In the title area or in the physical description area? Viewpoints on the location and terminology of the medium designator can be directly related to one's opinion of its primary function. If an "early warning device" is needed, such a device must be brief, generic in its expression, and should appear as soon as possible in the entry. Similar arguments could be advanced if the medium designator is to serve to distinguish different physical manifestations of works with the same title. If, on the other hand, one accords primacy to indicating the type of equipment needed for an item's use, the medium designator should be specific in nature and should provide a precise identification of the format. Since the purpose of such data is more to inform than to "warn," the information can be placed later in the order of bibliographic sequence, and take its place with other elements of the bibliographic record which describe physical characteristics.

The latter approach has the advantage of keeping distinct the different areas of bibliographic description; all statements pertaining to the physical description are in one place. On the other hand, an "early warning" device divides physical description information into two locations. The first location gives the type of medium (for example, "sound recording") and an alert that equipment may be needed; the second gives a more detailed description of the item, and some indication, at least by implication, as to the specific type of equipment needed (for example, "33⅓rpm, stereo"). It should be recognized, of course, that although their content may be similar, these two types of information nevertheless serve two distinctly different purposes.

Additional considerations arise in the organization of title data. The requirement that the medium designator be placed early in the entry poses a dilemma of sorts: the medium designator must appear after the title proper; otherwise, a lengthy subtitle could relegate the medium designator to a second or third line of the entry. At the same time, however, this location places the medium designator in uneasy proximity to bibliographic information which has been transcribed directly from the item or other chief source of information, and also results in the interruption of a single logical unit of information, the title. Locating the medium designator after the title proper was not prescribed until ISBD (G) and AACR 2. In pre-ISBD (G) codes (NBM 1, revised chapter 12 of AACR, and AECT 4), the "early warning" type of medium designator was placed after all title information. Some of these codes used as their model the ISBD (M), in which, of course, there was no provision for a medium designator. Therefore, such codes had to come up with their own ideas as to where the medium designator should be placed. In revised chapter 12 of AACR, the rules which prescribe the order of elements of bibliographic description are "to a certain extent derived from the analogous provisions of the revised chapter 6," which in turn was based on the ISBD (M). Such analogies have their limits, it is recognized, and accordingly the chapter supplies what it calls "innovative provisions dealing with the special characteristics of nonprint media" (pp. vii, viii). Presumably, one such "innovation" is the placement of the medium designator at the end of all title information.

In AACR 2, the medium designator is placed after the title proper, but before parallel titles and other title information. AECT 4's extension of the ISBD format to nonbook materials also differs from AACR 2, not only in the placement of the medium designator but also in the punctuation used.

The problem of where to place the medium designator might be circumvented by using some kind of early alerting device other than a formal element of bibliographic description. Various alternatives have been suggested. These include drawing attention to the specific medium designators in the physical description area through the use of underlining or capitalization. A more popular device is the provision of symbols or "media codes" which are part of the call number and indicate the particular medium type. "Color coding," the use of color in cards to indicate a specific medium, is used by some libraries but is now largely discouraged. Quite apart from other disadvantages attendant upon the use of these latter two devices is the problem that such methods are radical departures from recognized bibliographic standards. Recognized standards of this kind rely upon verbal expression to indicate informational content and upon sequence of informational elements to indicate order of importance.

As mentioned earlier, part of the controversy arising from the function and location of medium designators arises from the fact that no precise precedent for them can be found in the model for the bibliographic description of monographs. There is no problem, of course, if one argues that a medium designator should serve as a precise description of the physical item, rather than as an alerting device, for then it is clear that this purpose can be served more than adequately through the physical description or collation area. The NBMCR code, for example, included a requirement for a "physical form designator" in the physical description area. This designator was intended to state the physical characteristics of the item in order to facilitate its identification and use, and "to assist in distinguishing the different physical forms of a single work." These functions were assigned in other codes to general medium designators. As a standard part of the description, the physical form designator provided a specific statement of the physical character of the item described. This became more important, of course, in view of the absence of a general medium designation in NBMCR.

If, however, it is deemed important that the medium designator indicate the nature of the medium, then we are, as noted previously, faced with an information element not present in the model designed for the description of books. In large part this situation arises because books have for so long constituted the dominant medium in the holdings of libraries, and a medium designation was in fact implicit, since the nature of the medium was taken for granted. Such circumstances would of course prevail whenever a library's collection consisted for the most part of a single medium, regardless of the kind of medium involved. Thus, in AACR 2, the decision as to when a general material designation is appropriate for a given kind of material can be based in part upon whether most users are likely to make an implicit assumption of a specific medium of communication. While in most circumstances the printed book would be least likely to require a medium designation, it would be short-sighted to preclude the possibility of a medium designation for any one medium, and the framers of AACR 2 have made possible, though not mandatory, the provision of medium designations for all media.

This provision corrects at least one major inconsistency of AACR, which assigned general medium designators to some nonbook materials but made no provision for maps, microforms, and many types of pictorial materials.

TERMINOLOGY

Two separate lists of designations are given in AACR 2, one for British and one for North American use. The British list contains fewer terms, and uses generic categories to group together some of the more specific formats enumerated separately in the North American list. For example:

British	North American
cartographic material	map
	globe
graphic	art original
	chart
	filmstrip
	flashcard
	picture
	slide
	technical drawing
	transparency
object	diorama
	game
	microscope slide
	model
	realia

The terms in the North American list vary in specificity. Some media, such as sound recordings and realia, receive generic terms while terms for other media — such as flash cards, filmstrips, and microscope slides — are more specific and are in fact identical with specific material designations. A statement in the Library of Congress *Cataloging Service Bulletin* (No. 2, Fall 1978) views this as "a kind of accidental favoritism," resulting in unequal treatment of the media. This point is made as part of an argument that "ideally, [general material designations] should be discarded and the physical description relied upon for information about an item's nature."[7]

Two arguments can be made in support of the British preference for generic terms: 1) a clear distinction is made between general and specific material designations; 2) general terms, embracing a wider range of categories, are less confining than a list of specific terms which may not fit the item in hand. This point has been made by some map librarians who prefer the British term *cartographic material* to *map* or *globe*. It has also been suggested that the term *object* is more suitable for certain kinds of three-dimensional materials. For a three-dimensional object such as a stuffed animal or a doll, the designations of diorama, game, microscope slide, or model are obviously out of the question. The only term that can be used, therefore, is *realia*, which says, in effect, "none of the above."

Another point of possible controversy has been more easily resolved. The different codes are relatively uniform in their selection of terms to be used as general material designations. NBM 1, revised chapter 12 of AACR, and AECT 4 are in almost complete agreement with the North American list of AACR 2 with the exception of terms used for sound recordings. NBM 1 preferred the term *audiorecord*, and AECT 4, *audiorecording*. AACR had used specific terms: *phonodisc, phonotape, phonocylinder*, etc. Of lesser importance is the difference between NBM 1's term *videorecord* and the term *videorecording* used in AECT 4 and AACR 2.

The British NBMCR did not accept the concept of general material designations, but 12 of the terms used as "physical form designators," which appeared in the physical description area, correspond exactly to terms in the North American list of general material designations. These are:

art original	picture
diorama	slide
filmstrip	technical drawing
game	transparency
globe	microscope slide
model	

Most of the other terms are specific, and would be used as specific material designations in AACR 2.

THE CONCEPT OF EDITION

The cataloger is concerned with edition at two points. The first occurs when transcribing the edition statement, a relatively straightforward matter of recording statements relating to edition. The second, discussed in this chapter in greater detail, looks at what is meant by the term *edition* as applied to nonbook materials, and thus considers what constitutes a new edition, a decision which will often determine when a new bibliographic record is to be made.

Like most other elements of bibliographic description, *edition* was originally defined in terms of book-like materials. Such definitions of edition have undergone changes with time. Early definitions of edition had in mind copies of a publication printed from one setting of type. In AACR 2, the term *edition* as applied to book-like materials includes "all those copies of an item produced from substantially the same type image, whether by direct contact or by photographic methods" (p. 565). For nonbook materials, AACR 2 defines edition as "all the copies of an item produced from one master copy and issued by a particular agency or group of such agencies" (p. 565), a definition almost exactly the same as the one given in the *International Standard Bibliographic Description for Non-Book Materials* [ISBD (NBM)].[8] AECT 4 defines *edition* as "the whole number of copies of a work produced from the same master and issued at one time or at intervals." In all of these instances, the definition of edition is expressed in terms of production from a master copy, with an implicit recognition that the intellectual or artistic content of the original work as well as its physical representation have not been altered. What degree of alteration in the original work then constitutes a different edition? An examination of the terms *issue* and *reissue* can be helpful in this regard, because they indicate sub-categories that can be part of a given edition, and thus help in making a distinction between different editions and differences *within* an edition.

In AACR 2, an *issue* is "in the case of nonbook materials, those copies of an edition of an item forming a distinct group that is distinguished from other copies by well-defined variations." Presumably then, the variations could be intellectual, bibliographical, or physical in character, and whatever the case, a subjective judgment as to their significance will be involved. Such subjective judgment would not be required in the ISBD (NBM) definition of the term *reissue*: "a named or otherwise identified batch of copies of an item produced from the same master copy as an earlier issue in the same physical form, and emanating from the same publishing or production agency."[9] The requirement that the copies be produced from the same master ensures a sameness of intellectual content, and the requirement that the copies be "in the same physical form" leaves no doubt as to their relationship to the physical format of the original.

Intellectually, then, a distinction could be made among 1) successive issuances of items which reproduce exactly the intellectual content and physical form of the original, 2) successive issuances in which variations occur from the original, but are not significant enough in nature to warrant consideration as a new edition, and 3) issuances which differ enough to be considered a new edition.[10] For nonbook materials, these distinctions give rise to two important questions:

1) What differences in intellectual content, bibliographic characteristics, and physical format differentiate one edition from another?

2) What guidelines are to be used to determine when an item has been changed sufficiently for it to be considered a new edition?

In considering changes in intellectual content, there are clear analogies to be drawn from the conventions established for book-like materials. Some guidelines for determining substantive changes in intellectual content are suggested in the rules for choice of main entry. To be sure, these rules address a different bibliographic problem, that of determining authorship responsibility and thus choice of main access point, but some of the questions raised can be of some value in determining the most "obvious" cases of edition changes having to do with intellectual content.

Revised chapter 12 of AACR cautions that "the transfer to an audiovisual medium often involves additional intellectual and artistic responsibility which will make it necessary to consider that the original author's work has been significantly adapted." AECT 4, in considering the transfer from a visual to an aural medium in its entry rules for sound recordings, presents this idea in almost identical language. The question under consideration still has to do largely with making distinctions between different types and degrees of alteration of the intellectual content of a work. In its general rule for works that are modifications of other works, AACR 2 prescribes: "Enter a work that is a modification of another under the heading appropriate to the new work if the modification has substantially changed the nature and content of the original or if the medium of expression has been changed" (rule 21.9). A "reproduction" or reissuance of a work which results in a change of medium, then, would in all certainty result in the creation of a new bibliographic record.

Modifications which involve a new translator or illustrator, etc., will generally not require a change of main access point. However, resulting alterations in the statement of responsibility area would bring about a change in the bibliographic description which is significant enough to warrant consideration of the work as a new edition. Modifications which change the intellectual content of a work through revision, enlargement, or condensation would be similarly regarded.

In considering differences of physical format, it is important to remember that with nonbook media it is not uncommon for an item to be reproduced with the same intellectual content as the original but with a markedly different physical format. In many, if not most, cases, the difference in physical format will have a bearing upon the kind of equipment needed to use the item—as for example, in the change from a disc to a cassette format, from videotape to videodisc, or film reel to film loop.

The most familiar example of a change in physical format is that of microform reproductions of printed materials. In AACR, microform reproductions of a printed work were treated in the same manner as different issues of a given edition (rule 152 C of AACR and of revised chapter 6 of AACR). Information concerning the microform reproduction was added, in a note, to the bibliographic description for the original work. The note was given in the form known as a "dash entry," with two dashes representing the repetition of the author heading and the title.

Many have voiced the opinion that microform reproductions should be similarly treated in AACR 2. The controversy over the treatment of microforms in AACR 2 has brought into prominence two opposing viewpoints on the concept of edition as applied to microform reproductions.

The "edition" approach is reflected in AACR 2. Description of the item in hand is viewed as a "cardinal principle" in the code, and, in an attempt to treat all materials as consistently as possible, no exception is made for microforms in this regard. Since the reproduction is the item in hand and is markedly different from the original in its physical appearance and publication data, a separate bibliographic record must be made for the reproduction. In this sense, the reproduction is being considered as a different edition.

It is possible in theory to account for physical variations of a work in the physical description area, or, alternatively, in the note area. While AACR 2 does not address this question directly, a parallel of sorts might be found in the rules dealing with items which appear in more than one format. In the chapters on sound recordings and motion pictures and videorecordings, provision is made for the inclusion of a note indicating that other formats of the item are available. In the case of videorecordings, the code provides three alternatives for describing other formats of a work that is available in the library in two or more formats (rule 7.5B1). The first option allows the cataloger to use the more generic term *videorecording* in the physical description area and to give the specific alternative forms in the note area. The second option is to provide a multilevel description, in which the descriptive information is divided into two or more levels, with the first level recording only information relating to the multipart item as a whole, and a subsequent level relating to individual parts. The third option is to provide a separate description for each item. For sound recordings, motion pictures, and graphic materials, only the first option is explicitly stated, but the second and third alternatives would certainly seem to lend themselves to these kind of media as well.

AECT 4 states clearly that "each version of a work in the collection in the same or a different medium is cataloged separately. Other versions that are known to exist may be given in a note." An alternative is provided: "to minimize repetitive cataloging, the various versions in the collection may be listed on one card." This resembles AACR 2's first option for videorecordings, in that alternative formats are described in the notes area. The two options differ, however, in that in AECT 4 the physical description area describes one particular format of the item (e.g., 1 reel … 35mm), while in AACR 2 the generic term *videorecording* appears in the physical description, and the specific physical formats are described in a note.

TRANSCRIPTION OF THE EDITION STATEMENT

Rules for the transcription of an edition statement are contained in the major codes; however, not all codes agree that an edition statement is appropriate for all media.

In AACR 2, the general rules for transcription of the edition statement are to be applied to all media. While the British NBMCR code makes the observation that edition statements are not normally given for motion pictures and sound recordings, the rules do allow the edition to be recorded in those cases in which a "clear statement" actually does appear. Such statements are to be given in accordance with the general rules. AECT 4 is of the opinion that dioramas, models, and realia are not issued in different editions, and therefore the rules require no edition statement for these media.

While the decision as to what constitutes an edition is subject to different interpretations, little ambiguity exists as to how and when an edition statement should be recorded. AACR 2's general rules provide for the transcription of a statement relating to an edition of an item that contains differences from other editions or, as it is stated in many chapters, that is a named reissue of the item. Such statements are transcribed as found on the item. If no edition statement appears on the item, the cataloger need not hazard an opinion as to whether the item in hand is a new edition. For those more adventurous, an option allows for the provision of an edition statement supplied by the cataloger "if an item lacks an edition statement but is known to contain significant changes from previous editions" (rule 1.2B4). The Library of Congress decided at first not to apply this option in any of the chapters, as it was felt that "if the edition statement could be supplied by the cataloger, there would be too much danger of bibliographic 'ghosts'." It was felt instead that the notes area would be more appropriate for information of this type. Later it was decided that the option should be applied if differences are "manifest" rather than "merely supposed," and if the catalog records needed would otherwise "show exactly the same information in the areas beginning with the title and statement of responsibility area and ending with the series area."[11]

ISBD (NBM), in its rules for the edition statement, also provides an optional rule allowing for an edition statement supplied by the cataloger, but is more specific as to what is to be regarded as a new edition. These guidelines take into account both intellectual and physical variations. In one of its definitions of *edition*, ISBD (NBM) suggests that in cases of significant variations of an intellectual nature, an edition statement may be supplied:

> An issue or group of issues of a work in a particular form of presentation (e.g., sound cassette, sound disc, etc.) having significant differences in intellectual or artistic content from other issues in the same form of presentation, whether or not the item bears any formal statement to this effect.[12]

This can be contrasted with a rule applying to changes in physical format:

> A work reissued with unchanged content but in an altered physical form (e.g., a cassette version of a work originally released as a sound disc) is not regarded as a new edition unless the word "edition" (or a related term) appears in the item, its container or accompanying textual matter....[13]

The NBMCR code allows an edition statement to be recorded only if it appears on the item itself:

> When an item is known to be a member of a particular edition, give this information in the edition statement. The terms of the statement are those of the item or other source, and include the names of those (if any) having intellectual responsibility in respect of the edition.[14]

In AECT 4, the general rule similarly prescribes that an edition statement is recorded "according to the wording on the work itself."

THE CONCEPT OF PUBLISHER

Publication information is an obvious requirement for the description of both print and nonbook materials. However, it is equally manifest that the concepts of *publisher* and *publication* have to be defined so that they are appropriate for the description of nonbook materials. Another consideration is whether traditions in the production and distribution of certain nonbook media impose special requirements for the transcription of publication data. A third major question considers whether it is appropriate to include publication data for items which are not issued in "published" form. These three questions are addressed in the following discussion.

If publication data are to constitute one of the elements of bibliographic description for nonbook materials, the concept of *publisher* must be extended to include the different types of functions and activities which may occur in the production and distribution of nonbook materials. This extension is noticeable in the way that the terms *publisher* and *publication* are understood in current cataloging standards. A variety of functions are subsumed under the rubric "publication, distribution, etc., area" in AACR 2. In AACR 2 and NBM 2, the data for this publisher-analog can include the notation of names of persons or organizations such as distributor, publisher, producer, and production company. In addition to distributor, publisher, and producer, AECT 4 includes sponsor, as do the NBMCR rules. In ISBD (NBM), the term *publication, distribution, etc.* is applied to "all types of publication, distribution, issuing and release activities. These activities are distinct from those connected solely with the physical manufacture of the item...."[15]

It is obvious from the definitions of *producer* in some of the codes that the responsibilities of the producer can go beyond the mere issuance or release of an object. In the revised chapter 12 of AACR, and in AACR 2, producers of motion pictures can be noted in the statement of responsibility and thus can be recognized as having responsibility over the intellectual content of the work. In AACR 2, the producer of motion pictures is defined as "the person with final responsibility for the making of a motion picture, including business aspects, management of the production, and the commercial success of the film." A greater degree of responsibility is ascribed to the production company of a motion picture, which is defined as "the company or other organization that determines the content and form of a motion picture and is responsible for its manufacture and production. If there is, in addition, a sponsor, the production company is normally responsible only for the manufacture or production of the motion picture."

Ravilious agrees that a "multiplicity of roles may be masked by the single term 'publisher'," and that the publisher of a book can exercise a substantial degree of control over the intellectual content of a book, or, on the other hand, may be responsible for no more than the processing and marketing of an author's manuscript. However, it is implicit from the treatment accorded to producers in the codes that they are considered as enjoying a more powerful degree of control over the content of nonbook materials than is the case for the publishers of books.[16]

While on the one hand, the element of publisher has been recognized as appropriate for the bibliographic description of nonbook materials, and has indeed been considerably broadened, the other two elements of publication data — place and date — have until fairly recently been considered unnecessary in some instances. Some codes, such as NBM 1 and the third edition of the AECT rules, omitted place of publication from the required elements of imprint, with the exception of cases in which it was necessary to identify lesser-known producers. However, this is probably ascribed to the general tendency toward simplified cataloging exemplified in both of these codes.

Even in some of the more detailed codes, however, place of publication was not considered necessary or appropriate for some kinds of materials. In AACR, place of publication was omitted for most sound recordings, and exceptions were made if companies were not known primarily as record publishers. In the British NBMCR code, place of publication was omitted if no trademark name had been given. Ravilious observes this omission of place in a clear majority of the codes reviewed in his book, and explains that the trademark name under which most sound recordings are issued is usually sufficient for identification in a national context. (It may be noted, however, that in an international context, place may be needed to identify the nationality or viewpoint represented.) Ravilious also found that the trademark name was favored over the name of the manufacturer in almost all the codes he examined. This practice is continued in AACR 2, which calls for the trade name or brand name used by the company if the recording bears both the name of the publishing company and the trade name.

One element of information typically included in the publication area in the case of sound recordings was the manufacturer's catalog number. In the later codes, including AACR 2, this information is given in the area of the bibliographic record assigned to ISBN and other identifying numbers. While this placement of the manufacturer's number is in accordance with the ISBD pattern of description, there may be some disadvantage for the users who have come to regard the trademark name and catalog number as an inseparable unit of information.

In the case of films, traditions in the manufacture and marketing of the medium can likewise impose standards for description. In AACR, place of publication was omitted from the description of all films except foreign films. In the NBMCR code, the country of origin, rather than the city, was specified for most types of film. Ravilious suggests that the rationale for this rule was that "film archives tend to regard country of origin as the most meaningful unit of information, at least for feature films."[17] (It might also be noted that film archivists were well represented on the committee responsible for the NBMCR code.)

Some notation of date is required by all of the codes considered here; however, the date included can be the date of publication, issuance, release, copyright, creation, or even discovery, depending on the code and the type of item described.

Standards imposed by the ISBD have been largely responsible for AACR 2's requirement that all three elements of publication data be provided for most materials, including commercially produced sound recordings and films. However, there are still some types of "unpublished" materials for which certain of these elements can be omitted. For many of these types, one can well ask whether it is appropriate to provide publication information of any kind. Publication data are indicators as to how and when an item has been produced or distributed, but there are some works which have been issued in single copies and were never intended for distribution. Is it appropriate to use the term *producer* to refer only to those responsible for items intended for distribution? AACR 2 addresses this question implicitly in its treatment of certain materials such as art originals, realia, non-processed sound recordings, and manuscripts, but attention to this problem is sporadic rather than comprehensive. In the chapter on graphic materials, rules prescribe that the imprint consist of the date only for art originals and unpublished photographs; further, this date is the date of creation, not of publication or issuance. Manuscripts are another type of material requiring only the date in the publication area.

In the chapter on three-dimensional materials, "naturally occurring objects" (such as rocks, feathers, shells) receive no publication data at all, unless they have been mounted for viewing or presentation. For another category of materials, called "artefacts not intended primarily for communication," only the date of manufacture is recorded.

In the chapter on sound recordings, there is one type of "unpublished" material, nonprocessed sound recordings, for which no publication data of any kind are given. For these recordings, defined as "non-commercial instantaneous recordings, generally existing in unique copies," the date of recording is given in the note area.

AACR 2 thus provides special treatment for categories of materials which it implicitly recognizes as "unpublished." Logically, such treatment could be extended to "unpublished" materials of all kinds. Any of the media formats included in AACR 2 are capable of being produced on a non-commercial basis, and with the recent technological advances in videorecording and in motion pictures, it is by no means uncommon to find "nonprocessed" works produced by individuals in these formats.

AECT 4 is also less than thorough in its treatment of unpublished materials. Like AACR 2, it excludes art originals and realia from those materials requiring a publication statement. In the case of realia, however, the place and date of discovery may be recorded.

NBM 2 has created its own chapter for "locally-produced, noncommercial materials," and draws upon analogous sections of AACR 2 for models. NBM 2's rules apply to locally produced, non-commercial materials of all kinds, and state that only the date of manufacture is given "if the 'author' is also responsible for the manufacture of the item and is named in the statement of responsibility" (p. 99).

The revised chapter 12 of AACR considered imprint data as "inappropriate for material that is not released, published, or similarly issued in multiple copies as an edition." For such materials, the notes area was to provide information as to source of material and date of production or discovery.

In the NBMCR rules, unpublished graphic and three-dimensional materials receive only the date of production, and for naturally occurring objects ("specimens") no publication data of any kind are given. No provision is made for "unpublished" motion pictures or sound recordings.

ISBD (NBM) excludes from its scope all materials which have not been "published," and considers only those materials "having for their primary purpose the transmission of ideas, information or aesthetic content" and which are for the most part published in multiple copies. Excluded are "specimens or found objects, except in so far as such objects are packaged and marketed commercially, as well as original works of art," but not art prints published in a limited artist's edition.

A second problem area arises in applying the term *publication* to reproductions. AACR 2's "cardinal rule" requires that the starting point for description is the item in hand; thus information recorded in the *publication, distribution, etc.* area should relate to the "publisher," that is, reproducer, of the *copy* and not the *original*. This question becomes particularly problematic when the intellectual content of a work is reproduced exactly, but in a different physical format; this is typically the case with microform reproductions of print originals.

The same phenomenon can also be commonly found in videorecording copies of motion pictures, and tape recording copies of discs. Those who maintain that catalog descriptions of microform reproductions should give primacy to the original work rather than the copy have argued that the publication data of greatest significance is that which pertains to the original work whose intellectual content is the focus of attention, while the place, producer, and date of the reproduction are of marginal interest to the catalog user. A second major argument maintains that such information is not only of marginal interest but is also quite likely to change, since the "producer" can vary with each reproduction activity. The implications of this situation for multi-library data bases are especially noteworthy.

THE INTEGRATED APPROACH TO NONBOOK CATALOGING

The preceding discussion has looked at the ways in which standards for cataloging nonbook materials have been derived from concepts and standards developed for books. Although these concepts have had to be modified and extended, they have still served as effective models for the bibliographic description of nonbook materials.

If the same basic bibliographic concepts can be applied to both books and nonbook materials, then catalog codes should be able to use a single set of principles to achieve a uniform pattern of description and entry for all materials. This is certainly the case in AACR 2, where all materials are governed by the same basic rules.

The same is also true, to a more limited extent, in codes preceding AACR 2, although here the idea of a general framework for bibliographic description is much less clearly defined. Still, it was clear, even as early as the 1949 ALACR rules, that while special rules were needed for nonbook materials, the same type of bibliographic record could be used for both books and nonbook materials, and that bibliographic records for nonbook materials could be successfully integrated into a "multimedia" catalog.

An integrated approach to the cataloging of media was present to some extent in the ALA rules and supplements. Although the complete set of rules was comprised in part of separate, self-contained supplements for different types of materials, it was made clear that the rules for nonbook materials were designed to be compatible with the rules for books.

In AACR, there were further advances toward a uniform approach to the cataloging of print and nonprint materials. The combining, in a single code, of rules for nonbook media along with rules for books and book-like materials was a significant development in this regard.

Part 1 of AACR provided rules for the choice of entry and form of heading of book and book-like materials. Part 2 contained rules for the description of these materials, and part 3 gave rules for the choice of entry and description of nonbook materials. In theory, the section on nonbook materials was to be viewed as an extension of the rules for book-like materials, rather than as a self-contained unit. Part 3 included only modifications or extensions of the sections on books and book-like materials, and the relevant portions of parts 1 and 2 were to be used to supplement part 3 when necessary. In application, however, it was often difficult to determine which generalized elements of parts 1 and 2 of AACR were to be applied to the specific rules for nonbook media in part 3. In contrast to

AACR 2, there was no consistent system of numbering to facilitate the identification of analogous rules among the different chapters. Since the generalized rules which were to serve as a basis for nonbook media had been developed specifically with the predominant medium in mind, it was not always a simple matter to extend a concept from parts 1 or 2 to part 3.

Thus, in AACR, the rules for book-like materials served double duty as their own "specific" rules and as the "general" rules of models upon which rules for other media were to be based. The model posited by the general rules for books was at best an example, from which analogies were to be drawn for other media, rather than a comprehensive framework designed to encompass all media.

In AACR 2, in contrast, there is a chapter specifically set aside for the description of media in general. This chapter is applied to the several individual chapters covering specific media and thus serves to bring about an "integrated and standardized framework for the systematic description of all library materials" (p. viii). Within the structural framework of AACR 2, all media formats are treated alike. Nonbook materials are no longer assigned to a section of the code which is set apart from the rules for the predominant medium. Part 1 (description) and part 2 (choice and form of access points) apply to all media. There is no longer a part 3 which stands as a separate and not-so-equal section for nonbook materials.

AACR 2's inclusion of a general chapter for description is one of the more notable changes from the first edition of this code. Some precedents for a "general" chapter had already been established by two earlier codes for nonbook materials, NBMCR and AECT 4. In these codes as well were some of the elements of a system which directly links the general chapter to rules in specific chapters.

In NBMCR, rules outlining the general principles applicable to all of the materials covered by the code were presented in the first chapter. The code's numbering system linked the general rules with those in the individual chapters on specific media-groups. For example, the rules for the publication area were assigned the number 7 in the general section, and the notation GT7 in the chapter "Graphics and Three-Dimensional Representations." If one of the general rules was to be applied to a specific chapter without modification, the name and the number of the rule were given in square brackets in the specific chapter. Thus the only rules to appear in the specific chapters were those which extended or modified the general rules, as is true for the most part in AACR 2. Unlike AACR 2, the linkage in NBMCR also operated in the opposite direction: it was possible to see which of the general rules had been modified in specific chapters. For example, the notation [MP SR] appearing after the general rules for the edition statement indicated that the chapters on motion pictures and sound recordings contained special provisions for this element of description.

In AECT 4, a set of general rules in section 1 encompasses all elements of entry and description and contains the basic rationale and pattern underlying the rules as a whole. Section 2 presents the application of the rules to specific media; these are given in alphabetical order. The two sections are structurally integrated. The sequence of rules found in section 1 is maintained throughout all of the sub-sections in 2. The body of rules can sometimes explain how a basic rule is modified or extended to suit the requirements of the specific medium. Where no special commentary is needed, a brief reference is given to the basic rule, or, in certain instances, a statement explaining why a basic rule is not appropriate.

To a lesser extent, revised chapter 12 of AACR, NBM 1 and NBM 2 also contain general rules. In revised chapter 12, there was a single, general statement outlining a brief set of rules for choice of entry, and a general pattern to be applied to the description of materials.

In summary, an examination of codes for nonbook materials reveals that while most codes have as their objective an integrated catalog with a uniform pattern of description and entry for all materials, there are differences of degree in the way in which this objective is implemented. One key difference lies in the role played by general rules, and the way in which a code is structured to allow general rules to be applied to specific media.

THE INTERNATIONAL STANDARD BIBLIOGRAPHIC DESCRIPTION

A major step toward the establishment of a general standard for the description of materials was the International Standard Bibliographic Description (ISBD). The influence of the ISBD standard can largely be seen in the way in which a standard pattern of bibliographic description is imposed upon a wide variety of media formats. As mentioned earlier, the ISBD prescribes, in general terms, the types of information to be included in the bibliographic description, the order of these elements of information, and their punctuation.

The basic model of the ISBD was designed for books [ISBD (M)], but was applied to nonbook materials well before the development of the ISBD for nonbook materials [ISBD (NBM)] or the ISBD for materials in general [ISBD (G)]. There were some difficulties, however, in extending the ISBD model to nonbook materials. Not until the development of the ISBD (G) and its incorporation into AACR 2 could the ISBD serve as a full-fledged standard for nonbook materials. In the absence of such a standard, catalog codes did not always agree as to which elements of description should appear on a bibliographic record.

AACR was published well before the appearance of ISBD (M) and contained no list of bibliographic elements common to the description of media in general. There were also no generalized rules for punctuation. Since the section on nonbook materials was designed to be used in conjunction with the chapters on book-like materials, none of the chapters for nonbook materials contained rules covering all areas of description. For example, rules for publication data were not given for maps. Only the chapter on pictures contained rules for statement of authorship responsibility. None of the chapters in the nonbook section included rules for edition, or series statements. For any of these areas, the rules for books and book-like materials were to be applied "to the extent that they are pertinent." Medium designators were considered appropriate only for motion pictures, filmstrips, and phonorecords.

At the time of the publication of the NBM 1 code in 1971, the ISBD for monographs had been published, but its incorporation into the revised chapter 6 of AACR had not yet appeared.

In the revised chapter 12 of AACR, the rules for description were based to some extent on the revised chapter 6 of AACR, which covered the description of monographs. Like the revised chapter 6, the revised 12 introduced changes in bibliographic description which reflected the requirements prescribed in the ISBD.

Although published after the appearance of the ISBD (M), NBMCR made no specific reference to an ISBD format. Rules for description in this code departed from the standards in ISBD and in most other nonbook codes in one major respect: the introduction of a new area of description called *credits*. This area was placed between the edition and the publication areas. It acknowledged persons involved in what might be called secondary aspects of creative responsibility — compilers, translators, editors, scriptwriters, animators, etc. In addition, this statement recognized those involved in the production of an item, such as producers, directors, and performers.

In this way, the *credits* area, which would normally be included as part of the notes, was given a more prominent position. The code thus provided for three distinct levels of statement of responsibility: 1) the statement of primary responsibility, 2) the statement of credits, and 3) the notes area.

Also noteworthy in the pattern of description in NBMCR was the absence of provision for a medium designator and the inclusion instead of a requirement for a *physical form designator* in the physical description area. AACR 2 later incorporated this requirement into its *physical description area*, with the result that the statement of the character of the physical unit, such as *game* or *filmstrip*, is always included.

In AACR 2, the framework for the standard description of all bibliographic materials is the General International Standard Bibliographic Description [ISBD (G)]. Special requirements for particular media can be accommodated within the ISBD (G) without damage to the integrity of the framework. Some elements of description can be omitted if they are not suitable for a given type of material. Thus, for example, the elements of place of publication and name of publisher would not be appropriate in the description of naturally occurring objects, such as a seashell, or of artefacts not intended primarily for communication, such as a coin.

At the same time, there are aspects essential to the description of some media which would not be considered as part of a general pattern of description. The ISBD (G) addresses this situation by setting aside one area (area 3) to be used only "for details that are special to a particular class of material or type of publication." The code recognizes serials and cartographic materials as requiring such an area, and it is here that numerical and chronological designations are recorded for serials; for example, *vol. 1, no. 1- .* For cartographic materials, area 3 is the *mathematical data area*, and is comprised of statements for scale, for projection, and for coordinates and equinox.

The guidelines set down for the ISBD (G) serve not only as a basis for the rules of description in AACR 2, but also as a basis for the individual ISBDs to be developed by the International Federation of Library Associations. Thus the ISBD (G) sets up a uniform pattern within the internal structure of AACR 2, and imposes this same pattern as a superstructure to effect a uniformity among the various ISBDs and to achieve uniformity among the ISBDs and the AACR 2 code.

NOTES

1. Christopher Ravilious, *A Survey of Existing Systems and Current Proposals for the Cataloguing and Description of Non-Book Materials Collected by Libraries, with Preliminary Suggestions for Their International Co-ordination* (Paris: UNESCO, 1975), p. 33.

2. Antony Croghan, *A Code of Rules for, with an Exposition of, Integrated Cataloguing of Non-Book Media* (London: Coburgh Publications, 1972), p. 17.

3. *A.L.A. Cataloging Rules for Author and Title Entries* (Chicago: American Library Association, 1949), p. 26.

4. Croghan, *Code of Rules*, p. 46.

5. Peter Lewis, "Writing the NBM Rules," *Catalogue and Index* 34 (October 1973): 1.

6. Peter Lewis, "Early Warning Generic Medium Designations in Multimedia Catalogues," *Library Resources and Technical Services* 17 (Winter 1973): 67.

7. Library of Congress, Processing Services, *Cataloging Service Bulletin*, no. 2 (Fall 1978), p. 5.

8. *ISBD (NBM): International Standard Bibliographic Description for Non-Book Materials* (London: IFLA International Office for UBC, 1977), p. 2.

9. Ibid., p. 3.

10. See LC's rule interpretation on the difference between an edition and a copy. Library of Congress, Processing Services, *Cataloging Service Bulletin*, no. 13 (Summer 1981), p. 3.

11. Ibid., p. 7.

12. *ISBD (NBM)*, p. 22.

13. Ibid., p. 23.

14. *Non-Book Materials Cataloguing Rules*. NCET Working Paper No. 11 (London: National Council for Educational Technology with the Library Association, 1973), p. 23.

15. *ISBD (NBM)*, p. 25.

16. Ravilious, *A Survey of Existing Systems*, p. 22.

17. Ibid., p. 59.

3

INTRODUCTION TO
CHAPTERS OF CATALOGING EXAMPLES

The purpose of the following chapters is twofold: 1) to show how the cataloging rules in the AACR 2 and NBM 2 codes are applied, and 2) to illustrate, in part, some of the theoretical concepts and principles discussed in the two previous chapters.

The codes used in the examples are the two major nonbook cataloging standards which have been issued in recent editions.* Both of these codes have been discussed in detail in the two previous chapters.

To assist the reader in the use of the examples, this introduction describes first the way in which the two codes are organized, and then explains the procedure used to present the examples.

AACR 2—PART 1—ORGANIZATION

AACR 2's part 1 is divided into chapters which, for the most part, are arranged according to media groups. The chapters of media groups are:

cartographic materials
manuscripts
music
sound recordings
motion pictures

graphic materials
machine-readable data files
three-dimensional artefacts
  and realia
microforms

These media groups are comprised of diverse formats which have in common some basic characteristic underlying their physical form or intellectual content.

---

*A third major nonbook cataloging code, AECT, is scheduled to appear in a fifth edition, but was not yet available at the time of this writing.

The various media which make up the category of cartographic materials share the characteristic of "[representing] ... the earth or any celestial body." Another category of materials determined by intellectual content – or, more precisely, by the manner in which it communicates its message – is music.

Static two-dimensional visual representations form the category of "graphic materials." Dynamic visual materials include motion pictures and videorecordings. Three-dimensional artefacts and realia are included in a diverse assortment of materials ranging from natural objects to sculptures. The groups of materials included in the latter categories are related more by their physical format than by their intellectual content. The same can be said for the categories of microform and machine-readable data files.

In contrast to AACR, which allowed an item to be assigned to only one category, the categories in AACR 2 are not regarded as mutually exclusive and can be used in combination. This may occur when there is an intersection of content, form, or – in the case of serials – mode of issuance. Thus, it is inevitable that some types of materials which are independent of content, such as serials and microforms, will belong to more than one category. For example, a set of music scores reproduced in microform format and issued on a serial basis would fall under three categories.

The code assists the reader by suggesting possible combinations and indicating the chapter to serve as the basis for description. The introduction to the chapter on manuscripts points out that manuscript cartographic items belong in the chapter on cartographic materials. Likewise, direction is given as to the treatment of manuscript music, recorded music, microform reproductions of music, sound track film (not accompanied by visual material), and microform reproductions of printed texts.

The code also provides guidance by recognizing other bases for determining the organization of categories. For example, the term *graphic materials* might logically be construed as including maps, microforms, motion pictures, and microscope slides. *Three-dimensional artefacts* could logically include relief models and globes. In each of these cases, the reader is referred to the appropriate chapter.

The question of media combination also arises in instances in which there are multimedia items comprised of components from more than one media category; for example, a filmstrip with accompanying tape cassette. The general rules for description prescribe that multimedia items be described in terms of the predominant component, if there is one, with subsidiary components described as accompanying material. Another alternative provided for treatment of multimedia items is cataloging each item as a separate record.

AACR 2 – PART 2

While the chapters in part 1 of AACR 2 are divided up according to media categories, the chapters in part 2 are applied to all types of materials.

The two parts of AACR 2 address two distinct concerns of the bibliographic record – one concern is directed principally to the physical character of the item, and the second to the intellectual or artistic content. The classic distinction between *book* and *work* governs the division of the two parts of the code and determines the kinds of questions to be addressed by each part. In part 1, the physical form of the item determines the starting point for description and assigns the item to the appropriate chapter. In part 2, the rules "apply to works and not generally to physical manifestations of those works. [These rules] apply to all library materials, irrespective of the medium in which they are published or of whether they are serial or nonserial in nature" (rule 20.1).

NBM 2

While the substance of the NBM 2 rules is essentially similar to the parallel rules in AACR 2, NBM 2 follows a different pattern of organization. In the examples in this book, the NBM 2 rules will be cited according to the appropriate chapters in AACR 2. For example, rules from NBM 2's separate chapter on videorecordings have been placed in the chapter on motion pictures and video-recordings, which corresponds to AACR 2's chapter of that name.

In NBM 2, there is a set of general rules for the code as a whole, outlining the basic elements of description and the principles underlying the rules for entry. This is followed by separate chapters for the various media categories. Since NBM 2 was designed as a manual to AACR 2, the categories of materials covered are similar. However, the chapters in NBM 2 appear in alphabetical order and are drawn up around media categories that are more specific than the chapters found in AACR 2. For example, AACR 2's category of *Three-dimensional artefacts and realia* is divided up in NBM 2 into separate chapters for dioramas, models, realia, games, and microscope slides. The individual chapters contain, for the most part, those types of rules which are unique to a particular format—for example, sources of information and physical description, as well as a definition of the category, indication of its scope, and examples of catalog records. In contrast to some of the other codes (AACR 2, AECT 4, and NBMCR), there is no attempt to link the general and specific chapters with a common numbering system, but since the code is relatively compact, the reader will have little difficulty in locating the appropriate rule from the general section.

NBM 2 also parts company with AACR 2 by adding a separate chapter of its own for kits. In AACR 2, this category is included in the chapter on general rules for description. Separate chapters are also provided for "locally-produced, noncommercial materials" and technical drawings. A chapter on art-originals incorporates into one section the rules for two- and three-dimensional objects of this category. For the most part, NBM 2's additional chapters cover categories of materials that the code considered to be inadequately treated in AACR 2. In providing its own rules for these categories, NBM 2 has attempted, wherever possible, to locate an appropriate model in AACR 2, and if necessary, looks to other recognized codes for nonbook materials.

CATEGORIES OF MATERIALS COVERED
IN EXAMPLES

The following six categories are covered in separate chapters in this text:

cartographic materials
sound recordings
motion pictures and
   videorecordings

graphic materials
three-dimensional artefacts
   and realia
microforms

As previously noted, the categories named above correspond to chapters contained in AACR 2's part 1. In addition, a chapter on kits has been included. In an actual cataloging situation, of course, the cataloger will decide how to categorize the item in order to determine which chapters of the cataloging code are appropriate. This can sometimes be a rather difficult problem to resolve, since some items might logically fit into more than one category of material.

Some examples involve the use of a combination of chapters. The following combinations of categories are represented in examples:

music / microform   map / slide
serial / sound recording   music / kit
serial / microform   music / sound recording
map / microform   manuscript / microform

ORGANIZATION OF CATALOGING EXAMPLES

The following components are included for each example:

1) a description of the item to be cataloged

2) catalog record(s)

3) citation of rules used

4) commentary

CATALOG RECORDS

The catalog records reflect the application of AACR 2, level 2. If the application of NBM 2 would result in a variation, this version is also given. Examples reflect, for the most part, LC options, rule interpretations, and decisions. In the few cases where an LC policy is in conflict with AACR 2, both the AACR 2 and LC versions are given.

The reader should bear in mind that the LC rule interpretations are being constantly updated, and that the rule interpretations included in this text reflect only the interpretations available at this time (mid-1982). To keep current with rule interpretations, the cataloger should refer to the *Cataloging Service Bulletin*, issued quarterly by the Library of Congress. The spring 1982 issue (no. 16) contains an index which lists the interpretations by rule number.

The reader should also be aware that some of the LC policies and practices result from internal constraints rather than substantive theoretical differences with AACR 2. Other libraries may be able to be more flexible in the handling of nonbook materials. It should also be noted that at the Library of Congress, "data needed for the cataloging entries [for audiovisual materials] are supplied mainly by producers, manufacturers, film libraries, ... distributing agencies [and the National Audiovisual Center]" and that "in most cases, cataloging is done from the information thus provided, without actual viewing of the material itself."[1]

RULE CITATIONS

Order and Scope

The citation order follows the sequence in which rules would generally be considered:

a) scope/categorization (to determine which chapter of materials is used)

b) sources of information

c) areas of description from the title and statement of responsibility area through the standard number area

d) choice of access points

Included are all relevant rules for description and choice of main entry, as well as all relevant definitions from the glossary. Rules for form of heading are not given unless the heading is relatively complex—for example, a heading for a subordinate unit of a corporate body. Added entry rules are likewise cited only where noteworthy—for example, in the case of an added entry uniform title.

Procedure for Citations

Within each chapter, a rule (or excerpt therefrom) is first quoted in full. Each subsequent reference within the chapter is given as a rule number (in AACR 2) or page number (in NBM 2). (Definitions in AACR 2 are also identified by page number.) These subsequent citations may also contain a few key words from the rule, where appropriate. Subsequent citations always contain a reference to the example where the rule is quoted in full. The purpose of quoting the rules is to enable the reader to follow the cataloging procedure for each example without constantly referring back to the cataloging codes. It should be emphasized, however, that the quotations should in no way be used as a substitute for the rules themselves, and that the reader should consult the rules for the full details and context that only the original text can provide.

COMMENTARY

As appropriate, commentary is provided to:

a) point out differences among the two codes

b) provide background information

c) state LC options and rule interpretations

d) point out theoretical or practical issues involved in the application or interpretation of the rules.

The AECT 4 code has not been used as a source code in the cataloging examples because the code is scheduled to appear in a revised edition to be compatible with AACR 2. However, the commentary in the cataloging examples includes occasional references to AECT 4, since this code often contains useful definitions and makes theoretical points which can be useful in the application of the AACR 2 and NBM 2 codes.

NOTES

1. *Library of Congress Catalogs: Audiovisual Materials 1980* (Washington, DC: The Library, 1981), p. iii.

4

CARTOGRAPHIC MATERIALS

The category of cartographic materials includes media which have as their basic unity the characteristic of "[representing] in whole or in part, the earth or any celestial body." Among these media are atlases, globes, navigational charts, a wide variety of two- and three-dimensional maps, and even aerial photographs, if they have a cartographic purpose.

Major changes from AACR to AACR 2 include the provision for a general material designation and the inclusion of mathematical data (scale, projection, etc.) in the body of the catalog record. In AACR, such data were given in the note area.

The Library of Congress will not apply the option to supply the general material designation. The library will also interpret the rules for corporate main entry in such a way as to allow main entry under corporate body for maps in most cases. These interpretations will be reflected in the following examples.

In cataloging maps, technical expertise in the area of cartography becomes invaluable. Many terms and concepts referred to in AACR 2's chapter 3 are probably unfamiliar to the nonspecialist. A manual prepared by the Anglo-American Cataloguing Committee for Cartographic Materials should provide much-needed assistance: *Cartographic Materials: A Manual of Interpretation for AACR2* (Chicago: American Library Association, 1982). The manual elaborates on AACR 2, and provides a great deal of background information necessary for the cataloging of cartographic materials. Useful reference tools could also include fundamental cartography texts such as Arthur H. Robinson's *Elements of Cartography* (New York: Wiley, 1978). This work provides the map cataloger with an overview of the basic concepts and principles of cartography, including scale, projection, and grid. Phillip Muehrke's *Map Use: Reading, Analysis, and Interpretation* contains helpful examples of scale conversion and projections (Madison, WI: JP Publications, 1978). For definitions of terms, the cataloger might consult the *Multilingual Dictionary of Technical Terms in Cartography* (Wiesbaden: F. Steiner, 1973) and the *Glossary of Mapping, Charting, and Geodetic Terms*, 3rd ed. (Washington, DC: U.S. Government Printing Office, 1973).

4A   AERIAL PHOTOGRAPH

DESCRIPTION OF ITEM

Components: 1 aerial photograph; black and white
Dimensions: 22.8 x 22.8 cm., excluding border
             23.4 x 23.4 cm. with border
On photo is the following textual information:
   7-5-65   BEE-1FF-260

The item would be categorized as an aerial remote sensing image, and depicts a portion of Midland County, Michigan. The date is July 5, 1965. The scale, which has been determined by a comparison with a map of known scale, is 1:20,000.

CATALOG RECORD

[Midland County, Mich. aerial photograph].
     — Scale ca. 1:20,000. — [United States? : s.n.],
1965.
1 aerial remote sensing image ; 23 x 23 cm.
Shows portion of Midland County.
Title supplied by cataloger.
"BEE-1FF-260".

(Shows option to omit general material designation.)

SCOPE / CATEGORIZATION

AACR 2

3.0A.   "The rules in this chapter cover the description of cartographic materials of all kinds. Cartographic materials include all materials that represent, in whole or in part, the earth or any celestial body. These include two- and three-dimensional maps and plans ... aerial photographs with a cartographic purpose ..."

(Chapter on graphic materials)
8.0A.   "The rules in this chapter cover the description of graphic materials of all kinds ... For maps, see chapter 3 ..."

NBM 2

p. 48:
Chapter title: "Maps"
"*Map*: a flat representation of part or all of either the earth or the universe."

Comment

In AACR 2, the categorization of this item is determined by its intellectual content (cartographic information) rather than by its physical format (photograph).

SOURCES OF INFORMATION

AACR 2

3.0B2. "The chief source of information ... is:
a) the cartographic item itself ..."

NBM 2

p. 48:
"Information for the catalogue record is taken from the following sources in this order:
1. The item itself (Chief source of information)."

TITLE PROPER

AACR 2

3.1B4. "If the item lacks a title, supply one as instructed in 1.1B7. Always include the name of the area covered in the supplied title. [Map of Ontario]"

1.1B7. "If no title can be found in any source, devise a brief descriptive title. Enclose such a ... devised title in square brackets."

NBM 2

p. 17 (General rules):
"Sources of information
5. Information supplied by the cataloger. Such information is enclosed in square brackets. Supplied titles should be descriptive, reasonably concise, and if possible begin with a filing word which reflects subject content."

Comment

Note that NBM 2 provides more specific guidance than AACR 2 for the construction of supplied titles, and that the suggestions made are still within the bounds of AACR 2's rule, the example ("Map of Ontario") notwithstanding. The decision on whether to include the term "map" might be influenced by the decision on the inclusion of a general material designation.

GENERAL MATERIAL DESIGNATION

AACR 2

*3.1C1.   (Optional) "Add, immediately following the title proper, the appropriate general material designation as instructed in 1.1C."

1.1C1.   "If general material designations are to be used in cataloguing, ... North American agencies [should use] terms from list 2."

3.1A1.   "Enclose the general material designation in square brackets."

A.4G.   (Appendix A — Capitalization) "Lowercase the words making up a general material designation."

p. 567 (Glossary):
"**Map.** A representation, normally to scale and on a flat medium, of a selection of material or abstract features on, or in relation to, the surface of the earth or of another celestial body."

NBM 2

p. 9 (Chapter on cataloging policy for media centers):
"The North American list of general material designations is used in this book. Those electing [to omit the general material designation or to use] the British list ... or the ISBD list may use the rules on the following pages by disregarding the general material designation or by substituting the appropriate term from the British or ISBD lists."

*p. 18 (General rules):
"A general material designation is listed in lower case letters, in the singular, and its own square brackets immediately following the title proper."

p. 48:
"Maps ... are ... designated by the term 'map.' "

Comment

The Library of Congress will not display the general material designation for maps. The Anglo-American Cataloguing Committee for Cartographic Materials considered the matter of general material designations at length and voiced disapproval for the terms "map" and "globe" on the North American list, while preferring the more generic term "cartographic material" on the British list. It was the opinion of the committee that the North American terms were too specific and limiting, and that many other materials which might fall within the category of cartographic materials would not be comprehended by the terms "map" and "globe."[1]

---

*Option not applied in examples in this chapter.

The general material designation has not been included in the AACR 2 and NBM 2 examples in this chapter, to reflect the Library of Congress decisions on AACR 2 options.

MATHEMATICAL DATA AREA

AACR 2

3.3B1. "Give the scale of a cartographic item as a representative fraction expressed as a ratio (1:   ). Precede the ratio by the word *scale*."

"If no statement of scale is found on the item, ... compute a representative fraction ... by comparison with a map of known scale. Give the scale preceded by *ca*."

3.3A1. "**Punctuation** ... Precede this area by a full stop, space, dash, space."

NBM 2

p. 19 (General rules):
"**Mathematical Data or Material Specific Details Area**
This area is used only with cartographic materials and serials in the sections on globes, maps, and microforms."

p. 48:
"*Scale*. List the term 'Scale' and a representative fraction expressed as a ratio, e.g., Scale 1:1,000,000."

"If no scale is found, use a ... comparison with the scale of a similar map to determine one. Such a representative fraction is preceded by the term 'ca.' "

"Scale is always listed in the first level of description."

"*Punctuation*. Representative fraction scale information is separated from other scale information by a period-space (.) ..."

PUBLICATION, DISTRIBUTION, ETC., AREA

AACR 2

3.4C1. "Record the place of publication, distribution, etc., as instructed in 1.4C."

*1.4C6. "If no probable place can be given, give the name of the country, state, province, etc. If, in such a case, the country, state, province, etc., is not certain, give it with a question mark."

---

*i.e. *place* in terms of a city.

*"If no place or probable place can be given, give the abbreviation *s.l.* (sine loco), or its equivalent in nonroman scripts."

3.4D1.   "Record the name of the publisher, etc., ... as instructed in 1.4D."

1.4D6.   "If the name of the publisher, distributor, etc., is unknown, give the abbreviation *s.n.* (sine nomine) or its equivalent in nonroman scripts."

3.4F1.   "Record the date of publication, distribution, etc., as instructed in 1.4F."

1.4F1.   "If there is no edition statement, give the date of the first edition."

NBM 2

p. 20 (General rules):
**"If no probable place can be listed, give the name of the province, state, country, etc."

"If the place is unknown, list 'S.l.' in square brackets."

"If the publisher, etc. is unknown, list 's.n.' in square brackets ..."

"List the publication date of the item being catalogued."

Comment

If this item were not cartographic in purpose, and thus were to fall under the rules in chapter 8 in AACR 2, only the date would be given in the publication, distribution, etc., area, according to the special rule (8.4A2) for unpublished photographs. (Compare with the "Arlington Cemetery Photograph" example #7C.)

PHYSICAL DESCRIPTION AREA—EXTENT OF ITEM

AACR 2

***3.5B1. "Record the number of physical units of a cartographic item by giving the number of units in arabic numerals and one of the following terms, as appropriate.

> aerial remote sensing image
> globe
> map

---

*This sentence of rule considered but not applied.

**i.e. *place* in terms of a city.

***The terms listed in this rule citation include only those designations which are used for the examples in this chapter.

NBM 2

*p. 48:
"List the number of ... aerial remote sensing images, ... maps, ..."

Comment

This example underscores the need for consultation of appropriate reference sources in the selection of specific material designations, especially when the cataloger is unfamiliar with the terminology used for cartographic materials.

PHYSICAL DESCRIPTION AREA—OTHER PHYSICAL DETAILS

AACR 2

3.5C3. **"Colour. If the item is coloured or partly coloured, indicate this."

NBM 2

p. 49:
"List col. or b&w ..."

Comment

Note that the NBM 2 code, unlike AACR 2, requires a statement to be made for a black and white map.

PHYSICAL DESCRIPTION AREA—DIMENSIONS

AACR 2

3.5D1. **"Maps, plans, etc.** For two-dimensional cartographic items, give the height x width in centimetres, to the next whole centimetre up (e.g., if a measurement is 37.1 centimetres, record it as 38 cm.) ... Give the measurements of the face of the map, etc., measured between the neat lines.... If a map ... has no neat lines, ... give the greater or greatest dimensions of the map itself."

---

*The terms listed in this rule citation include only those designations which are used for the examples in this chapter.
**Rule must be considered, to determine that no color statement is made.

NBM 2

p. 49:
"Height x width of the face of the map between the neat lines are listed in centimetres."

The reader would refer to AACR 2.

NOTE AREA

AACR 2

3.7B1.   "**Nature and scope of the item.** If the nature or scope of a cartographic item is not apparent from the rest of the description, indicate it in a word or brief phrase."

3.7B3.   "**Source of title proper.** Make notes on the source of the title proper if it is other than the chief source of information."

3.7B19.   "**Numbers.** Give important numbers borne by the item other than ISBNs or ISSNs ..."

NBM 2

p. 22 (General rules):
"Other information which may be given in notes is listed in the following order:
    Nature, scope, or artistic form
    ...
    Source of title proper.
Numbers associated with item other than ISBNs or ISSNs ..."

Comment

In this instance, the designation "BEE-1FF-260" would identify the item as to the county, flight path, and frame number.

CHOICE OF ACCESS POINTS

AACR 2

21.1C.   "Enter a work under its title when:
1) the personal authorship is unknown ... or cannot be determined, and the work does not emanate from a corporate body"

NBM 2

The reader would consult AACR 2.

4B   CTA ROUTE MAP

DESCRIPTION OF ITEM

Components: 1 sheet map, colored

Size of sheet: 68 centimeters high; 49 centimeters wide. Folds to panel 23 x 10 cm.

The map is irregularly shaped and extends to the outer edges of the sheet. There are no neat lines. Map dimensions are 68 x 43 cm.

Inset shows central business district and "L" subway routes. There is a substantial amount of text on the reverse side of the map.

The scale of the map is 1:70,000. This has been computed using a natural scale indicator. The scale on the map is given as a bar graph.

Front panel:

>CTA Route Map
>Chicago Metropolitan Area
>Published by: Chicago Transit Authority
>Chicago, Ill.

Lower left-hand corner:

>CHICAGO
>TRANSIT MAP
>Showing CTA, Bus, "L" and Subway Lines and the Connecting Suburban Bus Routes

(The above information does not appear on the map itself)

Lower right-hand corner:

>©1967 Chicago Transit Authority
>Prepared and Lithographed in U.S.A. by Rand McNally & Co.

(The above information appears in very small print and is superimposed upon the map)

CATALOG RECORD

Chicago Transit Authority.
CTA route map : Chicago metropolitan area / prepared and lithographed in U.S.A. by Rand McNally & Co. — Scale ca. 1:70,000. — Chicago, Ill. : Chicago Transit Authority, c1967.
1 map : col. ; 68 x 43 cm. on sheet 68 x 49 cm. folded to 23 x 10 cm.
Title in lower left corner: Chicago transit map.
Text on verso.
Inset: Central business district, "L" subway routes.

I. Title. II. Title: Chicago transit map.

SCOPE / CATEGORIZATION

AACR 2

3.0A: chapter covers two-dimensional maps (Cited in #4A)

NBM 2

p. 48: "maps" chapter (Cited in #4A)

SOURCES OF INFORMATION

AACR 2

3.0B2: item itself (Cited in #4A)

NBM 2

p. 48: item itself (Cited in #4A)

TITLE PROPER

AACR 2

3.1B1.   "Record the title proper as instructed in 1.1B."

1.1B1.   "Transcribe the title proper exactly as to wording, order and spelling, but not necessarily as to punctuation and capitalization."

AACR 2 (cont'd)

3.1B3. "If the chief source of information bears more than one title, [and] if both or all of the titles are in the same language and script, choose the title proper on the basis of the sequence or layout of the titles. If these are insufficient to enable the choice to be made or are ambiguous, choose the most comprehensive title."

NBM 2

p. 18 (General rules):
"The title proper ... is copied exactly from the chief source of information. However, capitalization and punctuation follow prescribed rules."

p. 48:
"Sources of information
Information for the catalogue record is taken from the following sources in this order:[40]"
1. The item itself (Chief source of information). If two or more titles are given on the face of the map, preference is given in the following order:
a)   The most appropriate title,
b)   The title within the border of the map,
c)   The title in the margin;

p. 125 (Appendix A—Notes):
"40. Drawn from NBM/1 & [AECT 4]"

Comment

AACR 2's guidelines for choice of title proper still leave room for judgment on the part of the cataloger in this example. If the title proper is chosen "on the basis of the sequence or layout of the titles," a decision must be made between the title appearing in larger print ("Chicago Transit Map") or the title appearing on the panel, which may be regarded by some as analogous to a title page.

The "CTA Route Map" title has an accompanying subtitle, and these two may be regarded as more comprehensive than the single title. NBM 2 has provided guidelines for selection of titles among its rules for sources of information. In this example, the criteria cannot be applied since neither of the titles appears on the map itself; i.e., within the border or in the margin.

*GENERAL MATERIAL DESIGNATION

AACR 2

3.1C1: as in 1.1C

1.1C1: North American list

---

*Option to include general material designation not applied.

4B CTA Route Map / 79

3.1A1: square brackets

A.4G: lowercase

p. 567: definition of map
(Cited in #4A)

NBM 2

p. 9: North American list

p. 18: lower case, singular, square brackets; follows title proper

p. 48: map
(Cited in #4A)

OTHER TITLE INFORMATION

AACR 2

3.1E1.   "Record other title information as instructed in 1.1E."

1.1E1.   "Transcribe all other title information appearing in the chief source of information according to the instructions in 1.1B."

NBM 2

p. 18 (General rules):
"Other title information ... follows the general material designation and the title proper ... to which it pertains. [It is] listed in the exact wording found in the chief source of information."

STATEMENTS OF RESPONSIBILITY

AACR 2

3.1F1.   "Record statements of responsibility as instructed in 1.1F."

1.1F1.   "Record statements of responsibility appearing prominently in the item in the form in which they appear there."

(General introduction)
0.8   "The word *prominently* ... means that a statement to which it applies must be a formal statement found in one of the prescribed sources of information (see 1.0A) for areas 1 and 2 for the class of material to which the item being catalogued belongs."

NBM 2

p. 18 (General rules):
"The statement of responsibility is listed wherever possible in the wording and order found on the source(s) of information."

Comment

The explanation of the use of the term *prominently* indicates that the statement of responsibility should be recorded even though it is not readily visible.

MATHEMATICAL DATA AREA

AACR 2

3.3B1: give scale as representative fraction

3.3A1: punctuation
(Cited in #4A)

Rule 3.3B1 also includes:
"If no statement of scale is found on the item, ... compute a representative fraction from a bar graph ..."

NBM 2

p. 19: mathematical data area

p. 48: representative fraction; punctuation

Rule also includes:
"If no scale is found, use a bar graph ... to determine one."

"Natural scale indicators for conversion of graphic scales to representative fractions are commercially available, or the mathematically inclined can use the following method. If scale is given in terms of miles to an inch, multiply the number of miles per inch (1 in. = 43 mi.) by the number of inches in a mile (63,360 in.). For example, 43 x 63,360 = 2,724,480 is listed as Scale 1:2,724,480."

Comment

The rule beginning "If no statement of scale is found on the item" may be misleading if it is understood to include statements of *any* kind, including those in the form of a bar graph. If qualified to read "If no *verbal* scale statement is found on the item," the meaning becomes clearer. Since a computation of a scale involves some margin for error, the statement is regarded as "ca."

The manual prepared by the Anglo-American Cataloguing Committee for Cartographic Materials contains conversion tables and instructions for establishing the scale of a map with no scale statement.

PUBLICATION, DISTRIBUTION, ETC., AREA

AACR 2

3.4C1: as in 1.4C (Cited in #4A)

1.4C1.   "Record the place of publication, etc., in the form ... in which it appears."

3.4D1: as in 1.4D (Cited in #4A)

1.4D2.   "Give the name of the publisher, distributor, etc., in the shortest form in which it can be understood and identified internationally."

3.4F1: as in 1.4F (Cited in #4A)

1.4F6.   "If the dates of publication, distribution, etc., are unknown, give the copyright date ..."

1.4C3.   "Add the name of the country, state, province, etc., to the name of the place if it is considered necessary for identification, or if it is necessary to distinguish the place from others of the same name."

NBM 2

pp. 19, 20 (General rules):
"List the name of the place as it appears on the item and add the name of the province, state, country, etc., if it is necessary for identification."

"List the name of the publisher, producer, distributor, etc., in the shortest form that can be identified internationally."

"If the dates of publication or distribution cannot be ascertained, list the copyright date ..."

Comment

The name of the state has been added to the place of publication because of the following LC rule interpretation:

"1.4C3. ... If a place of publication and the name of its larger jurisdiction (e.g., country, state, or similar designation) appear together in the source from which they are being transcribed, generally transcribe both. Do this even if the place does not need to be identified or is clearly the best known one of that name."[2]

PHYSICAL DESCRIPTION AREA—EXTENT OF ITEM

AACR 2

3.5B1: map (Cited in #4A)

NBM 2

p. 48: map (Cited in #4A)

PHYSICAL DESCRIPTION AREA—OTHER PHYSICAL DETAILS

AACR 2

3.5C3: color (Cited in #4A)

NBM 2

p. 49: color (Cited in #4A)

PHYSICAL DESCRIPTION AREA—DIMENSIONS

AACR 2

3.5D1: height x width (Cited in #4A); Rule also includes:
"If a map ... is irregularly shaped, ... give the greater or greatest dimensions of the map itself."

"[If] there is substantial additional information on the sheet (e.g., text), give the sheet size as well as the size of the map ..."

"[If] the sheet itself contains a panel or section designed to appear on the outside when the sheet is folded, give the sheet size in folded form as well as the size of the map ..."

NBM 2

p. 49: height x width (Cited in #4A); Rule continues:
"For irregularly shaped maps list the greatest dimensions or, if these are difficult to determine, the dimensions of the sheet itself; e.g., on sheet 60 x 78 cm."

"Those wishing to describe precisely the dimensions of ... folded maps ... should consult the *Anglo-American Cataloguing Rules*, 2nd edition, rule 3.5D1.

Comment

Opinions will differ as to what amounts to "substantial additional information," also as to what would be considered an "irregularly shaped" map.

NOTE AREA

AACR 2

3.7B4.   **"Variations in title.** Make notes on title borne by the item other than the title proper."

3.7B10.   **"Physical description.** Indicate any physical details that are considered to be important and have not been included in the physical description area."

3.7B18.   **"Contents.** ... Make notes describing the contents of an item (either partially or fully), including: parts; insets ..."

NBM 2

p. 22 (General rules):
"Variations in title"
  ...
"Additional information concerning the physical description, particularly if such information affects the item's use."

p. 49:
"List mathematical and other cartographic data that is considered useful to the media centre's patrons."

"List insets."

CHOICE OF ACCESS POINTS

AACR 2

21.1B2.   "Enter a work emanating from one or more corporate bodies under the heading for the appropriate corporate body if it falls into one or more of the following categories:
 a)   those of an administrative nature dealing with the corporate body itself

  or its internal policies, procedures, and/or operations

  ...

 *f)   cartographic materials emanating from a corporate body other than a body that is merely responsible for the publication or distribution of the materials.

---

*New category included in AACR 2 revisions.

AACR 2 (cont'd)

˙ *"In case of doubt about whether a work falls into one or more of these categories, treat it as if it did not."

21.1B3. "When determining the main entry heading for works that emanate from one or more corporate bodies but that fall outside the categories given in 21.1B2, treat them as if no corporate body were involved. Make added entries under the headings for prominently named corporate bodies as instructed in 21.30E."

*21.1C. "Enter a work under its title when:

...

3)   it emanates from a corporate body but does not fall into one or more of the categories given in 21.1B2 and is not of personal authorship."

NBM 2

The reader would consult AACR 2.

Comment

Category *f* is an entirely new addition which did not appear in the original AACR 2. This category was added to rule 21.1B2 in the revisions of AACR 2 approved by the Joint Steering Committee for Revision of AACR (*Anglo-American Cataloguing Rules, Second Edition, Revisions*, Chicago: American Library Association, 1982). Under the original version of 21.1B2, most cartographic materials would have been entered under title rather than under corporate body. Strong opposition to the original 21.1B2 was voiced by the Anglo-American Cataloguing Committee for Cartographic Materials. The committee was successful in convincing the National Library of Canada and the Library of Congress to accept an interpretation of the original 21.1B2 which would "permit entry under corporate body for a large body of cartographic materials currently excluded from corporate main entry by AACR 2."[3] This "interpretation" eventually appeared as a rule revision.

In this example, corporate main entry could also be argued if one regards this map as an "administrative" document indicating the procedures and operations of the corporate body.

---

*Rule considered but not applied.

4C   OSAKA AND TOKYO MAPS

DESCRIPTION OF ITEM

Components: 1 colored silk sheet with maps printed on both sides; in
plastic container

Dimensions (height x width):

Map of Osaka   44.5 x 56 cm. - neat line to neat line
46.4 x 58.4 - border to border

Map of Tokyo   45.5 x 56.3 cm. - neat line to neat line
46.4 x 58.5 cm. - border to border

Sheet size: 63.3 x 67 cm.

Plastic container size: 18 x 10 cm.

Included on the map are a glossary of English and Japanese terms, a legend, and
indexes.

Map of Osaka:

Top border: EASTERN ASIA 1:1,000,000
OSAKA (very large type)
Restricted NI 53

Lower border (very small print):

A.M.S. 5301

First Edition 1942.

Second Edition 1943.

Prepared under the direction of the Chief of Engineers, U.S. Army,
by the Army Map Service (PT), U.S. Army, Washington, D.C.,
1943.

Redrawn from a Japanese Imperial Land Survey map dated 1937.

Communications revised to 1943 from intelligence reports.

Scale 1:1,000,000

Modified Polyconic Projection of the International Map of the World

Army Map Service, U.S. Army, Washington, D.C., 100141

1944

Osaka, Japan

Map of Tokyo:

The information is the same as above except that the name TOKYO appears
on the top border instead of OSAKA, the map number in the top right hand
corner is NI 54, and the bottom line in the bottom right hand corner reads:
Tokyo, Japan.

CATALOG RECORD
(Cataloged as a unit)

United States. Army Map Service.
    Osaka ; Tokyo / prepared under the direction of the Chief of Engineers, U.S. Army, by the Army Map Service (PT). — 2nd ed. 1943. — Scale 1:1,000,000 ; Modified polyconic proj. — Washington, D.C. : Army Map Service, 1943 [distributed 1944]
    2 maps on 1 sheet : col., silk ; 45 x 56 and 46 x 57 cm. in plastic case, 18 x 10 cm. — (Eastern Asia 1:1,000,000)
    Redrawn from a Japanese Imperial Land Survey map dated 1937. Communications revised to 1943 from intelligence reports.
    Army Map Service series: A.M.S. 5301.
    Printed on both sides.
    Includes glossary, legend, and indexes.
    "NI 53" and "NI 54".

    I. Title. II. Title: Tokyo. III. Series.

(Cataloged as a separate)

United States. Army Map Service.
    Osaka / prepared under the direction of the Chief of Engineers, U.S. Army, by the Army Map Service (PT). — 2nd ed. 1943. — Scale 1:1,000,000 ; Modified polyconic proj. — Washington, D.C. : Army Map Service, 1943 [distributed 1944]
    on 1 side of 1 map : col., silk ; 45 x 56 cm. in plastic case, 18 x 10 cm. — (Eastern Asia 1:1,000,000).
    Redrawn from a Japanese Imperial Land Survey map dated 1937. Communications revised to 1943 from intelligence reports.
    Army Map Service series: A.M.S. 5301.
    Includes glossary, legend, and indexes.
    "NI 53".
    With (on verso): Tokyo.

I. Title. II. Series.

SCOPE / CATEGORIZATION

AACR 2

3.0A: chapter covers two-dimensional maps (Cited in #4A)

NBM 2

p. 48: "maps" chapter (Cited in #4A)

SOURCES OF INFORMATION

AACR 2

3.0B2: item itself (Cited in #4A)

NBM 2

p. 48: item itself (Cited in #4A)

TITLE PROPER

AACR 2

3.1B1: as in 1.1B

1.1B1: transcribed exactly except for punctuation, capitalization

3.1B3: choose title on basis of sequence or layout (Cited in #4B)

3.1G1. "If a cartographic item lacks a collective title, *either* describe the item as a unit (see 3.1G2 and 3.1G3), *or* make a separate description for each separately titled part (see 3.1G4) ..."

(For the two maps cataloged as a unit):
3.1G2. "In describing a cartographic item lacking a collective title as a unit, record the titles of the individual parts as instructed in 1.1G."

1.1G2. "If, in an item lacking a collective title, no one part predominates, record the titles of the individually titled parts in the order in which they are named in the chief source of information, or in the order in which they appear in the item if there is no single chief source of information. Separate the titles of the parts by semicolons if the parts are all by the same person(s) or body (bodies), even if the titles are linked by a connecting word or phrase."

(For each map cataloged as a separate):
3.1G4. "If desired, make a separate description for each separately titled part of an item lacking a collective title. For the description of the extent in each of the descriptions, see 3.5B4. Link the separate descriptions with a note (see 3.7B21)."

NBM 2

p. 18: exactly from chief source, except for punctuation, capitalization (Cited in #4B)

p. 19 (General rules):
"Items without a collective title may be described in one of the following ways:

NBM 2 (cont'd)

...

2. If no work is predominant, list the titles ... in the order in which they appear in the chief source of information ...

Punctuation. If the works are all by the same author(s), the individual titles are separated by space-semicolon-space ...

3. Make a separate description for each part that has a distinctive title, and link the descriptions with a 'with' note ..."

Comment

Two decisions must be made when recording the title proper in AACR 2. The first decision determines the unit to be cataloged. Rule 3.1G presents the cataloger with essentially two choices in this example: 1) to catalog the two maps as a unit, or 2) to provide separate bibliographic records for each of the two maps. If the maps are cataloged as a unit, rule 3.1G2 is applied; our other choice is to treat each side of the sheet as a separate entity, in which case rule 3.1G4 would be applied.

The decision made on the unit to be cataloged will determine most aspects of the bibliographic record; in this example, title proper, date, physical description, and notes will differ according to whether the record describes the two maps as a unit or the two as separates. Thus, this decision should be the first one made in the cataloging process.

For most of the formats covered in AACR 2, the rules require that items without a collective title be treated as a unit. (See Art nouveau example, #8B). For three classes of materials, however, AACR 2 permits the cataloger to treat items without a collective title either as a unit, or as separate entities. This is the case with sound recordings (See Devienne example, #5F), motion pictures and videorecordings, and microforms. Only in the case of cartographic materials, however, is the cataloger allowed the additional choice of supplying a collective title (3.1G5). NBM 2, on the other hand, prefers that all classes of materials be treated equally in this regard. The Library of Congress will not follow the option to provide separate records.

Once the cataloger has decided on the unit to be cataloged, a second question must be settled in the selection of title. In this example, the question essentially involves whether the title(s) will include the term "Japan." AACR 2, in rule 3.1B3, prescribes that the choice be made "on the basis of the sequence or layout of the titles." In this example, the briefer title(s) is preferred, since it appears on the top margin, and in larger print than the more comprehensive title(s).

In recording the titles to be given for the collective unit, I am regarding the Osaka map as appearing "first" in the application of rule 1.1G2, based on the numbering sequence.

*GENERAL MATERIAL DESIGNATION

AACR 2

3.1C1: as in 1.1C

1.1C1: North American list

3.1A1: square brackets

A.4G: lowercase

p. 567: definition of map
(Cited in #4A)

NBM 2

p. 9: North American list

p. 18: lower case, singular, square brackets; follows title proper

p. 48: map
(Cited in #4A)

(For the two maps cataloged as a unit):
p. 19 (General rules):
"The general material designation is listed immediately after the last of a group of titles by one author."

STATEMENTS OF RESPONSIBILITY

AACR 2

3.1F1: as in 1.1F1

1.1F1: record statements appearing *prominently*

0.8: meaning of term *prominently*
(Cited in #4B)

NBM 2

p. 18: wording and order found on source
(Cited in #4B)

---

*Option to include general material designation not applied.

EDITION AREA

AACR 2

3.2B1. "Transcribe a statement relating to an edition of a work that contains differences from other editions, or that is a named revision of that work, as instructed in 1.2B.

> 2nd ed.
> 1974 new ed."

1.2B1. "Transcribe the edition statement as found on the item. Use standard abbreviations (see Appendix B) and numerals in place of words (see Appendix C)."

*3.2B5. "If an item lacking a collective title and described as a unit contains one or more parts with an associated edition statement, record such statements following the titles and statements of responsibility to which they relate, separated from them by a full stop."

NBM 2

p. 19 (General rules):
"The edition statement is listed as it appears on the item, using arabic numerals and standard abbreviations."

Comment

I am interpreting rule 3.2B5 in AACR 2 to mean that a separate edition statement would not have to be recorded for each title if the edition statements do not differ.

MATHEMATICAL DATA AREA

AACR 2

3.3B1: give scale as representative fraction

3.3A1: punctuation
(Cited in #4A)

Rule 3.3A1 continues:
"Precede the projection statement by a semicolon."

3.3C1. "Give the statement of projection if it is found on the item ... Use standard abbreviations (see Appendix B) ...
> Conic equidistant proj."

---

*Rule considered but not applied.

NBM 2

p. 19: mathematical data area

p. 48: representative fraction; punctuation (Cited in #4A)

p. 48:
"*Projection*. List projection if it is found in the first three sources of information."

"*Punctuation*. ... [Scale information is separated] from projection by a space-semicolon-space ..."

PUBLICATION, DISTRIBUTION, ETC., AREA

AACR 2

3.4C1: as in 1.4C (Cited in #4A)

1.4C1: record in form appearing on item

1.4C3: add name of larger jurisdiction (Cited in #4B)

3.4D1: as in 1.4D (Cited in #4A)

1.4D2: publisher's name in shortest form (Cited in #4B)

3.4F1: as in 1.4F (Cited in #4A)

1.4F1: "Give the date of publication, distribution, etc., of the edition named in the edition area."

1.4F4.   "If the publication date differs from the date of distribution, add the date of distribution if it is considered to be significant by the cataloguing agency. ...
London : Macmillan, 1971 [distributed 1973]"

NBM 2

pp. 19, 20: name of place; name of publisher in shortest form; publication date (Cited in #4A)

Comment

Since the date recorded is the date of the edition named in the edition area, the date of issue is added ("date of distribution").

PHYSICAL DESCRIPTION AREA — EXTENT OF ITEM

AACR 2

3.5B1: map (Cited in #4A)

(For the two maps cataloged as a unit):
3.5B2.   "If there is more than one map ... on a sheet, specify the number of maps ...
   6 maps on 1 sheet"

(For each map cataloged as a separate):
3.5B4:   "If the description is of a separately titled part of a cartographic item lacking a collective title (see 3.1G4) and if the part is not physically separate from the rest of the item, express the fractional extent in the form *on sheet 3 of 4 maps* (if the parts are numbered in a single sequence) or *on 1 side of 4 plans* (if there is no single numbering)."

NBM 2

p. 48: map (Cited in #4A)

Rule continues, pp. 48; 49:
"If there is more than 1 map on a sheet ... state this concisely, e.g., 3 aerial charts on 1 sheet ..."

Comment

Note how AACR 2 (in rule 3.5B2) and NBM 2 allow the *physical units* (i.e., the number of sheets) to be distinguished from the number of *units of content* (i.e., the number of maps) through the use of a phrase such as "2 maps on 1 sheet." Similar provisions for describing specific parts of a physical entity are made in the chapters for sound recordings and motion pictures (see Devienne example, #5F). In rule 3.5B4, however, AACR 2 is using the term *map* to refer to the physical unit. This use of the term *map* agrees with rule 3.5B1, which allows the term *map* to be used in recording the physical unit, but is not consistent with the use of the term in 3.5B2.

PHYSICAL DESCRIPTION AREA — OTHER PHYSICAL DETAILS

AACR 2

3.5C3: color (Cited in #4A)

3.5C4:   "**Material.** Record the material of which the item is made if it is considered to be significant (e.g., if a map is printed on a substance other than paper).
   ...
   1 map : col., silk"

NBM 2

p. 49:
"List col. or b&w, the material from which the map was made, if significant
..."

PHYSICAL DESCRIPTION AREA — DIMENSIONS

AACR 2

3.5D1: measure between neat lines (Cited in #4A)

(For the two maps cataloged as a unit):
Rule continues:
"If the maps ... in a collection are of two sizes, give both."

3.5D5. *Optional addition.* **Containers.** Add the dimensions of a
container, specified as such, to the dimensions of the item."

NBM 2

p. 49: measure between neat lines (Cited in #4A)

Rule continues:
"Those wishing to describe precisely the dimensions of ... maps of different
sizes, ... should consult the *Anglo-American Cataloguing Rules*, 2nd edition, rule
3.5D1."

p. 21 (General rules):
"Fractions are taken to the next number."

"If an item is housed in a container, the type of container may be listed
together with its dimensions.[13]"

p. 123 (Appendix A — Notes):
"13. Measuring the container drawn from 3.5D5 & 10.5D2. This may be
extended to all media if this is useful information."

Comment

As is true of the other elements of description, the statement of dimensions is
determined by the bibliographic unit being described. Measurement in AACR 2
and NBM 2 is made in terms of the neat lines; these are lines, usually grid or
graticule, which enclose the detail of a map. This is a change from AACR, which
measured according to the border or margin.

SERIES AREA

AACR 2

3.6B1. "Record each series statement as instructed in 1.6."

1.6B1. "If an item is one of a series, record the title proper of the series as instructed in 1.1B ..."

1.6B2. "If variant forms of the title of the series ... appear in the chief source of information, use the variant that identifies the series most adequately and succinctly."

3.1B2. "If the title proper includes a statement of scale, include it in the transcription."

NBM 2

p. 21 (General rules):
"If applicable, a series statement in parentheses follows the physical description area."

Comment

AMS 5301 is the numerical equivalent to *Eastern Asia 1:1,000,000.* Thus either statement might be considered as the title proper of the series. A map specialist would probably select *AMS 5301* as the "variant that identifies the series most adequately and succinctly," while a layperson might find that *Eastern Asia 1:1,000,000* provides a more useful identification.

Since the majority of maps are issued in series, familiarity with the various types of cartographic series commonly found in map collections is essential in the cataloging of these materials.

NOTE AREA

AACR 2

3.7B7. "**Edition and history.** Make notes relating to the edition being described or to the history of the cartographic item."

3.7B12. "Make notes on series data that cannot be given in the series area."

3.7B18: contents (Cited in #4B)

3.7B19. "**Numbers.** Give important numbers borne by the item other than ISBNs ..."

(For each map cataloged as a separate):

3.7B21. " **'With' notes.** If the description is of a separately titled part of a cartographic item lacking a collective title, make a note listing the other separately titled parts of the item in the order in which they appear there.

...

With (on verso): Motor road map of south-east England."

NBM 2

p. 22 (General rules):
"Edition and history"

"Additional information about series"

p. 22: contents (Cited in #4B)

p. 49: cartographic data (Cited in #4B)

p. 22 (General rules):
"Numbers associated with item other than ISBNs ..."

(For each map cataloged as a separate):
" 'With' notes are used when an item has separately titled parts and no collective title."

CHOICE OF ACCESS POINTS

AACR 2

21.1B2f: special rule for cartographic materials—corporate entry (Cited in #4B)

NBM 2

The reader would consult AACR 2.

FORM OF HEADING

AACR 2

24.24A. "Enter a principal service of the armed forces of a government as a direct subheading of the name of the government."

AACR 2 (cont'd)

"If the name of ... a component branch ... begins with the name or an indication of the name, of the principal service, enter it as a direct subheading of the name of the government.

United States. *Army Map Service"*

NBM 2

Outside the scope of this code. The reader would consult AACR 2.

4D   DYMAXION SKY-OCEAN WORLD

DESCRIPTION OF ITEM

Components: one "dymaxion" (a globe-like, three-dimensional representation of the earth made of 20 triangular faces); with base.

Colored, made of cardboard

18 centimeters high, 18 centimeters wide

Base:

DYMAXION SKY-OCEAN WORLD	The Fuller Projection R. Buckminster Fuller and Shoji Sadao Cartographers	Copyrighted 1967

SCALE VARIES APPROXIMATELY FROM 1:47,500,000 TO 1:57,000,000

Publisher's brochure:

Dymaxion Artefacts, Philadelphia, Pa.

A reference source explains that the dymaxion projection system divides the globe into twenty equilateral spherical triangles, which are then flattened to form the icosahedron.

CATALOG RECORD

Fuller, R. Buckminster.
Dymaxion sky-ocean world / R. Buckminster Fuller and Shoji Sadao, cartographers. — Scale 1:47,500,000-1:57,000,000 ; Fuller proj. — Philadelphia, Pa. : Dymaxion Artefacts, c1967.
1 globe : col., cardboard, mounted on cardboard stand ; 18 cm. in diam.
The dymaxion projection system divides the globe into twenty equilateral spherical triangles, which are then flattened to form the icosahedron.

I. Sadao, Shoji. II. Title.

─────────────

(Shows option to omit GMD)

─────────────

SCOPE / CATEGORIZATION

AACR 2

3.0A. (Cited in #4A)

Rule continues: "The rules in this chapter cover ... three-dimensional maps ... globes ..."

NBM 2

p. 38:
Chapter title: "Globes"
"*Globe*: a sphere representing the earth, other celestial bodies, or the universe."

Comment

While the scope of AACR 2's chapter 3 will encompass all three-dimensional cartographic materials, some compromise will have to be made with the chapter categorizations in NBM 2. Since the object in question here is not spherical, it will not fit the definitions for this format given in NBM 2; however, its three-dimensional nature would make it more similar to a globe than to a map.

SOURCES OF INFORMATION

AACR 2

3.0B2.: item itself (Cited in #4A)

Rule continues: "The chief source of information (in order of preference) is:
a) the cartographic item itself ...

AACR 2 (cont'd)

b)   container ... or case, the cradle and stand of a globe, etc.
If information is not available from the chief source, take it from any accompanying printed material (pamphlets, brochures, etc.)"

NBM 2

p. 38:
"Information for the catalogue record is taken from the following sources in this order[31]
1.   The item itself (Chief source of information)
2.   Cradle and stand (Chief source of information);"

p. 124 (Appendix A—Notes):
"31.   Container, cradle, and stand have not been given a hierarchy in 3.0B2. This seems a sensible order."

TITLE PROPER

AACR 2

3.1B1: as in 1.1B

1.1B1: transcribed exactly except for punctuation, capitalization (Cited in #4B)

NBM 2

p. 18: exactly from chief source except for capitalization, punctuation (Cited in #4B)

*GENERAL MATERIAL DESIGNATION

AACR 2

3.1C1: as in 1.1C

1.1C1: North American list

3.1A1: square brackets

A.4G: lowercase (Cited in #4A)

p. 566 (Glossary):
"**Globe.** The model of a celestial body, usually the earth or the celestial sphere, depicted on the surface of a sphere."

---

*Option to include general material designation not applied.

NBM 2

p. 9: North American list

p. 18: lowercase, singular, square brackets; follows title proper (Cited in #4A)

Comment

This example lends support to the argument that the terms for cartographic materials in the North American list of general material designations are too limited in scope. As long as maps are commonly understood to be two-dimensional, and globes defined as spherical in shape, neither term will be a precise fit in this case. As suggested earlier in the discussion on scope/categorization, the term *globe* would appear to be preferable because it implies three-dimensionality. The Library of Congress will not display the general material designation for globes.

STATEMENTS OF RESPONSIBILITY

AACR 2

3.1F1: as in 1.1F

1.1F1: record in form appearing on item (Cited in #4B)

NBM 2

p. 18: wording and order found on source (Cited in #4B)

MATHEMATICAL DATA AREA

AACR 2

3.3B1: give scale as representative fraction

3.3A1: punctuation (Cited in example #4A, amplified by #4C)

3.3B3. "If the scale within one area varies and the outside values are known, give both scales connected with a hyphen."

3.3C1: projection (Cited in #4C)

NBM 2

p. 38:
"Mathematical data area
Scale. See Maps pages 48-53"

p. 48 (Rules for scale cited in example #4A, projection in #4C)

Comment

It is stated on the item that the scale varies approximately; however, I have decided against indicating this fact with the term *ca.* since this term is used in cases in which the scale has been estimated by the cataloger.

PUBLICATION, DISTRIBUTION, ETC., AREA

AACR 2

3.0B3. "Prescribed sources of information....

AREA	PRESCRIBED SOURCES OF INFORMATION
Publication, distribution, etc.	Chief source of information, accompanying printed material"

3.4C1: as in 1.4C (Cited in #4A)

1.4C1: place of publication in form on item

1.4C3: add name of state (Cited in #4B)

3.4D1: as in 1.4D (Cited in #4A)

1.4D2: name of publisher (Cited in #4B)

3.4F1: as in 1.4F (Cited in #4A)

1.4F6: copyright date (Cited in #4B)

NBM 2

pp. 19, 20: name of place as given on item; add state; name of publisher, copyright date (Cited in #4B)

Comment

Rule 3.0B2 of AACR 2 states that "accompanying printed material" can include brochures; thus the place and publisher are not bracketed here.

PHYSICAL DESCRIPTION AREA — EXTENT OF ITEM

AACR 2

3.5B1 (Cited in example #4A)

Rule continues:
*"If the cartographic item is not comprehended by one of the above terms, use an appropriate term (preferably taken from rule 5.B of one of the chapters of Part I)."

NBM 2

p. 38:
"List the number of globes ..."

Comment

As with the use of the term *globe* as a general material designation, one could again raise the question as to the appropriateness of this term for an object that is not spherical. Presumably, AACR 2 would allow a more appropriate term to be substituted, if one could be determined.

PHYSICAL DESCRIPTION AREA—OTHER PHYSICAL DETAILS

AACR 2

3.5C3: color (Cited in example #4A)

3.5C4: material (Cited in example #4C)

3.5C5. "**Mounting.** If the item is mounted or has been mounted subsequent to its publication, indicate this.

> 1 globe : col. wood, mounted on brass stand"

NBM 2

p. 38:
"List col. or b&w, the material from which the globe was made, if significant, and the mounting."

Comment

It would seem appropriate to note the material here, since most globes are not made of cardboard.

PHYSICAL DESCRIPTION AREA—DIMENSIONS

AACR 2

3.5D4. "**Globes.** For globes, give the diameter, specified as such."

---

*Rule considered but not applied.

NBM 2

p. 38:
"List the diameter in centimetres followed by the phrase 'in diam.' "

NOTE AREA

AACR 2

1.7A5. "When appropriate, combine two or more notes to make one note."

3.7B1: nature and scope (Cited in example #4A)

3.7B10: physical description (Cited in example #4B)

NBM 2

p. 22:
nature, scope (Cited in example #4A)

physical description (Cited in example #4B)

CHOICE OF ACCESS POINTS

AACR 2

21.1A1. "A personal author is the person chiefly responsible for the creation of the intellectual or artistic content of a work. For example, ... cartographers are the authors of their maps ..."

21.6C1. "If responsibility is shared between two or three persons or bodies and principal responsibility is not attributed to any of them by wording or layout, enter under the heading for the one named first. Make added entries under the headings for the others.

NBM 2

p. 18 (General rules):
"A work for which authorship can be clearly established is entered under author. ... For example, ... cartographers are the authors of their maps ..."

NOTES

1. Minutes of the first meeting of the Anglo-American Cataloguing Committee for Cartographic Materials, Ottawa, October 1-5, 1979, pp. 5, 6.

2. Library of Congress, Processing Services, *Cataloging Service Bulletin*, no. 12 (Spring 1981), p. 10.

3. *CSB*, no. 7 (Winter 1980), p. 3.

5

SOUND RECORDINGS

Aural media in AACR 2 are grouped together in the chapter on sound recordings, and include recordings on discs, tapes, rolls, and film. For sound recordings of musical works, the cataloger must also consult the chapter on music scores (5) and the chapter on uniform titles (25).

AACR 2 introduced a major change in the rules for main entry of sound recordings by allowing, in some instances, for the performer to be considered as the "author" of a work. Notable changes occur also in the transcription of publication data. The copyright date is no longer recorded with the designation "p", and the publisher's number is no longer given after the publisher's name. Instead, the transcription of publication data and numbers is made more consistent with the description of other materials.

Policy statements issued by the Library of Congress on the cataloging of sound recordings are documented in the *Music Cataloging Bulletin*. These policy statements are frequently updated and revised.

Recent articles on the description of sound recordings include:

1. C. P. Ravilious, "AACR 2 and Its Implications for Music Cataloguing," *Brio* 16 (Spring 1979).

2. Sam Richmond, "Problems in Applying AACR 2 to Music Materials," *Library Resources and Technical Services* 26 (April/June 1982).

3. Ben R. Tucker, "Some Miscellaneous Notes about AACR 2 Rule Interpretations Being Developed at the Library of Congress," *Music Cataloging Bulletin* 11 (February 1980).

4. Ben R. Tucker, "More AACR 2 Rule Interpretations Being Developed at the Library of Congress," *Music Cataloging Bulletin* 11 (September 1980).

The catalog records in the following examples will reflect AACR 2. It should be noted that the Library of Congress has decided to give the publisher's number as the first note, instead of the last as prescribed by AACR 2.

5A POWER!

DESCRIPTION OF ITEM

Components: 1 tape cassette, in container
Dimensions of cassette: 3⅞ x 2½ inches (height x width)
Tape width: ⅛ inch

No indication of number of tracks, playing speed, or number of sound channels (e.g., mono., stereo.).

Cassette label:

Success Motivation® Cassette Tapes

POWER! HOW TO GET IT,
HOW TO USE IT

By Michael Korda

05588

Performing Rights℗1976, Success Motivation® Institute, Inc.
P.O. Box 7614, Waco, Texas 76710
Condensed from the book Copyright© 1975, Michael Korda and Paul Gitlin

---

Container label:

Success Motivation Cassette Tapes

Presents

POWER!
How to get it,
How to use it

MICHAEL KORDA

SMI

Success Motivation Institute, Inc.
5000 Lakewood Dr., Waco, Texas 76710

Packaging label:

Running Time: 60 minutes

Promotional brochure:

Analyzes uses and abuses of power in the business world.

CATALOG RECORD

> Korda, Michael.
> Power! [sound recording] : how to get it, how to use it / by Michael Korda. — Waco, Tex. : Success Motivation Institute, c1976.
> 1 sound cassette (60 min.) : 1 ⅞ ips, 2 track, mono.
> Condensed from the book of the same title, c1975.
> Summary: Analyzes uses and abuses of power in the business world.
> Success Motivation Institute: 05588.
>
> I. Title.

LC policy differences:

1. LC will not include *mono.* if not indicated on item.

2. LC will give publisher's number as the first note.

SCOPE / CATEGORIZATION

AACR 2

6.0A. "The rules in this chapter cover the description of sound recordings in all media, i.e., discs, tapes (open reel-to-reel, cartridges, cassettes) ..."

NBM 2

p. 80:
Chapter title: "Sound recordings"
"*Sound recording*: a recording on which sound vibrations have been registered by mechanical or electronic means so. that the sound may be reproduced."

"Discs, ... tapes (open reel-to-reel, cartridge, and cassette), ... are included under this heading ..."

SOURCES OF INFORMATION

AACR 2

6.0B1. "Chief source of information. ...

TYPE	CHIEF SOURCE
...	...
Tape cassette	Cassette and label

If information is not available from the chief source, take it from the following sources (in this order of preference):
accompanying textual material
container (sleeve, box, etc.)
other sources"

Footnote:
"In this list *label* means any permanently affixed paper, plastic, etc., label as opposed to the container itself, which may have data embossed or printed on it."

NBM 2

p. 80:
"Information for the catalogue record should be taken from the following sources in this order:
1. The item itself (Chief source of information), e.g., the permanently affixed labels on discs, tape reels, cassettes, and cartridges;
2. Accompanying textual material;
3. Container;
4. Other sources."

TITLE PROPER

AACR 2

6.1B1. "Record the title proper as instructed in 1.1B."

1.1B1. "Transcribe the title proper exactly as to wording, order, and spelling, but not necessarily as to punctuation and capitalization."

1.0C. "When punctuation occurring within or at the end of an element is retained, give it with normal spacing. Prescribed punctuation is always added, even though double punctuation may result."

NBM 2

p. 18 (General rules):
"The title proper ... is copied exactly from the chief source of information. However, capitalization and punctuation follow prescribed rules."

GENERAL MATERIAL DESIGNATION

AACR 2

6.1C1. (Optional). "Add immediately following the title proper the appropriate general material designation (see 1.1C)."

1.1C1. "If general material designations are to be used in cataloguing, ... North American agencies [should use] terms from list 2."

6.1A1. "Enclose the general material designation in square brackets."

(Appendix A — Capitalization):
A4G. "Lowercase the words making up a general material designation."

p. 570 (Glossary):
"**Sound recording.** A recording on which sound vibrations have been registered by mechanical or electrical means so that the sound may be reproduced."

NBM 2

p. 9 (Chapter on cataloging policy for media centers):
"The North American list of general material designations is used in this book. Those electing [to omit the general material designation or to use] the British list ... or the ISBD list may use the rules on the following pages by disregarding the general material designation or by substituting the appropriate term from the British or ISBD lists."

p. 18 (General rules):
"A general material designation is listed in lower case letters, in the singular, and in its own square brackets immediately following the title proper."

p. 80:
"[Tapes] (... cassette) ... are ... designated by the term 'sound recording.' "

Comment

The Library of Congress will display the general material designation for sound recordings.

OTHER TITLE INFORMATION

AACR 2

6.1E1. "Record other title information as instructed in 1.1E."

1.1E1. "Transcribe all other title information appearing in the chief source of information according to the instructions in 1.1B."

NBM 2

p. 18 (General rules):
"Other title information ... follows the general material designation and the title proper ... to which it pertains. [It is] listed in the exact wording found in the chief source of information."

STATEMENTS OF RESPONSIBILITY

AACR 2

6.1F1. "Record statements of responsibility relating to writers of spoken words ... as instructed in 1.1F."

1.1F1. "Record statements of responsibility appearing prominently in the item in the form in which they appear there."

NBM 2

p. 81:
"*Statements of responsibility.* Persons or groups are listed in this area if they are authors of spoken sound recordings ..."

p. 18 (General rules):
"The statement(s) of responsibility is listed wherever possible in the wording and order found on the source(s) of information."

PUBLICATION, DISTRIBUTION, ETC., AREA

AACR 2

6.4C1. "Record the place of publication, distribution, etc., as instructed in 1.4C."

1.4C1. "Record the place of publication, etc., in the form ... in which it appears."

*1.4C3. "Add the name of the country, state, province, etc., to the name of the place if it is considered necessary for identification, or if it is considered necessary to distinguish the place from others of the same name."

6.4D1. "Record the name of the publisher, etc., as instructed in 1.4D."

1.4D2. "Give the name of a publisher, distributor, etc., in the shortest form in which it can be understood and identified internationally."

6.4F1. "Record the date of publication, distribution, etc., as instructed in 1.4F."

---

*For LC rule interpretation, see example #4B, p. 81.

1.4F6. "If the dates of publication, distribution, etc., are unknown, give the copyright date ... in its place."

NBM 2

pp. 19, 20 (General rules):
"List the name of the place as it appears on the item and add the name of the province, state, country, etc., if it is necessary for identification."

"List the name of the publisher, producer, distributor, etc., in the shortest form that can be identified internationally."

"If the dates of publication or distribution cannot be ascertained, list the copyright date ..."

Comment

The copyright date for sound recordings is usually indicated on an item by the symbol "p". In the revised chapter 14 of AACR, the cataloger was instructed to use this symbol in recording the copyright date for sound recordings. In AACR 2, however, the notation of copyright date for sound recordings is made consistent with the treatment of other materials.***

The LC rule interpretations include the following:

"6.4F1. All copyright dates must be preceded by the 'c' symbol. This means that if the cataloger wishes to use a copyright date in the publication, distribution, etc., area (in accordance with 1.4F6) record 'p1980' as 'c1980.' "[1]

PHYSICAL DESCRIPTION AREA—EXTENT OF ITEM

AACR 2

*6.5B1. "Record the number of physical units of a sound recording by giving the number of parts in arabic numerals and one of the following terms as appropriate:

sound cartridge	sound tape reel
sound cassette	...
sound disc	"

**"*Optionally*, if general material designations are used and the general material designation includes the word *sound*, drop the word *sound* from all of the above terms except [sound track film]."

---

*The terms listed in this rule citation include only those designations which will be used for the examples in this chapter.

**Option not applied in this example.

***Currently being reconsidered by the Joint Steering Committee.

AACR 2 (cont'd)

6.5B2. "Add to the designation the stated total playing time of the sound recording in minutes (to the next minute up) unless the duration is less than 5 minutes ..."

NBM 2

p. 81:
*"List the number of sound cartridges, sound cassettes, sound discs ..."

**"*Option.* If a general material designation is used, the word 'sound' may be omitted from all specific material designations except 'sound page' ..."

"List in parentheses after the specific material designation the total playing time stated on the item, its packaging, or its accompanying material."

p. 109 (Glossary):
"Cassette—An enclosed container for film or magnetic tape in reel-to-reel format."

Comment

The Library of Congress will not apply option 6.5B1.

PHYSICAL DESCRIPTION AREA—OTHER PHYSICAL DETAILS

AACR 2

6.5C3. "**Playing speed.** ... Give the playing speed of a tape in inches per second (ips)."

6.5C6. "**Number of tracks.** For tape cartridges, cassettes, and reels, give the number of tracks, unless the number of tracks is standard for that item.[1]"

Footnote:
"1. The standard number of tracks for a cartridge is 8, for a cassette 4."

6.5C7. "**Number of sound channels.** Give one of the following terms as appropriate:

      mono.
      stereo."

---

*The terms listed in this rule citation include only those designations which will be used for the examples in this chapter.
**Option not applied in this example.

NBM 2

p. 81:
"*Tapes.* List playing speed in inches per second (ips). List number of tracks only if it is not standard for the item. List mono., stereo. ... as appropriate."

Comment

The recording mode and number of tracks are not indicated on the item; however, a spoken word recording is not likely to be issued in stereo, and the presence of stereo is usually so indicated. A monaural recording will usually have two tracks. A playing speed of 1⅞ is standard for the format.

The *Music Cataloging Bulletin* (March 1981) notes that the Music Section at the Library of Congress has made the following decision: "6.5C7. When the number of sound channels is not stated explicitly, do not record any term."

PHYSICAL DESCRIPTION AREA—DIMENSIONS

AACR 2

*6.5D5. "**Sound cassettes.** Give the dimensions of the cassette if they are other than the standard dimensions (3⅞ x 2½ in.) in inches, and the width of the tape if other than the standard width (⅛ in.) in fractions of an inch."

NBM 2

p. 81:
*"*Cassettes.* List the dimensions in inches only if they are other than 3⅞ x 2½ in.

*List the width of the tape in fractions of an inch only if it is other than ⅛ in."

NOTE AREA

AACR 2

6.7B7. "**Edition and history.** Make notes relating ... to the history of the recording."

6.7B17. "**Summary.** Give a brief objective summary of the content of a sound recording (other than one that consists entirely or predominantly of music) unless another part of the description provides enough information."

---

*Rule must be considered, to determine that no statement of dimensions is given.

AACR 2 (cont'd)

6.7B19. **"Notes on publishers' numbers.** Give the publisher's alphabetic and/or numeric symbol as found on the item. Precede the number(s) by the label name and a colon."

NBM 2

p. 22 (General rules):
"[I]nformation which may be given in notes is listed in the following order:

...

Edition and history

...

Summaries.* These are not necessary for media which can be readily examined or adequately described by title and/or series statement."

p. 81:
"List label name and publishers' numbers."

Comment

The Library of Congress will record the note on publishers' numbers as the first note.[2]

CHOICE OF ACCESS POINTS

AACR 2

21.23A. "Enter a sound recording of one work (music, text, etc.) under the heading appropriate to that work."

21.12A. "Enter an edition that has been revised, ... condensed, etc., under the heading for the original if the person or body responsible for the original is named in a statement of responsibility ..."

21.4A. "Enter a work ... by one personal author ... under the heading for that person ..."

NBM 2

p. 80:
"1. The work(s) of one composer or author are entered under the name of that composer or author ..."

p. 18 (General rules):
"1. A reproduction of a work originally produced in another medium is entered in the same manner as the original work."

---

*Rule considered but not applied.

5B   HOPKINS

DESCRIPTION OF ITEM

Components: 1 tape cassette, in container
1 instruction booklet

Dimensions of cassette: 3⅞ x 2½ inches (height x width)
Tape width: ⅛ inch

No indication of number of tracks, playing speed, or number of sound channels.

Cassette label, front:

Classification
Exercise - Dewey 800's

Cassette label, back:

By Judith Hopkins

Container label:

Classification   Exercise

Instruction booklet:

Self-Instructional Unit: Classifying With Dewey System - The 800's
[Literature]
Unit Contents: Three printed pages of instructions and sample problems; One cassette tape recording
Time: Running time of tape recording - 21 minutes
Additional Items Needed: One cassette tape recorder (or playback unit), a copy of the Dewey Schedules, and a copy of the Dewey Tables, (18th ed.)

CATALOG RECORD

Hopkins, Judith.
Classification exercise [sound recording] : Dewey 800's / by Judith Hopkins.
1 sound cassette (21 min.) : 1⅞ ips, 2 track, mono. + 1 booklet.
Summary: Instructions on the classification of literature according to the 800's section of the Dewey Decimal System, 18th ed. Sample problems included.

I. Title.

SCOPE / CATEGORIZATION

AACR 2

6.0A: chapter covers tape cassettes (Cited in #5A)

NBM 2

p. 80: "Sound recordings" chapter; includes tape cassettes (Cited in #5A)

p. 99:
Chapter title: "Locally-Produced, Noncommercial Materials[64]"
"A media centre's collection may include locally-produced, noncommercial materials. These may be ... items which are produced by the students or staff of, and for use in, an institution."

p. 126 (Appendix A — Notes):
"64. This section has been drawn from 6.11, 8.4A2, 10.4C2, 10.4D2, and 10.4F2."

SOURCES OF INFORMATION
AACR 2

6.0B1: cassette and label, accompanying material, container (Cited in #5A)

NBM 2

p. 80: item itself and label, accompanying material, container (Cited in #5A)

TITLE PROPER

AACR 2

6.1B1: as in 1.1B

1.1B1: transcribed exactly except for punctuation, capitalization (Cited in #5A)

NBM 2

p. 18: exactly from chief source, except for punctuation, capitalization (Cited in #5A).

GENERAL MATERIAL DESIGNATION

AACR 2

6.1C1: follows title proper

1.1C1: North American list

6.1A1: square brackets

A.4G: lowercase

p. 570: definition of sound recording (Cited in #5A)

NBM 2

p. 9: North American list

p. 18: lowercase, singular, brackets; follows title proper

p. 80: sound recording (Cited in #5A)

OTHER TITLE INFORMATION

AACR 2

6.1E1: as in 1.1E

1.1E1: transcribe as in 1.1B (Cited in #5A)

NBM 2

p. 18: exact wording found in source (Cited in #5A)

STATEMENTS OF RESPONSIBILITY

AACR 2

6.1F1: as in 1.1F

1.1F1: record in form appearing on item (Cited in #5A)

NBM 2

p. 81: list authors of spoken sound recordings

p. 18: record wording and order found on source (Cited in #5A)

PUBLICATION, DISTRIBUTION, ETC., AREA

AACR 2

Footnote, p. 163:
"Nonprocessed sound recordings are noncommercial instantaneous recordings, generally existing in unique copies."

6.11A.   "Follow the rules for sound recordings (6.1-6.10) as far as possible in describing nonprocessed recordings."

6.11C.   "Do not give any information in the publication, etc., area."

NBM 2

p. 99 (Chapter on locally produced, noncommercial materials):
"If the 'author' is also responsible for the manufacture of the item and is named in the statement of responsibility, the name, together with the place, is not repeated in the publication/distribution area."

Comment

Noncommercial sound recordings are regarded in AACR 2 as "unpublished"; thus no publication data are given. NBM 2's chapter on locally produced materials is applied here in conjunction with the chapter on sound recordings.

The date of recording, if known, would be given in a note. In this example, the information given in the publication area is the same in NBM 2 as in AACR 2. Note, however, that NBM 2 is more restrictive in the application of its rule than is AACR 2 in the corresponding rule (6.11C) for omission of publication data. NBM 2's rule continues:

"If the author is not responsible for the production or manufacture of the item, the name of the manufacturer is given in parentheses following the date ..."

PHYSICAL DESCRIPTION AREA—EXTENT OF ITEM

AACR 2

6.5B1: sound cassette

6.5B2: playing time (Cited in #5A)

NBM 2

p. 81: sound cassette; playing time

p. 109: definition of cassette (Cited in #5A)

PHYSICAL DESCRIPTION AREA — OTHER PHYSICAL DETAILS

AACR 2

6.5C3: playing speed

6.5C6: number of tracks only if not standard

6.5C7: sound channels — mono.

(Cited in #5A)

NBM 2

p. 81: playing speed, number of tracks only if not standard, mono. (Cited in #5A)

PHYSICAL DESCRIPTION AREA — DIMENSIONS

AACR 2

6.5D5: cassette dimensions and tape width given only if other than standard (Cited in #5A)

NBM 2

p. 81: cassette dimensions and tape width given only if other than standard (Cited in #5A)

PHYSICAL DESCRIPTION AREA — ACCOMPANYING MATERIAL

AACR 2

6.5E1.   "Record the name, and *optionally** the physical description, of any accompanying material as instructed in 1.5E."

1.5E1.   "There   are   four   ways   of   recording   information   about accompanying material:

a)   record the details ... in a separate entry
or   b)   record the details ... in a multilevel description ...
or   c)   record the details ... in a note ...
or   d)   record the name of accompanying materials at the end of the physical description."

6.5A1.   "**Punctuation.** ... Precede a statement of accompanying material by a plus sign."

---

*Option not applied in this example.

NBM 2

p. 21 (General rules):
"If an item contains two or more media, one of which is clearly predominant, it is catalogued by the dominant medium and the subordinate accompanying material may be listed after the dimensions."

"*Punctuation.* The statement of accompanying material is preceded by a space-plus sign-space (+)."

Comment

The Library of Congress rule interpretations include the following:

Generally record material at the end of the physical description area when the item satisfies all the following conditions:
  a) It is issued at the same time and by the same publisher as the main work and essentially is of use only in conjunction with the main work.
  b) It is by the same author as the main work ...
  c) The title is a general term (e.g., 'teacher's manual') or is otherwise dependent on the title of the main work ...[3]

NOTE AREA

AACR 2

6.7B17: summary (Cited in #5A)

NBM 2

p. 22: summaries (Cited in #5A)

CHOICE OF ACCESS POINTS

AACR 2

21.23A: if one work, under heading appropriate to the work

21.4A: single personal authorship, under heading for person (Cited in #5A)

NBM 2

p. 80: work of one author under name of author (Cited in #5A)

5C SINATRA

DESCRIPTION OF ITEM

Components: 1 reel of tape, in container

Diameter of tape reel: 7 inches

Tape width: ¼ inch

_____

Tape label:

reprise 4 track
7½ ips

MY KIND OF BROADWAY
FRANK SINATRA

STEREO   Reprise
                                                FS1015

Side 1

1. I'll only miss her when I think of her 2:50
2. They can't take that away from me 2:40
3. Yesterdays 3:45
4. Nice work if you can get it 2:33
5. Have you met Miss Jones? 2:30
6. Without a song 3:37

Side 2

1. Ev'rybody has the right to be wrong! 2:05
2. Golden moment 3:01
3. Luck be a lady 5:15
4. Lost in the stars 4:08
5. Hello, Dolly! 2:45

Duplicated exclusively on American recording tape
Manufactured and distributed by Stereotape, Inc.

_____

Tape container, side:

Reprise 4 Track 7½ ips   My Kind of Broadway
                                 Frank Sinatra
                                 Reprise   FS 1015

_____

Tape container, back:

FRANK SINATRA Sings the Greatest Songs from Musical Comedy
MY KIND OF BROADWAY

....

Manufactured and Distributed by Stereotape. Beverly Hills, Calif.

[Tape container on back also gives program notes, and the titles of the individual songs, with durations.]

CATALOG RECORD

Sinatra, Frank.
My kind of Broadway [sound recording]. — [United States?] :
Reprise ; Beverly Hills, Calif. : Manufactured and distributed by
Stereotape, [196-?]
1 sound tape reel (36 min.) : 7½ ips, 4 track, stereo. ; 7 in.
Program notes and durations on container.
Eleven songs from musical comedy, sung by Frank Sinatra with
orchestral accompaniment.
Reprise: FS 1015.

I. Title.

SCOPE / CATEGORIZATION

AACR 2

6.0A: chapter covers reel-to-reel tapes (Cited in #5A)

NBM 2

p. 80: "sound recordings" chapter; includes reel-to-reel tapes (Cited in #5A)

SOURCES OF INFORMATION

AACR 2

6.0B1: container if information not available from chief source (Cited in #5A)

Rule continues:

" TYPE	CHIEF SOURCE
...	...
Tape (open reel-to-reel)	Reel and label"

NBM 2

p. 80: label on tape reel; container (Cited in #5A)

TITLE PROPER

AACR 2

6.1B1: as in 1.1B

1.1B1: transcribed exactly except for punctuation, capitalization (Cited in #5A)

NBM 2

p. 18: exactly from chief source, except for punctuation, capitalization (Cited in #5A)

GENERAL MATERIAL DESIGNATION

AACR 2

6.1C1: follows title proper

1.1C1: North American list

6.1A1: square brackets

A.4G: lowercase

p. 570: definition of sound recording (Cited in #5A)

NBM 2

p. 9: North American list

p. 18: lowercase, singular, brackets; follows title proper (Cited in #5A)

p. 80:
"[T]apes (open reel-to-reel ...) ... are ... designated by the term 'sound recording.' "

STATEMENTS OF RESPONSIBILITY

AACR 2

*6.1F1: "If the participation of the person(s) or body (bodies) named in a statement found in the chief source of information goes beyond that of performance, execution, or interpretation of a work (as is commonly the case with 'popular,' rock, and jazz music), record such a statement as a statement of responsibility. If, however, the participation is confined to performance, execution, or interpretation (as is commonly the case with 'serious' or classical music and recorded speech), give the statement in the note area (see 6.7B6)."

NBM 2

p. 81: *"[Persons or groups are listed ... if they are] persons who have contributed more to the recording than performance, execution, or interpretation. Those who function solely as performers, etc., are listed in the note area."

Comment

AACR 2 requires the cataloger to make a judgment as to the nature of the performer's contribution. It was decided in this case not to regard Sinatra's performance as involving more than interpretation, but opinions will certainly differ. Some types of performers are relatively easy to categorize; for example, jazz artists, whose work involves a considerable degree of improvisation. Performers of classical music and recorded speech, for the most part, perform the work as written by the composer or author. However, in the case of a "popular" performer like Sinatra, who lends his own unmistakable style to all his performances, it is difficult to determine whether the contribution goes beyond mere interpretation. The Library of Congress has decided to "accept only the most obvious cases as qualifying for the statement of responsibility" in its application of this rule.[4]

PUBLICATION, DISTRIBUTION, ETC., AREA

AACR 2

6.4C1: as in 1.4C (Cited in #5A)

1.4C6. "If no probable place can be given, give the name of the country, state, province, etc. If, in such a case, the country, state, province, etc., is not certain, give it with a question mark."

*"If no place or probable place can be given, give the abbreviation s.l. (sine loco) ..."

---

*Rule considered but not applied.

6.4D1: as in 1.4D

1.4D2: publisher's name (Cited in #5A)

Rule 6.4D1 continues:
"*Optionally*, record the name of the distributor as instructed in 1.4D."
...

    London : Gandolf Records : Distributed by Middle Earth Co."

1.4D7. "In case of doubt about whether a named agency is a publisher or a manufacturer, treat it as a publisher."

1.4D1. "Give the name of the publisher, distributor, etc., following the place(s) to which it relates."

1.4D3. "Do not omit from the phrase naming a publisher, distributor, etc.:
a) words or phrases indicating the function (other than solely publishing) performed by the person or body"

6.4F1: as in 1.4F (Cited in #5A)

1.4F7. "If no date of publication, distribution, etc., copyright date, or date of manufacture can be assigned to an item, give an approximate date of publication."

NBM 2

p. 20:
*"If the place is unknown, list 'S.l.' in square brackets."

"When more than one publisher appears on the item, list place and corresponding publisher in the following order:
    the first named place and publisher ..."

"If the bodies named perform different functions, e.g., producer and distributor, both are listed."

"If no date can be found, give an approximate date. (See the *Anglo-American Cataloguing Rules*, 2nd edition, rule 1.4F7.)"

Comment

AECT 4 notes that "frequent changes in the existence, organization, names, and locations of recording companies often make it difficult to ascertain where the producer's business office is located." (p. 38).

---

*Rule considered but not applied.

The Library of Congress will apply the following rule interpretation for 1.4C6: "If no probable place can be given, give the name of the country (in its well established English form if there is one."[5]

Stereotape is both a distributor and manufacturer, and is being treated as a distributor here, based on a broad application of rule 1.4D7.

The Library of Congress will apply the option in 6.4D1 for recording the name of the distributor.

PHYSICAL DESCRIPTION AREA—EXTENT OF ITEM

AACR 2

6.5B1: sound tape reel

6.5B2: playing time

(Cited in #5A)

Rule 6.5B2 continues:
"If no indication of duration appears on the item [or] its container ..., give an approximate time if it can be readily established."

NBM 2

p. 81: sound tape reel; playing time (Cited in #5A)

Rule continues:
"If duration is not stated, an approximate time, e.g., (ca. 30 min.), is listed if it can be ascertained easily."

Comment

Since the exact durations are listed for each piece, the total playing time has been calculated from the individual durations. Note the following LC rule interpretation for 6.5B2:

"**6.5B2.** When the total playing time of a sound recording is not stated on the item but the durations of its parts (sides, individual works, etc.) are, if desired add the stated durations together and record the total, rounding off to the next minute if the total exceeds 5 minutes.

Precede a statement of duration by "ca." only if the statement is given on the item in terms of an approximation. Do not add "ca." to a duration arrived at by adding partial durations or by rounding off seconds."[6]

PHYSICAL DESCRIPTION AREA — OTHER PHYSICAL DETAILS

AACR 2

6.5C3: playing speed

6.5C6: number of tracks

6.5C7: number of sound channels — stereo.

(Cited in #5A)

NBM 2

p. 81: playing speed, number of tracks, stereo. (Cited in #5A)

PHYSICAL DESCRIPTION AREA — DIMENSIONS

AACR 2

6.5D6. **"Sound tape reels.** Give the diameter of the reel in inches, *and the width of the tape if other than the standard width (¼ in.) in fractions of an inch."

NBM 2

p. 81:
"*Tape reels.* List the diameter of the reel in inches. *If the tape is other than ¼ in., list the width in fractions of an inch."

NOTE AREA

AACR 2

1.7A5: "When appropriate, combine two or more notes to make one note."

6.7B6. **"Statements of responsibility.** Give the names of performers and the medium in which they perform if they have not already been named in the statements of responsibility and if they are judged necessary for the bibliographic description."

6.7B11. **"Accompanying material.** Make notes on the location of accompanying material if appropriate. ...

Programme notes on container"

6.7B17: summary

6.7B19: publishers' numbers (Cited in #5A)

---

*Rule must be considered, to determine that no statement of width is given.

NBM 2

p. 81:
"List performers and their medium of performance if not given elsewhere in the description, or if appropriate, combine these with a contents note."

p. 22 (General rules):
"Accompanying materials ..."

p. 22: summary (Cited in #5A)

p. 81: publishers' numbers (Cited in #5A)

Comment

The individual songs and their durations can be listed in a contents note, but since the songs are extensive in number, a summary note has been provided instead.

CHOICE OF ACCESS POINTS

AACR 2

21.1A1. "[I]n certain cases performers are the authors of sound recordings ..."

21.23C. "Enter a sound recording containing works by different persons under the heading for the person or body represented as principal performer."

Footnote:
"Principal performers are those given prominence (by wording or layout) in the chief source of information."

NBM 2

p. 80:
"A sound recording which contains musical or literary works composed or written by two or more persons is entered under the principal performer, whether a person or performing group, if up to three principal performers are given prominence in the chief source of information ..."

Comment

Note the following LC rule interpretation for rule 21.23C:

For recordings containing works by different composers or writers, follow the guidelines below in 1) deciding whether or not there are principal performers and 2) identifying the principal performers, if any. Then, if there are one, two, or three principal performers, apply 21.23C; if there are four or more, or if there are none, apply 21.23D.

The use of the term "principal performer" in 21.23C-D can lead to confusion since the term implies a performer who is more important (or, in the words of footnote 5 on p. 314, given greater prominence) than other performers. This interpretation, however, would often produce undesirable results: it would make main entry under the heading for a performer impossible under 21.23C when there is only one performer or when there are only two or three performers who are given equal prominence. It is, therefore, necessary to consider a performer's prominence in relation not only to that given other performers but also to the prominence given other entities, particularly the works performed.

Consider that a recording has a principal performer or principal performers when one or more performers are named in the chief source of information and the wording, layout, typography, etc., of the labels, container, accompanying material, etc., clearly present the activity of the performer(s), rather than the presentation of particular musical or written content, as the major purpose of the recording.[7]

AECT 4 was among the first codes to recognize the performer as an author, and gives the following rationale for this innovation:

> In general, an audiorecording of a work originally produced in another medium is entered in the same manner as the original work. It should be emphasized, however, that the audiorecording is a new work which must be analyzed independently from the original. The transfer from a visual to an aural medium may involve additional significant intellectual and artistic contributions extensive enough to warrant a main entry different from that of the original work, for example, a musical composition in which improvisation is such that the audiorecording is considered an adaption of the original composer's work ... (p. 36).

In contrast to AACR 2, AECT 4 requires the cataloger to judge the importance of the artistic interpretation of the performer or the degree to which the performer is important in identifying the work:

> An audiorecording may be entered under the name of a performer or performing group when the artistic interpretation of a work is considered of prime importance and the name is significant in identifying the work.... Entry under performer may frequently occur in recordings of popular music and in improvisations since the requestor usually identifies them by performer and expects to find the renditions of each performer kept together (p. 37).

5D SGT. PEPPER

DESCRIPTION OF ITEM

Components: 1 tape cartridge; duration not indicated
Dimensions of cartridge: 5¼ x 3⅞ inches (height x width)
Tape width: ¼ inch

Cartridge label, front:

Music from the Movie
As Performed by Abbey Road '78

SGT. PEPPER'S
LONELY HEARTS CLUB
BAND

Springboard
America's Best Buy in Recorded Music

Side label:

Springboard Records
A Product of Springboard International
8295 Sunset Blvd., Los Angeles, CA 90046
© ℗ 1978 Springboard International Records, Inc.

Packaging label:

8-Track Stereo Tape

Another side label:

Music from the movie
SGT. PEPPER'S LONELY HEARTS CLUB BAND   Springboard

As performed by Abbey Road '78   8T-SPB-4111

Back label:

1   Sgt. Pepper's Lonely Hearts Club Band/
With a little help from my friends (Medley)
Strawberry fields forever

Back label: (cont'd)

2   Come together
    Get back
    Got to get you into my life

3   Got to get you into my life (Cont'd)
    Getting better
    The long and winding road

4   The long and winding road, (Cont'd)
    Here comes the sun
    Lucy in the sky with diamonds

CATALOG RECORD

Sgt. Pepper's Lonely Hearts Club Band [sound recording] : music from the movie / as performed by Abbey Road '78. — Los Angeles, CA : Springboard Records, c1978.
1 sound cartridge : 3¾ ips, stereo.
Music and lyrics by John Lennon, Paul McCartney, and George Harrison.
Contents: Sgt. Pepper's Lonely Hearts Club Band / With a little help from my friends (Medley) — Strawberry fields forever — Come together — Get back — Got to get you into my life — Getting better — The long and winding road — Here comes the sun — Lucy in the sky with diamonds.
Springboard: 8T-SPB-4111

I. McCartney, Paul. II. Lennon, John. III. Harrison, George. IV. Abbey Road '78.

SCOPE / CATEGORIZATION

AACR 2

6.0A: chapter covers tape cartridges (Cited in #5A)

NBM 2

p. 80: "sound recordings" chapter; includes tape cartridges (Cited in #5A)

SOURCES OF INFORMATION

AACR 2

6.0B1. **"Chief source of information**

" TYPE	CHIEF SOURCE
...	...
Tape cartridge	Cartridge and label"

NBM 2

p. 80: label on cartridge (Cited in #5A)

TITLE PROPER

AACR 2

6.1B1: as in 1.1B

1.1B1: transcribed exactly except for punctuation, capitalization (Cited in #5A)

NBM 2

p. 18: exactly from chief source, except for punctuation, capitalization (Cited in #5A)

GENERAL MATERIAL DESIGNATION

AACR 2

6.1C1: follows title proper

1.1C1: North American list

6.1A1: square brackets

A.4G: lowercase

p. 570: definition of sound recording (Cited in #5A)

NBM 2

p. 9: North American list

p. 18: lowercase, singular, brackets; follows title proper (Cited in #5A)

p. 80:
"[Cartridge tapes] are ... designated by the term 'sound recording.' "

OTHER TITLE INFORMATION

AACR 2

6.1E1: as in 1.1E

1.1E1: transcribe as in 1.1B (Cited in #5A)

NBM 2

p. 18: exact wording found in source (Cited in #5A)

STATEMENTS OF RESPONSIBILITY

AACR 2

*6.1F1: give statement in note area if participation is confined to performance (Cited in #5A, amplified by #5C)

1.1F12.   "Treat a noun phrase occurring in conjunction with a statement of responsibility as other title information if it is indicative of the nature of the work.

> Characters from Dickens [GMD] : dramatised adaptations / by
> Barry Campbell"

1.1E4.   "If the other title information includes a statement of responsibility ..., and the statement ... is an integral part of the other title information, transcribe it as such."

NBM 2

*p. 81: groups functioning solely as performers listed in note area (Cited in #5A, amplified by #5C)

Comment

Although the contribution of the performing group is limited to performance or execution of the work, AACR 2's rule 6.1F1 has not been applied here. Rule 1.1F12 suggests that the noun phrase is to be treated as other title

---

*Rule considered but not applied.

information, and since the statement of responsibility is considered here as an integral part of the other title information, it is retained, according to 1.1E4.

The Library of Congress provides the following rule interpretation for 1.1F12:

> This statement offers guidance in dealing with one part of the problem caused by having to categorize a statement appearing in the chief source as either "statement of responsibility" or as "other title information."
>
> 1) In some situations it is useful to distinguish between statements of responsibility and other title information on the premise that verbs indicate responsibility and that nouns indicate other title information. If there is no clear demarcation between other title information and a word or phrase indicative of the person's or body's function, place the slash between noun and verb (usually a past participle).

> a report / presented by

> textes / choisis et presentés par

> Text and photographs / prepared by

> a study / conducted by[8]

PUBLICATION, DISTRIBUTION, ETC., AREA

AACR 2

6.4C1: as in 1.4C

1.4C1: place of publication in form on item

1.4C3: add name of state

6.4D1: as in 1.4D

(Cited in #5A)

6.4D2. "If a sound recording bears both the name of the publishing company and the name of a subdivision of that company ..., record the name of the subdivision ... as the name of the publisher."

6.4F1: as in 1.4F

1.4F6: copyright date

Cited in #5A)

NBM 2

pp. 19, 20: name of place as given on item; add state; name of publisher; copyright date (Cited in #5A)

p. 81:
"If the item has both the name of the publisher and a subdivision with a distinctive name or trade name, list the subdivision or trade name rather than that of the parent company."

PHYSICAL DESCRIPTION AREA—EXTENT OF ITEM

AACR 2

6.5B1: sound cartridge

6.5B2: approximate playing time if readily established (Cited in #5A, amplified by #5C)

NBM 2

p. 81: sound cartridge (Cited in #5A, amplified by #5C)

p. 109 (Glossary):
"Cartridge—An enclosed container for film or magnetic tape in an endless loop format."

Comment

The term *cassette* is frequently used to include all types of permanently encased tape formats. The definition provided in NBM 2 aids the cataloger in the selection of the appropriate specific material designation. AECT 4 also gives a definition for *cartridge*: "A permanently encased single reel of film or tape which has the ends joined together to form a loop that provides playback without rewinding ..." (p. 213).

While AACR 2 indicates that an approximate time can be given if it can be readily established, the Library of Congress has decided on the following interpretation of 6.5B2:

> If no durations are stated on the item ..., do not give a statement of duration. Do not approximate durations from the ... type of cassette, etc."[9]

PHYSICAL DESCRIPTION AREA—OTHER PHYSICAL DETAILS

AACR 2

6.5C3: playing speed

6.5C6: number of tracks only if not standard

6.5C7: number of sound channels—stereo. (Cited in #5A)

NBM 2

p. 81: playing speed, number of tracks only if not standard, stereo. (Cited in #5A)

PHYSICAL DESCRIPTION AREA—DIMENSIONS

AACR 2

6.5D4. "**Sound cartridges.** Give the dimensions of the cartridge if they are other than the standard dimensions [(5¼x3⅞ in.)]* in inches, **and the width of the tape if other than the standard width (¼ in.) in fractions of an inch."

NBM 2

p. 81:
*"*Cartridges.* List the dimensions in inches only if they are other than [5¼x3⅞ in.]

**List the width of the tape in fractions of an inch only if it is other than ¼ in."

Comment

NBM 2's general rules on dimensions (p. 21) state that fractions are taken to the next number. This would not be consistent with AACR 2's example in rule 6.5D5 (similar in purpose to the rule considered here for cartridges), in which the dimensions of a cassette are given as "7¼ x 3½ in."

NOTE AREA

AACR 2

6.7B6: statements of responsibility (Cited in #5C)

---

*Incorrectly given as "5¼x7⅞ in."; later corrected in *Cataloging Service Bulletin.*[10]
**Rule must be considered, to determine that no statement is given.

Rule continues:
"Give also statements relating to any other persons or bodies connected with a work that are not named in the statements of responsibility if they are considered important."

6.7B18. "**Contents.** Give a list of the titles of individual works contained on a sound recording."

6.7B19: publishers' numbers (Cited in #5A)

NBM 2

p. 22 (General rules):
"Statements of responsibility. This may include ... statements of responsibility not taken from the chief source of information ..."

"Contents"

p. 81: publishers' numbers (Cited in #5A)

Comment

In this example, a contents note has been given, but a summary note would have been just as appropriate, as in example #5C.

CHOICE OF ACCESS POINTS

AACR 2

21.0B.   "**Sources for determining access points**
Determine the access points for the item being catalogued from the chief source of information for that item ... Use information ... appearing outside the item only when the statements appearing in the chief source of information are ambiguous or insufficient."

21.23D.   "Enter under title a sound recording containing works by different persons or bodies performed by more than three principal performers or having no principal performers."

NBM 2

p. 80:
"A sound recording which contains musical or literary works composed or written by two or more persons and has no principal performers or more than three principal performers is entered:
   (a) Under title, if the sound recording has a collective title for the component parts"

Comment

It was necessary in this case to consult sources outside the item to determine the authorship responsibility situation. While AACR 2's rule 21.0B allows outside sources to be consulted when information in the chief source is "insufficient," the decision as to what constitutes "insufficient" information, and the subsequent decision to pursue the necessary reference sources to uncover the missing data, appear to be left to the cataloger. The songs on this recording were written by members of the Beatles group, but not by the group as a collective body. John Lennon and Paul McCartney, individually, are responsible for all of the songs with the exception of "Here comes the sun," written by George Harrison. Since this example contains works by different persons, rule 21.23C would apply. Another possible approach would be to regard the entire collection of songs as a single work in which three composers have shared responsibility.

This recording has no "principal performer," as defined by LC's rule interpretation of 21.23C, since the activity of the performers is not presented as the major purpose of the recording. Note the following example:

Chief source of information:

SONGS OF THE WOBBLIES
with
Joe Glazer

(Sung by Glazer, with instrumental ensemble; no principal performers)

Main entry under title[11]

5E   DISEASE A MONTH

DESCRIPTION OF ITEM

Components: 1 tape cassette, in container

Dimensions of cassette: 3⅞x2½ inches (height x width)

Tape width: ⅛ inch

No indication of number of tracks, playing speed, or number of sound channels.

This is the first issue of the audio version of the serial.

Tape label:

The Glycogen Storage Diseases

Allan Drash
James Field

October

Disease   Ⓟ1971

a   Year Book Medical Publishers, Inc.

Month   Chicago

Letter from the publisher:

    1. DISEASE A MONTH is being issued in both a printed and tape-cassette version.

    2. The taped version is a condensation of the printed version. However, before the April 1979, issue, the taped version contained the exact reproduction of the text, minus tables and figures.

    The printed version bears the title: DM; Disease-a-month and has an ISSN number of 0011-5029. It began publication in October 1954.

CATALOG RECORD

    Disease-a-month [sound recording]. — Oct. 1971-   . — Chicago : Year Book Medical Publishers, 1971-
    sound cassettes : 1 ⅞ ips, 2 track, mono.
    Each issue has a distinctive title.
    Audio version of the printed serial: DM : Disease-a-month, Oct. 1954-   . ISSN 0011-5029.
    "The taped version is a condensation of the printed version. However, before the April 1979 issue, the taped version contained the exact reproduction of the text, minus tables and figures." — Publisher.

SCOPE / CATEGORIZATION

AACR 2

(Introduction):
    0.23. "The chapters in Part I can be used alone or in combination as the specific problem demands. For example, a difficult problem in describing a serial sound recording might lead the user to consult chapters 1, 6, and 12."

AACR 2 (cont'd)

0.24. "In describing serials, chapter 12 should be used in conjunction with the chapter dealing with the physical form in which the serial is published."

(Chapter on serials):
12.0A. "The rules in this chapter cover the description of serial publications of all kinds and in all media."

p. 570 (Glossary):
"**Serial.** A publication in any medium issued in successive parts bearing numerical or chronological designations and intended to be continued indefinitely."

6.0A: chapter covers tape cassettes (Cited in #5A)

NBM 2

p. 80: "sound recording" chapter; includes tape cassettes (Cited in #5A)

Comment

This item is both a serial and a sound recording. The AACR 2 rules have been organized to allow both aspects of such an item to be described fully. Properties of the item relative to its serial nature can be described using chapter 12. Note that "serial" refers to mode of issuance and is independent of physical format, which is dealt with here in the chapter on the description of sound recordings. NBM 2 includes a few references to serial publications in the chapter on microforms, but the reader would have to consult AACR 2 for fuller detail.

Let us assume in this example that the cataloger expects the library to receive subsequent issues; therefore, the item is treated as a serial.

SOURCES OF INFORMATION

AACR 2

12.0B2. "**Sources of information. Nonprinted serials**
Follow the instructions given at the beginning of the relevant chapter in Part I (e.g., for sources of information for a serial sound recording, see chapter 6)."

6.0B1: cassette and label (Cited in #5A)

1.0H. "**Items with several chief sources of information ...**
"**Single part items.** Describe an item in one physical part from the first occurring chief source of information or that one that is designated as first ..."

NBM 2

p. 80: item itself and label (Cited in #5A)

Comment

Note that AACR 2 refers the reader to the relevant chapter dealing with the physical aspects of a nonprint serial. The rule governing the determination of chief source for the *serial* aspect of the item, however, is contained in the general rules, and corresponds to the rule given for the chief source of information for printed serials (12.0B1). The latter rule states that the first issue of the serial is to be preferred as the chief source.

The Library of Congress has issued the following rule interpretations:

1.0H. Only the subrule "Single part items" applies to serials. Note that it is the first issue published ... that is the basis for the description (cf. 12.0B1), and that this first issue is then a "single part item." (The subrule "Multipart items" is not applicable to serials because the glossary definition of "multipart item" excludes serials.)[12]

12.0B1. The basis for the description is the first issue, not the latest as in pre-AACR 2 rules.

Note that when later issues are received showing differences in the data recorded, one or more details in the record may seem "obsolete" *vis-à-vis* a current issue, but still the record would stand as originally formulated.[12a]

TITLE PROPER

AACR 2

6.1B1: as in 1.1B

1.1B1: transcribed exactly except for punctuation, capitalization (Cited in #5A)

(Chapter on serials):
12.1B1.   "Record the title proper as instructed in 1.1B."

NBM 2

p. 18: exactly from chief source, except for punctuation, capitalization (Cited in #5A)

GENERAL MATERIAL DESIGNATION

AACR 2

6.1C1: follows title proper

1.1C1: North American list

AACR 2 (cont'd)

6.1A1: square brackets

A.4G: lowercase

p. 570: definition of sound recording (Cited in #5A)

NBM 2

p. 9: North American list

p. 18: lowercase, singular, brackets; follows title proper

p. 80: sound recording (Cited in #5A)

NUMERIC AND/OR ALPHABETIC, CHRONOLOGICAL, OR OTHER DESIGNATION AREA

AACR 2

(Chapter on serials):
12.3C1. "If the first issue of a serial is identified by a chronological designation, record it in the terms used in the item. Use standard abbreviations ..."

12.3A1. "**Punctuation.** ... Follow the ... date of the first issue of a serial by a hyphen."

NBM 2

p. 19 (General rules):
"*Mathematical Data or Material Specific Details Area*
*This area is used only with cartographic materials and serials in the sections on globes, maps, and microforms."

p. 125 (Appendix A—Notes):
"It is possible to reproduce cartographic material, and serials (though less likely), in [media other than microforms], e.g., a map on a transparency. If descriptive cataloguing is to be truly consistent, this area should be applied to maps and serials in any format. *However, AACR 2 does not allow this."

---

*Rule considered but not applied.

Comment

At the time of its writing, NBM 2 was under the impression that Area 3 could be applied only to printed materials and microforms. It is readily apparent, however, that NBM 2 would be in full agreement with the idea of allowing Area 3 to be applied to all media formats. AACR 2 is somewhat inconsistent in the way in which it refers to Area 3 in the specific chapters. Rule 6.3 in the chapter on sound recordings states that the material (or type of publication) specific details area is not used for sound recordings. The same rule is given for all other formats except cartographic materials and microforms. What the code meant to imply was that this area is not used for sound recordings in terms of their description as sound recordings; however, Area 3 can be used to describe any format issued as a serial, and chapter 12 on serials applies to all serial aspects of such a publication. This concept may be a bit obscured, however, by rule 11.3B in the chapter on microforms, which instructs the reader to "record the numeric and/or chronological or other designation of a serial microform or a serial reproduced in microform as instructed in 12.3." Thus the reader might easily be led to infer that Area 3 is to be applied to microforms, but not to any other nonprint format.

PUBLICATION, DISTRIBUTION, ETC., AREA

AACR 2

6.4C1: as in 1.4C

1.4C1: place of publication in form on item

1.4C3: add name of state

6.4D1: as in 1.4D

1.4D2: name of publisher

6.4F1: as in 1.4F

1.4F6: copyright date (Cited in #5A)

Chapter on serials):
12.4C1. "Record the place of publication, distribution, etc., as instructed in 1.4C."

12.4D1. "Record the name of the publisher, distributor, etc., as instructed in 1.4D."

12.4F1. "Record the date of publication of the first issue as instructed in 1.4F. Follow the date with a hyphen and four spaces."

NBM 2

pp. 19, 20: name of place as given on item; add state; name of publisher in shortest form; copyright date (Cited in #5A)

PHYSICAL DESCRIPTION AREA—EXTENT OF ITEM

AACR 2

(Chapter on serials):
12.5B1. "For a serial that is still in progress, give the relevant specific material designation (taken from rule 5B in the chapter dealing with the type of material to which the serial belongs, e.g., 11.5B for microform serials) preceded by three spaces."

6.5B1: sound cassette (Cited in #5A)

NBM 2

p. 81: sound cassette

p. 109: definition of cassette (Cited in #5A)

Comment

A statement of duration would be inappropriate, since the serial is still ongoing.

PHYSICAL DESCRIPTION AREA—OTHER PHYSICAL DETAILS

AACR 2

(Chapter on serials):
12.5C1. "Give the other physical details appropriate to the item being described as instructed in rule 5C in the chapter dealing with the type of material to which the serial belongs (e.g., 2.5C for printed serials)."

6.5C3: playing speed

6.5C6: number of tracks only if not standard

6.5C7: sound channels—mono. (Cited in #5A)

NBM 2

p. 81: playing speed, number of tracks only if not standard, mono. (Cited in #5A)

PHYSICAL DESCRIPTION AREA—DIMENSIONS

AACR 2

12.5D1.   "Give the dimensions of the serial as instructed in rule .5D in the chapter dealing with the type of material to which the serial belongs ..."

6.5D5: cassette dimensions and tape width only if other than standard (Cited in #5A)

NBM 2

p. 81: cassette dimensions and tape width only if other than standard (Cited in #5A)

NOTE AREA

AACR 2

1.7A5: notes can be combined (Cited in #5C)

(Chapter on serials):
*12.7B1.   **"Frequency.** Make notes on the frequency of the serial unless it is apparent from the content of the title ..."

12.7B4.   **"Variations in title.** ... If individual issues of a serial (other than a monographic series) have special titles, make a note about this. ...

Each issue has a distinctive title"

12.7B7.   **"Relationships with other serials.** Make notes on the relationships between the serial being described and any immediately preceding, ... or simultaneously published serial.

...

   h)   **Edition.** If a serial is a subsidiary edition differing from the main edition in partial content ..., give the name of the principal edition."

12.7B16.   **"Other formats available.** Make notes on other formats in which a serial is available."

NBM 2

p. 22 (General rules):
"Edition and history"

---

*Rule must be considered, to determine that no frequency note is given.

CHOICE OF ACCESS POINTS

AACR 2

21.23D: title main entry if works by different persons and no principal performers (Cited in #5D)

NBM 2

p. 80: title main entry if works by two or more persons and no principal performers (Cited in #5D)

5F   DEVIENNE

DESCRIPTION OF ITEM

Components: 1 twelve-inch disc, microgroove, 33⅓ rpm, in container.

Disc label:

HNH
Records
Francois Devienne
Concerto No. 2 in D Major for Flute

(P) 1977 HNH Records   1   HNH 4015   STEREO
Incorporated   33⅓

  1. Allegro vivace (9'12")
  2. Adagio cantabile—Rondo (Allegretto) (10'24")

PETER-LUKAS GRAF, flute
ENGLISH CHAMBER ORCHESTRA
RAYMOND LEPPARD, Conductor & Harpsichord

Disc label, side 2:

HNH
Records
Jacques Ibert
Concerto for Flute

(P) 1977 HNH Records   2   HNH 4015   STEREO
Incorporated   33⅓

  1. Allegro (4'55")
  2. Andante (6'30")
  3. Allegro scherzando (8'37")

PETER-LUKAS GRAF, Flute
ENGLISH CHAMBER ORCHESTRA
RAYMOND LEPPARD, Conductor

Container, front:

Devienne   HNH
Concerto No. 2 for Flute & Orchestra   Records
Ibert
Concerto for Flute & Orchestra
PETER-LUKAS GRAF
ENGLISH CHAMBER ORCHESTRA
RAYMOND LEPPARD

Container, back:

Francois Devienne
(1759-1803)
Concerto No. 2 in D Major for Flute
Side 1:
  [Lists movements and durations]

Jacques Ibert
(1890-1962)
Concerto for Flute
Side 2:
  [Lists movements and durations]

1977 HNH Records Incorporated
Post Office Box 222, Evanston, Illinois 60204

(Container, back also includes program notes about the compositions and the performers.)

Container, side:

HNH 4015 Devienne: Flute Concerto No. 2 . Ibert: Flute Concerto - Stereo
Graf . English Chamber Orchestra . Leppard

CATALOG RECORD

(Cataloged as a unit)

Graf, Peter-Lukas.
    Concerto no. 2 in D major for flute / Francois Devienne. Concerto for flute / Jacques Ibert [sound recording]. — Evanston, Ill. : HNH Records, 1977.
    1 sound disc (39 min.) : 33⅓ rpm, stereo. ; 12 in.
    Peter-Lukas Graf, flute ; English Chamber Orchestra, Raymond Leppard, conductor.
    Durations: 19 min., 36 sec.; 19 min., 22 sec.
    HNH Records: HNH 4015

    I. Devienne, Francois, 1759-1803. Concertos, flute, orchestra, no. 2, D major. II. Ibert, Jacques, 1890-1962. Concertos, flute, orchestra. III. Leppard, Raymond. IV. English Chamber Orchestra.

(Cataloged as a separate):

Devienne, Francoise, 1759-1803.
    [Concertos, flute, orchestra, no. 2, D major]
    Concerto no. 2 in D major for flute [sound recording] / Francois Devienne. — Evanston, Ill. : HNH Records, 1977.
    on side 1 of 1 sound disc (20 min.) : 33⅓ rpm, stereo. ; 12 in.
    Peter-Lukas Graf, flute ; English Chamber Orchestra, Raymond Leppard, conductor.
    HNH Records: HNH 4015.
    With: Concertos, flute, orchestra / Jacques Ibert. Evanston, Ill. : HNH Records, 1977.

    I. Graf, Peter-Lukas. II. English Chamber Orchestra. III. Leppard, Raymond.

SCOPE / CHARACTERIZATION

AACR 2

6.0A: chapter covers discs (Cited in #5A)

NBM 2

p. 80: "sound recordings" chapter; includes discs (Cited in #5A)

SOURCES OF INFORMATION

AACR 2

6.0B1: chief source, accompanying material, container (Cited in #5A)

Rule continues:

TYPE	CHIEF SOURCE
"	
...	...
Disc	Label "

"If there are two or more chief sources of information as defined above (e.g., two labels on a disc) treat these as a single chief source."

NBM 2

p. 80: disc label, accompanying material, container (Cited in #5A)

TITLE PROPER

AACR 2

6.1B1: as in 1.1B

1.1B1: transcribed exactly except for punctuation, capitalization (Cited in #5A)

*Rule 6.1B1 continues:
"For data to be included in titles proper for musical items, see 5.1B1."

*5.1B1.   "Record the title proper as instructed in 1.1B. If a title consists of the name(s) of one or more types of composition and one or more of the following statements — medium of performance, key, date of composition, and/or number — record those elements as the title proper."

6.1G1.   "If a sound recording lacks a collective title, *either* describe the item as a unit (see 6.1G2 and 6.1G3) *or* make a separate description for each separately titled work (see 6.1G4)."

(Cataloged as unit):
6.1G2.   "In describing as a unit a sound recording lacking a collective title, record the titles of the individual works as instructed in 1.1G."

1.1G2.   "If, in an item lacking a collective title, no one part predominates, record the titles of the individually titled parts in the order in which they are named in the chief source of information, or in the order in which they appear in the item if there is no single chief source of information."

---

*Altered rule appears in AACR 2 revisions.

AACR 2 (cont'd)

(Cataloged as separates):
6.1G4.   "If desired, make a separate description for each separately titled work on a sound recording. For the description of the extent in each of the descriptions, see 6.5B3. Link the separate descriptions with a note (see 6.7B21). For instructions on sources of information, see 6.0B."

NBM 2

p. 18: exactly from chief source, except for punctuation, capitalization (Cited in #5A)

p. 80:
"4. Items without a collective title may be described in either of two ways:

a)   As a unit ...

b)   In separate entries for each work. These entries are linked by a 'With' note (see *Note area* below ...)"

p. 19 (General rules):
"Items without a collective title may be described in one of the following ways:

...

2.   If no work is predominant, list the titles (and statements of responsibility, if works are by different authors) in the order in which they appear in the chief source of information ...

Punctuation ... If the works are by different authors, the title and statement of responsibility area for each work is separated from the one previously listed by a period and 2 spaces (.).

3.   Make a separate description for each part that has a distinctive title, and link the descriptions in a 'with' note ...

*4.   Supply a collective title[9] and state the reason and/or source of the supplied title in a note ... This method is most useful when there is a large number of parts or when the parts have separate titles which are non-distinctive ..."

p. 123 (Appendix A—Notes):
"9.   1.0A2, 3.1G1 & 3.1G5, and 8.1B2 have been extended to all materials."

Comment

In AACR 2, the cataloger has a choice of describing the recording as one unit or as two separate works, with individual entries for each. NBM 2 provides an additional option (for supplying a collective title) modeled on rules in AACR 2 for cartographic materials and for graphic materials. In applying rule 6.1G1, the

---

*Option not applied in this example.

Library of Congress will describe the item as a unit. For an analogous example, see #4C in the chapter on cartographic materials.

GENERAL MATERIAL DESIGNATION

AACR 2

6.1C1: follows title proper

1.1C1: North American list

6.1A1: square brackets

A.4G: lowercase

p. 570: definition of sound recording (Cited in #5A)

(Chapter on uniform titles):
*25.5E. "*Optionally*, if general material designations are used ..., add the designation at the end of the uniform title."

NBM 2

p. 9: North American list

p. 18: lowercase, singular, brackets; follows title proper

p. 80: sound recording (Cited in #5A)

Rule on p. 18 continues:
"An exception to the placement and bracketing of the general material designation is made for items which are catalogued with a uniform title. The cataloguer has the option of placing a general material designation after the uniform title, capitalized and separated from the uniform title by a period and one space (.). If the uniform title is enclosed in square brackets, the general material designation is included in these brackets."

(Cataloged as unit):
p. 19 (General rules):
**"If an item [without a collective title] has works by different authors, the general material designation is listed after the last statement of responsibility."

Comment

AACR 2 and NBM 2 make optional a practice which was the rule in both the original and the revised chapter 14 of AACR. The Library of Congress will not apply this option.

---

*Option not applied in this example.
**This is indicated through examples in AACR 2's rules 6.12 and 1.1G2.

STATEMENTS OF RESPONSIBILITY

AACR 2

(Cataloged as separates):
6.1F1: as in 1.1F (Cited in #5A)

Rule also includes:
"Record statements of responsibility relating to ... composers of performed music ... as instructed in 1.1F."

1.1F1: record in form appearing on item (Cited in #5A)

(Cataloged as unit):
6.1F1: give statement in note area if participation is confined to performance (Cited in #5A, amplified by #5C)

1.1G2.   "If the individual parts [of an item lacking a collective title] are by different persons ..., follow the title of each part by its ... statements of responsibility and a full stop followed by two spaces."

NBM 2

p. 81: groups functioning solely as performers listed in note area (Cited in #5A, amplified by #5C)

Rule also includes:
"Persons or groups are listed in this area if they are ... composers ..."

PUBLICATION, DISTRIBUTION, ETC., AREA

AACR 2

6.4C1: as in 1.4C

1.4C1: place of publication in form on item

1.4C3: add name of state

6.4D1: as in 1.4D

1.4D2: name of publisher

6.4F1: as in 1.4F (Cited in #5A)

NBM 2

pp. 19, 20: name of place as given on item; add state; name of publisher; date (Cited in #5A)

PHYSICAL DESCRIPTION AREA — EXTENT OF ITEM

AACR 2

6.5B1: sound disc; duration (Cited in #5A, amplified by #5C)

(Cataloged as separates):
6.5B3.   "If the description is of a separately titled part of a sound recording lacking a collective title (see 6.1G4), express the fractional extent in the form *on side 3 of 2 sound discs* ... (if the physical parts are numbered or lettered in a single sequence) ... Follow such a statement by the duration of that part."

NBM 2

p. 81: sound disc (Cited in #5A)

Rule continues:
"Duration for an item without a collective title described as a unit ... is listed in the note area."

Comment

The physical description for this item is determined by the decision made as to the unit to be cataloged. Compare this with example #4C in the chapter on cartographic materials. In both NBM 2 and AACR 2, the duration for the item described as a unit is given in the note area. NBM 2 indicates this procedure in its rules for extent of item, while in AACR 2, the appropriate rule appears in the note area (6.7B10).

PHYSICAL DESCRIPTION AREA—OTHER PHYSICAL DETAILS

AACR 2

6.5C3: playing speed

6.5C7: sound channels—stereo (Cited in #5A)

*6.5C4. "**Groove characteristic.** Give the groove characteristic of a disc if it is not standard for the type of disc.

> 1 sound disc (7 min.) : 78 rpm, microgroove"

NBM 2

p. 81: playing speed, stereo. (Cited in #5A)

Comment

AECT 4 notes that "discs of 33.3 and 45 rpm. are cut in microgroove. Discs of 78 rpm. are cut in standard groove" (p. 41).

NOTE AREA

AACR 2

6.7B6: statements of responsibility (Cited in #5C)

(Cataloged as unit):
6.7B10. "**Physical description.** Indicate important physical details that are not already included in the physical description area.

...

Give the duration of each part of a multipart item without a collective title and described as a unit (see 6.1G2-6.1G3).

> Durations: 17 min. ; 23 min. ; 9 min."

6.7B11: accompanying material (Cited in #5C)

6.7B19: publishers' numbers (Cited in #5A)

(Cataloged as separates):
6.7B21. " **'With' notes.** If the description is of a separately titled part of a sound recording lacking a collective title, make a note beginning *With:* and listing the other separately titled parts of the item in the order in which they appear there. ...

> With: Peer Gynt (Suite) no. 1-2 / Edvard Grieg — Till Eulen-
> spiegels lustige Streiche / Richard Strauss"

---

*Rule considered but not applied.

NBM 2

p. 81: list performers (Cited in #5C)

p. 22 (General rules):
"Additional information concerning the physical description ..."

p. 22: accompanying materials (Cited in #5C)

p. 81: publishers' numbers (Cited in #5A)

(Cataloged as separates):
p. 22 (General rules):
" 'With' notes are used when an item has separately titled parts and no collective title"

Comment

Note the following LC rule interpretations: *1.7B21. "For each item listed in a 'with' note, give the title proper (or uniform title if one has been assigned, the statement of responsibility, and the entire publication, distribution, etc., area."[13]

6.7B10. ... If the individual works in a collection are identified in the title and statement of responsibility area, list the durations of the works in a note.

When recording individual durations in the note area, give them as they appear on the item (e.g., in minutes and seconds if so stated). If only the durations of the parts of a work are stated (e.g., the movements of a sonata), if desired, add the stated durations together and record the total for the work in minutes, rounding off to the next minute.

Do not add "ca." to a duration arrived at by adding partial durations or by rounding off seconds.[14]

CHOICE OF ACCESS POINTS

AACR 2

(Cataloged as unit):
21.1A1: performers can be authors

21.23C: works by different persons under heading for principal performer

(Cited in #5C)

Rule continues:
"If there are two or three persons or bodies [represented as principal performer], enter under the heading for the first named and make added entries under the headings for the others."

---

*A "with" note would be inappropriate in an LC version of this example, since LC would not catalog the item as separates.

AACR 2 (cont'd)

21.30J.   "**Titles.** Make an added entry under the title proper of every work entered under a personal heading ... unless:

...

4)   a conventionalized uniform title has been used in an entry for a musical work (see 25.25-25.36)."

21.30M.   "**Analytical entries.** Make an added entry (analytical) under the heading for a work contained within the work being catalogued ..."

"Make such entries in the form of the heading for the person ... under which the work contained is, or would be, entered. Unless the entry is under title, make the added entry in the form of a name-title heading."

"When appropriate, substitute a uniform title (see chapter 25) for a title proper in a name-title or title analytical entry heading."

(Cataloged as separates):
21.23A: if one work, under heading appropriate to the work

Rule continues:
"Make added entries under the headings for the principal performers ... unless there are more than three."

21.4A: single personal authorship, under heading for person (Cited in #5A)

21.1A1.   "[C]omposers of music are the authors of the works they create ..."

NBM 2

(Cataloged as unit):
p. 80: works by two or more persons, under principal performer (Cited in #5C)

Rule continues:
"[Enter under principal performer] if up to three principal performers are given prominence in the chief source of information."

p. 81:
"If the work for which an added entry is made requires a uniform title, the uniform title must be used in the added entry ..."

"Title added entries are never made for nondistinctive uniform titles which require the name of the composer for accurate identification, e.g., Scherzo, piano, op. 20, A major."

(Cataloged as separates):
p. 80: work of one composer under name of composer (Cited in #5A)

Comment

The choice of main entry is determined according to whether the item is described as a unit, or described separately with one record for each work. In AACR 2, the rule which offers these two options is included among the rules for title proper, but since it is this rule which will determine the choice of main entry, title, statements of responsibility, and many other aspects of description, the decision on whether to catalog the item as a unit or as separates must be the first decision made. In this example, a decision to catalog the item as a unit will result in main entry under heading for the performer, since the disc contains works by two different composers and there are principal performers. According to the criteria in the LC rule interpretation, principal performers are named in the chief source, and the layout and typography of the labels and container present the activity of the performer as the major purpose of the recording:

> Once it has been decided that a recording has principal performers, consider to be principal performers, from among the performers named, those given the greatest prominence in the chief source of information. If all are given equal prominence, consider all to be principal performers.[15]

If cataloged as separates, however, main entry will be under the headings for the individual composers, since in this case each of the items described is the work of a single composer.

Note also the following rule interpretation for the added entries:

> Do not consider a conductor or accompanist to be a member of the body he or she conducts or accompanies.[16]

UNIFORM TITLE

Note: If the recording is cataloged with separate descriptions for each work, uniform titles would be constructed for each of the works. The following citations will identify the rules to be used in constructing the uniform title for the Devienne composition.

AACR 2

(Chapter on uniform titles):
25.1. "Uniform titles provide the means for bringing together all the catalogue entries for a work when various manifestations (e.g., editions, translations) of it have appeared under various titles."

25.27B. "If the title ... consists solely of the name of one type of composition, use the accepted English form of name if there are cognate forms in English, French, German, and Italian, or if the same name is used in all these languages. Give the name in the plural ... unless the composer wrote only one work of the type."

AACR 2 (cont'd)

25.29A1. "Add a statement of the medium of performance if the title consists solely of the name of a type, or the names of two or more types, of composition."

25.29D1. "Use English terms whenever possible [for individual instruments]."

25.29G. "For works for one solo instrument and accompanying ensemble, use the name of the solo instrument followed by the name of the accompanying ensemble.

...

[Concertos, piano, orchestra ...]"

25.31A1. "If the title consists solely of the name(s) of type(s) of composition, add as many of the following identifying elements as can readily be ascertained. Add following the statement of medium of performance and in the order given:

a)   serial number

*b)   opus number or thematic index number

c)   key

Precede each element by a comma."

25.31A2. **"Serial numbers.** If works with the same title and the same medium of performance are consecutively numbered, add the number."

25.31A5. **"Key.** Include the statement of key in the uniform title for pre-twentieth century works. If the mode is major or minor, add the appropriate word."

NBM 2

p. 80:
"A uniform title is necessary to bring together various versions, editions, and arrangements of a work ..."

"Uniform titles are formulated according to the rules outlined in the *Anglo-American Cataloguing Rules*, 2nd edition, chapter 25."

---

*Rule considered but not applied.

NOTES

1.   Library of Congress, Processing Services, *Cataloging Service Bulletin*, no. 11 (Winter 1981), p. 15.

2.   Ibid., p. 15.

3.   Ibid., p. 10.

4.   Ibid., p. 15.

5.   *CSB*, no. 13 (Summer 1981), p. 9.

6.   Ibid., p. 14.

7.   Ibid., p. 22.

8.   *CSB*, no. 12 (Spring 1981), p. 6.

9.   *CSB*, no. 13 (Summer 1981), p. 14.

10.   *CSB*, no. 6 (Fall 1979), p. 2.

11.   *CSB*, no. 13 (Summer 1981), p. 24.

12.   *CSB*, no. 11 (Winter 1981), p. 5.

12a.   Ibid., p. 16.

13.   *CSB*, no. 12 (Spring 1981), p. 15.

14.   *CSB*, no. 13 (Summer 1981), pp. 14-15.

15.   Ibid., pp. 22-23.

16.   Ibid., p. 22.

6

MOTION PICTURES
AND VIDEORECORDINGS

Motion pictures and videorecordings are typically the result of collaborative effort. There has been little agreement as to which of the authorship functions is primary, and as a result, main entry for films is usually under title. However, the problem of determining levels of authorship responsibility involves more than the selection of access points: responsibility can also be ascribed in the statement of responsibility and in the notes areas. The cataloger will find that AACR 2 explicitly allows a great deal of leeway in deciding which of these two areas is to be selected for purposes of ascription. To some extent, there is also leeway—of an implicit kind—in determining main entry, since the authorship for any type of material is defined in terms of the person principally responsible for the intellectual or artistic content of the work, and since views may differ as to whether any one person is primarily responsible for the creation of a given film.

In describing the physical aspects of a film, the cataloger will need to have some familiarity with the various formats in which motion pictures and video-recordings can be issued. Particularly in the case of videorecordings, there is a lack of standardization of formats which often makes it necessary for the cataloger to specify the brand name of an item in order to inform the user of the type of equipment needed for playback.

6A   BONE CRUNCHERS

DESCRIPTION OF ITEM

Components: 1 reel of super 8 millimeter film, color, silent
1 booklet
Both of above in container
Dimensions of container: 8 centimeters (height and width)

Title frame:

National Football League
"Bone Crunchers"
Presented by gaf and the NFL

Container front:

NFL Films'

"Bone Crunchers"

presented by gaf

40 feet
Super 8

Container side:

A super 8 color film of selected NFL action highlights GAF prepared by
Columbia Films for GAF Corporation   NFL

Other side of container:

GAF Corporation
New York, N.Y. 10020

From booklet:

Scene 1

Rams at Packers, Conference Playoff

Long kick-off return by Tom Brown of the Packers. Packers' Jim
Flanigan blocks Jon Kilgore of the Rams, who still manages to make
the tackle.

Publisher's brochure indicates that the film is three minutes, twenty seconds in
length.

CATALOG RECORD

"Bone crunchers" [motion picture] / presented by gaf and the
   NFL. — New York, N.Y. : GAF, [197-?]
   1 film reel (3 min., 20 sec.) : si., col. ; super 8 mm. + 1
guide.
   "A super 8 color film of selected NFL action highlights prepared by
Columbia Films for GAF Corporation" — container.
   Film: 40 feet.
   Summary: Ten scenes of tackles, tumbles, fumbles, and the
like.

   I. National Football League. II. GAF Corporation

SCOPE / CATEGORIZATION

AACR 2

7.0A. "The rules in this chapter cover the description of motion pictures and videorecordings of all kinds ..."

NBM 2

p. 64:
Chapter title: "Motion Pictures"
"*Motion picture*: film, with or without sound, bearing a sequence of images which creates the illusion of movement when projected."

SOURCES OF INFORMATION

AACR 2

7.0B1. "The chief source of information for motion pictures and videorecordings is the film itself (e.g., the title frames) and its container (and its label) if the container is an integral part of the piece (e.g., a cassette).

If the information is not available from the chief source, take it from the following sources (in this order of preference):

> accompanying textual material (e.g., scripts, shot lists, publicity material)
> container (if not an integral part of the piece)
> other sources"

NBM 2

p. 17 (General rules):
"Cataloguing information for the title and statement of responsibility area, the edition area, the publication/distribution, etc., area, and the series area should be taken from the following sources in the order indicated:

1. The material itself ...
2. Accompanying data ...
3. The container, where it is not an integral or unifying part of the item ... and, therefore, may be discarded."

TITLE PROPER

AACR 2

7.1B1. "Record the title proper as instructed in 1.1B."

1.1B1. "Transcribe the title proper exactly as to wording, order, and spelling, but not necessarily as to punctuation and capitalization."

NBM 2

p. 18 (General rules):
"The title proper ... is copied exactly from the chief source of information. However, capitalization and punctuation follow prescribed rules."

GENERAL MATERIAL DESIGNATION

AACR 2

7.1C1. (Optional). "Add immediately following the title proper the appropriate general material designation as instructed in 1.1C."

1.1C1. "If general material designations are to be used in cataloguing, ... North American agencies [should use] terms from list 2."

7.1A1. "Enclose the general material designation in square brackets."

(Appendix A – Capitalization)
A.4G. "Lowercase the words making up a general material designation."

p. 568 (Glossary):
"**Motion picture.** A length of film, with or without recorded sound, bearing a sequence of images that create the illusion of movement when projected in rapid succession."

NBM 2

p. 9 (Chapter on cataloging policy for media centers):
"The North American list of general material designations is used in this book. Those electing [to omit the general material designation or to use] the British list ... or the ISBD list may use the rules on the following pages by disregarding the general material designation or by substituting the appropriate term from the British or ISBD lists."

p. 18 (General rules):
"A general material designation is listed in lower case letters, in the singular, and in its own square brackets immediately following the title proper."

Comment

The Library of Congress will display the general material designation for motion pictures.

STATEMENTS OF RESPONSIBILITY

AACR 2

7.1F1. "Record statements of responsibility relating to those persons or bodies credited in the chief source of information with participation in the production of a film (e.g., as producer, director, animator) who are considered to be of major importance to the film and the interests of the cataloguing agency. Give all other statements of responsibility in notes."

NBM 2

p. 64:
"List those persons or bodies who are considered to be of major importance to the work or to the media centre's patrons. Other persons or bodies who have contributed to the work may be listed in the note area ..."

Comment

GAF and the NFL are indicated as "presenters" of the film, and it is not clear whether they were actually involved in the film's production. Even those qualifying as producers can be relegated to a note, if not considered to be of major importance to the film. Thus an argument could be made for omitting this statement from the statement of responsibility area, and including it in a note instead.

Note, however, the LC interpretation of rule 7.1F1:

> When deciding whether to give names in the statement of responsibility ... or in a note, generally give the names in the statement of responsibility when the person or body has some degree of overall responsibility ...[1]

PUBLICATION, DISTRIBUTION, ETC., AREA

AACR 2

7.4C1. "Record the place of publication, distribution, etc., as instructed in 1.4C."

1.4C. "Record the place of publication, etc., in the form ... in which it appears."

*1.4C3. "Add the name of the country, state, province, etc., to the name of the place if it is considered necessary for identification, or if it is considered necessary to distinguish the place from others of the same name."

7.4D1. "Record the name of the publisher, distributor, releasing agency, etc., and of a production agency or producer not named in the statements of responsibility (see 7.1F) as instructed in 1.4D."

---

*For LC rule interpretation, see example #4B, p. 81.

1.4D2.   "Give the name of a publisher, distributor, etc., in the shortest form in which it can be understood and identified internationally."

7.4F1.   "Record the date of publication, distribution, release, etc., as instructed in 1.4F."

1.4F7.   "If no date of publication, distribution, etc., copyright date, or date of manufacture can be assigned to an item, give an approximate date of publication.

...

, [197-?]   *Probable decade*"

NBM 2

p. 19 (General rules):
"List the name of the place as it appears on the item and add the name of the province, state, country, etc., if it is necessary for identification."

p. 64:
"The publisher, distributor, releasing agent, etc., is listed. A producer or production agency which has not been named in the statement of responsibility is also given."

p. 20 (General rules):
"If no date can be found, give an approximate date. (See the *Anglo-American Cataloguing Rules*, 2nd edition, rule 1.4F7.)"

Comment

Although the producer was named in the statement of responsibility, it is included here since it is the only "publisher" indicated (cf. 7.4D1).

Football buffs acquainted with the players named in the guide will probably be able to give a more precise date.

PHYSICAL DESCRIPTION AREA—EXTENT OF ITEM

AACR 2

*7.5B1.   "Record the number of physical units of a motion picture or videorecording by giving the number of parts in arabic numerals and one of the following terms as appropriate:

film cartridge   videocassette
...   ...
film reel"

---

*The terms listed in this rule citation include only those designations which are used for the examples in this chapter.

AACR 2 (cont'd)

*"*Optionally*, if general material designations are used and the general material designation indicates that the item is a motion picture or videorecording, drop *film* or *video* from all of the above terms."

7.5B2. "Add to the statement of extent the stated total playing time of the item in minutes unless the duration is less than five minutes, in which case give the duration in minutes and seconds."

NBM 2

p. 64:
**"List the number of film cartridges, ... film reels."

*"*Option*. If a general material designation is used, the word 'film' may be omitted from the specific material designation ..."

"List in parentheses after the specific material designation the total playing time stated on the item, its packaging, or its accompanying material."

Comment

The Library of Congress will not apply the option in 7.5B1 to omit the terms *film* or *video*.

PHYSICAL DESCRIPTION AREA—OTHER PHYSICAL DETAILS

AACR 2

7.5C3. "**Sound characteristics.** Indicate the presence or absence of a sound track by the abbreviations *sd.* (sound) or *si.* (silent)."

7.5C4. "**Colour.** Indicate whether an item is in colour or black and white (using the abbreviations *col.* or *b&w.*"

NBM 2

p. 64:
"List sd., si., ..."

"List b&w or col."

---

*Option not applied in this example.

**The terms listed in this rule citation include only those designations which are used for the examples in this chapter.

PHYSICAL DESCRIPTION AREA – DIMENSIONS

AACR 2

7.5D2. "Give the gauge (width) of a motion picture in millimetres. If 8 mm., state whether single, standard, super, or Maurer."

NBM 2

p. 64:
"List width in millimetres. For 8 mm., preface the dimensions with one of the following: Maurer, single, standard, super.

Media centres, which have chosen 1st level description and which contain more than one motion picture format, must have enough information listed in the physical description area to enable the patron to identify necessary equipment. Whether a film is sound or silent and the gauge of the film are essential data for the selection of equipment ..."

p. 21 (General rules):
*"If an item is housed in a container, the type of container may be listed together with its dimensions."

Comment

AECT 4 notes:

For 8mm films it is essential to distinguish between standard and super 8mm formats since each requires a different type of equipment for projection. The super 8 format has smaller sprocket holes and a sixty percent larger image, and the cartridge of a super 8 film differs from that of a standard 8. Super 8mm is always designated ... The notation '8mm' indicates standard 8mm format ... (pp. 154, 155).

PHYSICAL DESCRIPTION AREA – ACCOMPANYING MATERIAL

AACR 2

7.5E1. "Record the name, and *optionally* the physical description,** of any accompanying material as instructed in 1.5E."

1.5E1. "There are four ways of recording information about accompanying material:

(Rule continues on page 166)

---

*Rule considered but not applied.
**Option not applied.

AACR 2 (cont'd)

a) record the details ... in a separate entry

or b) record the details ... in a multilevel description ...

or c) record the details ... in a note ...

or d) record the name of the accompanying material at the end of the physical description."

7.5A1. **"Punctuation.** ... Precede a statement of accompanying material by a plus sign."

NBM 2

p. 21 (General rules):
"If an item contains two or more media, one of which is clearly predominant, it is catalogued by the dominant medium and the subordinate accompanying material may be listed after the dimensions."

"Punctuation. The statement of accompanying material is preceded by a space-plus sign-space (+)."

NOTE AREA

AACR 2

7.7B5. **"Parallel titles and other title information.** Give ... other title information not recorded in the title and statement of responsibility area if they are considered to be important."

7.7B10. **"Physical description.** Make the following notes on the physical description when appropriate and if this level of detail is desired:

...

b) *Length of film or tape.* Give the length in feet of a motion picture (from first frame to last) ..."

7.7B17. **"Summary.** Give a brief objective summary of the content of an item unless another part of the description provides enough information."

NBM 2

p. 22 (General rules):
"Parallel titles and other title information (if not listed in the title and statement of responsibility area)"

p. 64:
"List other physical details which affect use ..."

"*Summary.* An objective and succinct summary of the content and intended use is necessary for many films."

CHOICE OF ACCESS POINTS

AACR 2

21.1C.   "Enter a work under its title when:

...

3)   it emanates from a corporate body but does not fall into one or more of the categories given in 21.1B2 and is not of personal authorship"

NBM 2

The reader would consult AACR 2.

6B   HOW A COW IS MILKED

DESCRIPTION OF ITEM

Components: 1 super 8 millimeter film loop cartridge, color, silent

———————————

Title frame:

> HOW A COW IS MILKED
> > Film 2 from series
> > > THE STORY OF MILK
> > Copyright MCMLXVII
> Society for Visual Education, Inc.

———————————

Label on container front:

> SINGER
> Education & Training Products
> SVE

———————————

Label on container back:

> SU-6
> HOW A COW
> IS MILKED
> SUPER 8MM

———————————

Stamped onto the container is the term "Technicolor."*

Publisher's order catalog:

> The Story of Milk
>
> Full-Color 8mm Loops
>
> Upper Primary-Intermediate
>
> Delightful motion picture films present the story of milk. Each film approx. 4 minutes long.
>
> ...
>
> SU-6-HOW A COW IS MILKED
>
> SU-7-HOW MILK IS PROCESSED
>
> ...
>
> Each Super 8mm Loop $24.00
>
> ...
>
> Society for Visual Education
> Chicago, Ill.

CATALOG RECORD

> How a cow is milked [motion picture]. — Chicago, Ill. : Society for
>   Visual Education, c1967.
>   1 film cartridge (ca. 4 min.) : Technicolor, si., col. ; super
> 8 mm. — (The story of milk ; film 2)
>   Loop film mounted in cartridge.
>   Intended audience: Upper primary-intermediate.
>   "SU-6"
>
> I. Society for Visual Education. II. Series.

Differences in the NBM 2 version (publication and physical description areas):

> How a cow is milked [motion picture]. — [Chicago] : Society for
>   Visual Education, c1967.
>   1 film cartridge (Technicolor) (ca. 4 min.) : si., col. ; super
> 8 mm. — (The story of milk ; film 2)

---

*The term *Technicolor*, in this instance, refers to the brand name of a film cartridge. Thus the term can serve to indicate the type of playback equipment needed.

SCOPE / CATEGORIZATION

AACR 2

7.0A: chapter covers motion pictures (Cited in #6A)

NBM 2

p. 64: "motion pictures" chapter (Cited in #6A)

Rule continues:
"Loops, cartridges ... are included under this heading ..."

SOURCES OF INFORMATION

AACR 2

7.0B1: film itself; publicity material (Cited in #6A)

NBM 2

p. 17: material itself (Cited in #6A)

Rule continues:
"4.   Outside sources, such as ... producer's brochures, etc. If the source of the information is not stated in the note area, the information is enclosed in square brackets."

TITLE PROPER

AACR 2

7.1B1: as in 1.1B

1.1B1: transcribed exactly except for punctuation, capitalization (Cited in #6A)

NBM 2

p. 18: exactly from chief source, except for punctuation, capitalization (Cited in #6A)

GENERAL MATERIAL DESIGNATION

AACR 2

7.1C1: follows title proper

1.1C1: North American list

AACR 2 (cont'd)

7.1A1: square brackets

A.4G: lowercase

p. 568: definition of motion picture (Cited in #6A)

NBM 2

p. 9: North American list

p. 18: lowercase, singular, brackets; follows title proper (Cited in #6A)

p. 64:
"Loops, cartridges ... are ... designated by the term 'motion picture.' "

PUBLICATION, DISTRIBUTION, ETC., AREA

AACR 2

7.0B2. **"Prescribed sources of information. ...**

AREA	PRESCRIBED SOURCES OF INFORMATION
...	...
Publication, distribution, etc.	Chief source of information and accompanying material"

7.0B1: *Accompanying material* includes publicity material (Cited in *sources of information* section of #6A)

7.4C1: as in 1.4C

1.4C1: place of publication in form on item

1.4C3: add name of state

7.4D1: as in 1.4D

1.4D2: name of publisher in shortest form

7.4F1: as in 1.4F (Cited in #6A)

1.4F1.   "Give dates in Western-style arabic numerals."

1.4F6.   "If the dates of publication, distribution, etc., are unknown, give the copyright date ... in its place."

NBM 2

p. 17: information from producer's brochures enclosed in brackets (Cited in *sources of information* section of this chapter)

p. 64: list publisher (Cited in #6A)

p. 20 (General rules):
"If the dates of publication or distribution cannot be ascertained, list the copyright date ..."

Comment

In AACR 2's chapter on motion pictures and videorecordings, the producer's brochure is included among the prescribed sources of information for publication data; thus, the place of publication is not enclosed in brackets. In NBM 2, however, the general rules, which apply to motion pictures, stipulate that data from producers' brochures are to be bracketed.

PHYSICAL DESCRIPTION AREA—EXTENT OF ITEM

AACR 2

7.5B1: film cartridge

7.5B2: playing time (Cited in #6A)

NBM 2

p. 64: film cartridge; playing time (Cited in #6A)

Rule also includes:
"List in parentheses a trade name[46] if the use of the item is conditional upon this information (see sample cards 70 ...)"

p. 65 (Sample card 70, captioned as "sound motion picture loop," has following physical description area):

"1 cartridge (Technicolor) (18 min.) : sd., col. ; super 8 mm. —
(Red China series)."

Footnote for sample card 70:
" '(Technicolor)' [in this example] is a projection requirement for a Technicolor projector, not a statement of colour process."

NBM 2 (cont'd)

p. 125 (Appendix A—Notes):
"46. 7.5B1 applies this only to videorecordings. A trade name is also necessary for motion picture loop cartridges."

p. 109 (Glossary):
"Cartridge—An enclosed container for film or magnetic tape in an endless loop format."

Comment

Although described in the producer's catalog as a film loop, this item falls into the category of "cartridge" because of its enclosed container. The term *loop* is frequently used in common parlance to indicate film tapes in loop format. AACR 2 does not include a definition of this and many other terms used as specific material designations. Note NBM 2's definition of *cartridge*. AECT 4 also gives a definition of this term: "*Cartridge*. A permanently encased single reel of film or tape which has the ends joined together to form a loop that provides playback without rewinding" (p. 213).

AECT 4 also distinguishes a *cartridge* from a *cassette*: "A *cartridge* film is a loop film enclosed in a cartridge; a *cassette* film is mounted in reel-to-reel format and enclosed in a cassette; a *loop* is a short section of film, not enclosed, which has the ends spliced together and is designed to run continuously; ..." (p. 150).

NBM 2 makes a departure from the rules in AACR 2 by allowing the inclusion of a trade name in the statement of extent. The use of the motion picture cartridge is indeed conditional upon the identification of a trade name, since the latter indicates the type of playback equipment needed. Since, in the case of videorecordings, AACR 2 requires that such essential information be given in the statement of extent area, it might be said that NBM 2's interpretation is within the spirit of AACR 2. The only question that might be raised here is whether this information could also be considered as a statement of special projection requirements; if so, the information can be given in the *other physical details* section of the physical description.

The statement of time is recorded here in minutes, even though it is less than five minutes, because the duration given is only an estimate.

PHYSICAL DESCRIPTION AREA—OTHER PHYSICAL DETAILS

AACR 2

7.5C2. "**Aspect ratio and special projection characteristics.** If a film has special projection requirements, record them as succinctly as possible (e.g., Cinerama, Panavision, multiprojector, etc. ...)"

7.5C3: sound

7.5C4: color

(Cited in #6A)

NBM 2

p. 64: sound, color (Cited in #6A)

*Rule on p. 64 also includes:
"If appropriate, list the aspect ratio and special projection characteristics, for example, Cinerama ..."

PHYSICAL DESCRIPTION AREA—DIMENSIONS

AACR 2

7.5D2: width; super 8 mm (Cited in #6A)

NBM 2

p. 64: width; super 8 mm (Cited in #6A)

SERIES AREA

AACR 2

7.6B1. "Record each series statement as instructed in 1.6."

1.6B1. "If an item is one of a series, record the title proper of the series as instructed in 1.1B ..."

1.6G1. "Record the numbering of the item within the series in the terms given in the item."

NBM 2

p. 21 (General rules):
"If applicable, a series statement in parentheses follows the physical description area. The series area in 3rd level cataloguing could include:

title proper of series

...

numbering within series"

---

*Rule considered but not applied.

NOTE AREA

AACR 2

7.7B14. "**Audience.** Make a brief note of the intended audience for a motion picture if one is stated on the item, its container, or accompanying material."

7.7B19. "**Numbers borne by the item.** Give important numbers borne by the item other than ISBNs or ISSNs ..."

NBM 2

p. 22 (General rules):
"Audience level as stated on the item is listed. Such information may not be desirable in a public catalogue, particularly for juvenile and youth collections."

...

"Numbers associated with item other than ISBNs or ISSNs ..."

CHOICE OF ACCESS POINTS

AACR 2

21.1C3: corporate body falls outside 21.1B2—title entry (Cited in #6A)

NBM 2

The reader would consult AACR 2.

6C   LET'S LEARN

DESCRIPTION OF ITEM

Components: 1 reel of 16 millimeter film, colored, sound, approximately
16 minutes in length

1 discussion guide

Both of above in container.

———————————

Title frame at beginning of film:

Let's Learn

The Library and Alternative Learning

———————————

Frame at end of film:

> Writer: Helene Slavens
> Camera / ed. : Charles Slavens
> Sound: Boris Boden
> Sponsor: Ramapo Catskill Library System
> In Cooperation with the New York State Library

Back cover of discussion guide:

> Film and Discussion Guide
> produced by
> Ramapo Catskill Library System
> Middletown, New York 10940

Title on container:

> Let's Learn

Excerpts from discussion guide:

> The 16mm film was directed, written and filmed by Charles and Helene Slavens of Winterscreen, Inc., of New York City. The entire staff of RCLS participated in interpreting the System's functions and those of the public library systems of New York State to Winterscreen ...
> *Let's Learn* depicts how one particular system, the Ramapo Catskill Library System, is responding to ... the movement toward lifelong learning. Only those services available to adult learners through the Ramapo Catskill System and its member libraries are described in the film.

A bibliography is provided. Two of the items cited in the bibliography have an imprint date of 1979.

(Catalog record appears on page 176)

CATALOG RECORD

Ramapo Catskill Library System.
　Let's learn [motion picture] : the library and alternative learning / writer: Helene Slavens. — Middletown, N.Y. : Produced by Ramapo Catskill Library System, [1979?].
　1 film reel (ca. 16 min.) : sd., col. ; 16 mm. + 1 discussion guide.
　Credits: Camera and editing, Charles Slavens ; sound, Boris Boden.
　Summary: Shows how public library systems can respond to needs of adult learners, as illustrated by the services available through the Ramapo Catskill Library System and its member libraries. Made in cooperation with the New York State Library.

　I. Slavens, Helene.　II. Title.

SCOPE / CATEGORIZATION

AACR 2

7.0A: chapter covers motion pictures (Cited in #6A)

NBM 2

p. 64: "motion pictures" chapter (Cited in #6A)

SOURCES OF INFORMATION

AACR 2

7.0B1: film itself; accompanying textual material; container (Cited in #6A)

NBM 2

p. 17: material itself; accompanying data; container (Cited in #6A)

TITLE PROPER

AACR 2

7.1B1: as in 1.1B

1.1B1: transcribed exactly except for punctuation, capitalization (Cited in #6A)

NBM 2

p. 18: exactly from chief source, except for punctuation, capitalization (Cited in #6A)

GENERAL MATERIAL DESIGNATION

AACR 2

7.1C1: follows title proper

1.1C1: North American list

7.1A1: square brackets

A.4G: lowercase

p. 568: definition of motion picture (Cited in #6A)

NBM 2

p. 9: North American list

p. 18: lowercase, singular, brackets; follows title proper (Cited in #6A)

OTHER TITLE INFORMATION

AACR 2

7.1E1. "Record other title information as instructed in 1.1E."

1.1E1. "Transcribe all other title information appearing in the chief source of information according to the instructions in 1.1B."

NBM 2

p. 18 (General rules):
"Other title information ... follows the general material designation and the title proper ... to which it pertains. [It is] listed in the exact wording found in the chief source of information."

STATEMENTS OF RESPONSIBILITY

AACR 2

7.1F1: list only persons or bodies of major importance (Cited in #6A)

1.1F1. "Record statements of responsibility appearing prominently in the item in the form in which they appear there."

(General introduction)
0.8. "The word *prominently* (used in such phrases as *prominently named* and *stated prominently*) means that a statement to which it applies must be a formal statement found in one of the prescribed sources of information ... for

AACR 2 (cont'd)

areas 1 and 2 for the class of material to which the item being catalogued belongs."

NBM 2

p. 64: list only persons or bodies of major importance (Cited in #6A)

Comment

The use of the term *prominently* in AACR 2's rule 1.1F1 is explained in rule 0.8. While the film credits are not "prominent" in terms of layout (i.e., they occur at the end of the film), they do appear as a formal statement in a prescribed source. The decision is left to the cataloger, however, as to whether the people listed in the credits are "of major importance to the film and the interests of the cataloguing agency."

PUBLICATION, DISTRIBUTION, ETC., AREA

AACR 2

7.0B2: prescribed sources of information are chief source and accompanying material (Cited in #6B)

7.4C1: as in 1.4C

1.4C1: place of publication in form on item

1.4C3: add name of state

7.4D1: as in 1.4D

1.4D2: name of publisher in shortest form (Cited in #6A)

1.4D3.   "Do not omit from the phrase naming a publisher, distributor, etc.:

a) words or phrases indicating the function (other than solely publishing) performed by the person or body"

7.4F1: as in 1.4F

1.4F7: approximate date (Cited in #6A)

NBM 2

p. 19: name of place as given on item; add state

p. 64: list publisher

p. 20: approximate date (Cited in #6A)

Comment

The year 1979 is given as the probable date since the film was acquired in that year, and two of the items in the bibliography contained in the guide have a date of 1979.

PHYSICAL DESCRIPTION AREA—EXTENT OF ITEM

AACR 2

7.5B1: film reel

7.5B2: playing time (Cited in #6A)

NBM 2

p. 64: film reel; playing time (Cited in #6A)

PHYSICAL DESCRIPTION AREA—OTHER PHYSICAL DETAILS

AACR 2

7.5C3: sound

7.5C4: color

(Cited in #6A)

NBM 2

p. 64: sound, color (Cited in #6A)

PHYSICAL DESCRIPTION AREA—DIMENSIONS

AACR 2

7.5D2: width (Cited in #6A)

NBM 2

p. 64: width (Cited in #6A)

PHYSICAL DESCRIPTION AREA—ACCOMPANYING MATERIALS

AACR 2

7.5E1: as in 1.5E

1.5E1: four ways of recording information

7.5A1: punctuation (Cited in #6A)

NBM 2

p. 21: subordinate materials listed after dimensions (Cited in #6A)

NOTE AREA

AACR 2

7.7B6. **"Statements of responsibility. ... Credits.** List persons (other than

AACR 2 (cont'd)

the cast) who have contributed to the artistic and technical production of a motion picture or videorecording and who are not named in the statements of responsibility (see 7.1F). Do not include ... persons making only a minor contribution. Preface each name or group of names with a statement of function."

7.7B17: summary (Cited in #6A)

NBM 2

p. 64:
"List featured performers or other participants not given elsewhere in the record. The names are prefaced by an appropriate term such as Cast, Presenter, Narrator, Credits, and, if appropriate, a statement of function."

p. 64: summary (Cited in #6A)

Comment

Note the following LC rule interpretation:

7.7B6 ... For audiovisual items, generally list persons (other than producers, directors, and writers) who have contributed to the artistic and technical production of a work in a credits note (see 7.1F1...)
Give the following persons in the order in which they are listed below. Preface each name or group of names with the appropriate term(s) of function.
photographer(s); camera; cameraman/men ...
film editor(s) ...
music ..."[2]

CHOICE OF ACCESS POINTS

AACR 2

21.1B2. "Enter a work emanating from one or more corporate bodies under the heading for the appropriate corporate body if it falls into one or more of the following categories:

a)   those of an administrative nature dealing with the corporate body itself
or   its internal policies, procedures, and/or operations

...

or   its officers and/or staff

or   its resources (e.g., catalogues, inventories, membership directories) ..."

NBM 2

The reader would consult AACR 2.

Comment

This work falls under category 21.1B2a of AACR 2's conditions for main entry under corporate body. In describing "only those services available to adult learners through the Ramapo Catskill System and its member libraries," the film deals with policies, procedures, and operations of the corporate body from which it emanates.

The Library of Congress notes the following about category 21.1B2a:

> "*Category a.* To belong to this category the work must deal with the body itself.
>
> The words 'administrative nature' indicate works dealing with the management or conduct of the affairs of the body itself, including works that describe the activities of the body either in general terms or for a particular period of time.... Normally, such works are intended in the first instance for internal use, although they may be available to others.... Other works, particularly general descriptions of objectives and/or activities, may be generally available for purposes of public relations."[3]

NBM 2 has a rule calling for title main entry for "a work for which authorship cannot be established because of the extent and nature of collaborative authorship" (p. 18). A similar rule appeared in AACR, but is not present in AACR 2.

6D   ATTILA THE HUN

DESCRIPTION OF ITEM

Components: 1 reel of standard 8 millimeter film, color, 5 minutes in length, silent, in container.

Container:

ATTILA THE HUN STORMS THE MIDWAY
OR,
THE BEAST IN SEARCH OF A HUMORETTE
by
Michael Northcott and Richard Halston

The film itself contains no bibliographic information. Michael Northcott and Richard Halston wrote the scenario and did the camera work. The film was created in Chicago in 1975, when Northcott and Halston were high school students. Northcott and Halston are the only cast members in the film, which depicts Attila the Hun on a rampage through the University of Chicago campus. The wild man is finally pacified by a Good Humor bar, acquired from a vendor stationed outside the University's Library.

CATALOG RECORD

> Northcott, Michael.
> Attila the Hun storms the Midway, or, The beast in search of a Humorette [motion picture] / by Michael Northcott and Richard Halston. — [Chicago : M. Northcott and R. Halston, 1975]
> 1 film reel (ca. 5 min.) : si., col. ; standard 8 mm.
> Title from container.
> Credits: Northcott and Halston form the cast, and are responsible for the scenario and camera work.
> Summary: Attila the Hun storms through the University of Chicago campus, and is eventually pacified by a Good Humor bar.
>
> I. Halston, Richard. II. Title. III. Title: The beast in search of a Humorette.

Differences in the NBM 2 version (publication area):

> Attila the Hun storms the Midway, or, The beast in search of a Humorette [motion picture] / by Michael Northcott and Richard Halston. — [1975]

SCOPE / CATEGORIZATION

AACR 2

7.0A: chapter covers motion pictures (Cited in #6A)

NBM 2

p. 64: "motion pictures" chapter (Cited in #6A)

p. 99:
Chapter title: "Locally-Produced, Noncommercial Materials[64]"
"A media centre's collection may include locally-produced, noncommercial materials. These may be ... items which are produced by the students or staff of, and for use in, an institution."

p. 126 (Appendix A—Notes):
"64.   This section has been drawn from 6.11, 8.4A2, 10.4C2, 10.4D2, and 10.4F2."

Comment

NBM 2, unlike AACR 2, provides a general set of rules for locally produced materials. The separate chapter for "locally-produced, noncommercial materials" would be used in conjunction with the chapter on motion pictures in cataloging this example.

SOURCES OF INFORMATION

AACR 2

7.0B1: use container if information is not available from film itself (Cited in #6A)

NBM 2

p. 17: material itself, container (Cited in #6A)

Comment

The rules indicate that the container is to be used as a source of information if the necessary data is not available from the film itself. Presumably, the container is to be regarded as a "substitute chief source" in much the same way that rule 2.0B1 considers the cover or the half title page as substitute chief sources for books. In rule 2.0B1, however, such sources are explicitly identified as substitutes. If analogous rules in other chapters are to be applied in a similar fashion, the rules should contain a more explicit indication as to what the substitute chief sources are to be.

TITLE PROPER

AACR 2

7.1B1: as in 1.1B

1.1B1: transcribed exactly except for punctuation, capitalization (Cited in #6A)

· Rule 1.1B1 continues:
"An alternative title is part of the title proper (see Glossary, Appendix D). Follow the first part of the title and the word *or* (or equivalent) with commas and capitalize the first word of the alternative title."

p. 563 (Glossary):
"*Alternative title.* The second part of a title proper that consists of two parts, each of which is a title; the parts are joined by the word *or* or its equivalent in another language, e.g., *The tempest, or, The enchanted island.*"

NBM 2

p. 18: exactly from chief source, except for punctuation, capitalization (Cited in #6A)

NBM 2 (cont'd)

Rule also includes:
"The following will provide guidance for the cataloguing of many nonbook items. When these brief rules will not suffice, see *Anglo-American Cataloguing Rules*, 2nd edition, rule 1.1."

GENERAL MATERIAL DESIGNATION

AACR 2

7.1C1: follows title proper

1.1C1: North American list

7.1A1: square brackets

A.4G: lowercase

p. 568: definition of motion picture (Cited in #6A)

NBM 2

p. 9: North American list

p. 18: lowercase, singular, brackets; follows title proper (Cited in #6A)

STATEMENTS OF RESPONSIBILITY

AACR 2

7.1F1: list persons of major importance (Cited in #6A)

NBM 2

p. 64: list persons of major importance (Cited in #6A)

PUBLICATION, DISTRIBUTION, ETC., AREA

AACR 2

7.0B2: prescribed sources (Cited in #6B)

Rule continues:
"Enclose information taken from outside the prescribed source(s) in square brackets."

7.4C1: as in 1.4C

1.4C1: place of publication

7.4D1: as in 1.4D

1.4D4: "If the name of the publisher ... appears in a recognizable form in the title and statement of responsibility area [and if the publisher is a person,] give the initials and the surname of the person."

7.4F1: as in 1.4F

1.4F7: approximate date (Cited in #6A)

NBM 2

p. 99 (Chapter on locally produced, noncommercial materials):
"If the 'author' is also responsible for the manufacture of the item and is named in the statement of responsibility, the name, together with the place, is not repeated in the publication/distribution area."

"The date of manufacture is listed."

p. 17: supplied information enclosed in brackets (Cited in *sources of information* section of #6B)

Comment

It would be useful to differentiate "published" items from those that are not published, i.e., those that have not been issued in multiple copies and made available for distribution. For certain categories of "unpublished" materials, such as art originals, non-processed sound recordings, naturally occurring objects which have not been mounted for viewing, and unpublished photographs, AACR 2 makes special provisions for omission of some of the publication data elements. However, some other categories, such as locally produced motion pictures and videorecordings, have no such provisions, and since there are no general rules covering these kinds of publications, a strict interpretation of the rules would suggest that place, publisher, and date be recorded. The question remains as to whether, in this case, Northcott and Halston are to be regarded as "publishers." NBM 2, on the other hand, allows the place and "publisher" to be omitted for locally produced items. If locally produced motion pictures and videorecordings were to be cataloged by analogy using appropriate rules from the chapter on sound recordings, no publication data would be given in the publication, distribution, etc., area; instead, a date would be given in the note area.

Richard Thaxter, head of the Audiovisual Cataloging Section at the Library of Congress, advises that chapter 6's rules for nonprocessed sound recordings (6.11) be used as a guide in cataloging unpublished locally produced videorecordings. Presumably, the same would apply for locally produced motion pictures.[4]

PHYSICAL DESCRIPTION AREA—EXTENT OF ITEM

AACR 2

7.5B1: film reel

7.5B2: playing time

(Cited in #6A)

Rule continues:
"If no indication of duration appears on the item, its container, or its accompanying textual material, give an approximate time if it can be readily established."

NBM 2

p. 64: film reel; playing time (Cited in #6A)

Rule continues:
"If duration is not stated, an approximate time, e.g., (ca. 50 min.), is listed if it can be ascertained easily."

PHYSICAL DESCRIPTION AREA—OTHER PHYSICAL DETAILS

AACR 2

7.5C3: sound

7.5C4: color

(Cited in #6A)

NBM 2

p. 64: sound, color (Cited in #6A)

PHYSICAL DESCRIPTION AREA—DIMENSIONS

AACR 2

7.5D2: width (Cited in #6A)

NBM 2

p. 64: width (Cited in #6A)

NOTE AREA

AACR 2

7.7B3. **"Source of title proper.** Make notes on the source of the title proper if it is other than the chief source of information."

7.7B6: statements of responsibility (Cited in #6C)

7.7B17: summary (Cited in #6A)

NBM 2

p. 22 (General rules):
"Source of title proper"

p. 64: featured performers or participants (Cited in #6C)

p. 64: summary (Cited in #6A)

Comment

Although Northcott and Halston appear in the statement of responsibility area, it was considered useful to indicate the nature of their contributions in a note.

CHOICE OF ACCESS POINTS

AACR 2

21.1A1. "A personal author is the person chiefly responsible for the creation of the intellectual or artistic content of a work."

21.6C1. "If responsibility is shared between two or three persons ... and principal responsibility is not attributed to any of them by wording or layout, enter under the heading for the one named first. Make added entries under the headings for the others."

NBM 2

p. 18 (General rules):
"A work for which authorship can be clearly established is entered under author." (Quotes AACR 2's definition of authorship.)

Comment

AECT 4 notes that it is difficult to establish "a creativity priority among the many functions performed in the production of a film." None of the major codes sets up a ranking of creativity functions which would indicate clearly the person who is to be regarded as "author" in the production of a film. At the same time, however, most codes make it clear that any person chiefly responsible for the intellectual or artistic content of the film can be regarded as author. Thus the question of authorship here is not tied to a specific kind of function, as say the writing of a text, the composing of a musical composition, the compiling of a bibliography, or, as proponents of the *auteur* theory would suggest, the directing of a film. Rather, the decision is based on the extent and significance of the intellectual or artistic responsibility. In this case, Northcott and Halston are regarded as "authors" not because they were responsible for any one particular function or functions, but because, as the only persons participating in the creation of the film, there is no question as to their being chiefly responsible.

AECT 4 has observed that "creator main entry will occur more frequently in 8mm films which are less complicated to produce than are 16mm pictures ..." (p. 151).

6E   CREATIVE STORYTELLING

DESCRIPTION OF ITEM

Components: 1 videotape cassette, color, sound, ¾ inch tape, 30 minutes in length, second generation show copy

---

Title frame at beginning of film:

Creative Storytelling Techniques
Mixing the Media with
Dr. Caroline Feller Bauer

Frame at end of film:

Directed by Ken Yandle
Production supervisor: Guy March
Produced by Mobile Video Productions
1979 Copyright ALA

Based on Bauer's book *Handbook for Storytellers* 1977 ALA
Original music by Edmund Soule

Content:

Bauer is responsible for the content and presentation of the recording. She describes and demonstrates ways in which storytelling can be enhanced through the use of aids such as puppets and graphic displays.

Label on cassette:

CREATIVE STORYTELLING TECHNIQUES
"MIXING THE MEDIA"
with Dr. Caroline Feller Bauer   U-Matic

MEMOREX
Video Cassette

Promotional brochure:

Available for purchase or rental from
                    the Public Television Library
      ...
Address all orders to: The Public Television Library
                    475 L'Enfant Plaza, S.W.
                    Washington, D.C. 20024

CATALOG RECORD

Bauer, Caroline Feller.
Creative storytelling techniques [videorecording] : mixing the
media / with Caroline Feller Bauer ; produced by Mobile Video
Productions. — Washington, D.C. : Public Television Library
[distributor], c1979.
1 videocassette (U-matic) (30 min.) : sd., col. ; ¾ in.
Credits: Director, Ken Yandle ; production supervisor, Guy
March ; original music, Edmund Soule.
Second generation, show copy.
Based on: Handbook for storytellers. Chicago : American
Library Association, 1977. The author describes and then demon-
strates ways in which storytelling can be enhanced through the use
of aids such as puppets and graphic displays.

I. Bauer, Caroline Feller. Handbook for storytellers. II. Title.

Differences in NBM 2 version (publication, physical description, and note areas):

Creative storytelling techniques [videorecording] : mixing the
media / with Caroline Feller Bauer ; produced by Mobile Video
Publications. — [Washington, D.C. : Public Television Library,
distributor], c1979.
1 videocassette (ca. 30 min.) : sd., col. ; ¾ in.
Credits: Director, Ken Yandle ; production supervisor, Guy
March ; original music, Edmund Soule.
      U standard.

(Remainder of NBM 2 note area follows AACR 2.)

SCOPE / CATEGORIZATION

AACR 2

7.0A: chapter covers videorecordings (Cited in #6A)

NBM 2

p. 95:
Chapter title: "Videorecordings"
"*Videorecording*: a recording designed for television playback on which both pictures and sound have been registered electronically."

"[Cassettes] are included under this heading ..."

"The rules for Motion pictures on pages 64 to 70 apply to videorecordings with the following additions and exceptions."

SOURCES OF INFORMATION

AACR 2

7.0B1: film itself, container, publicity material (Cited in #6A)

NBM 2

p. 17: material itself, producer's brochure considered "outside source" (Cited in #6A, amplified by #6B)

TITLE PROPER

AACR 2

7.1B1: as in 1.1B

1.1B1: transcribed exactly except for punctuation, capitalization (Cited in #6A)

NBM 2

p. 18: exactly from chief source, except for punctuation, capitalization (Cited in #6A)

GENERAL MATERIAL DESIGNATION

AACR 2

7.1C1: follows title proper

1.1C1: North American list

7.1A1: square brackets

A.4G: lowercase (Cited in #6A)

p. 572 (Glossary):
"**Videorecording.** A recording on which visual images, usually in motion and accompanied by sound, have been registered; designed for playback by means of a television set."

NBM 2

p. 9: North American list

p. 18: lowercase, singular, brackets; follows title proper (Cited in #6A)

p. 95:
"[Cassettes] are ... designated by the term 'videorecording.' "

OTHER TITLE INFORMATION

AACR 2

7.1E1: as in 1.1E

1.1E1: transcribe as in 1.1B (Cited in #6C)

NBM 2

p. 18: exact wording found in source (Cited in #6C)

STATEMENTS OF RESPONSIBILITY

AACR 2

7.1F1: list persons and bodies of major importance (Cited in #6A)

1.1F76. "If there is more than one statement of responsibility, record them in the order indicated by their sequence on, or by the layout of, the chief source of information."

1.1F7. "Include titles and abbreviations of titles of nobility, address, honour, and distinction ... with the names of persons in statements of responsibility if:

a)   such a title is necessary grammatically

...

AACR 2 (cont'd)

b)   the omission would leave only the person's given name or surname

...

c)   the title is necessary to identify the person

...

Omit all other titles, etc., from the names of persons in statements of responsibility. Do not use the mark of omission."

NBM 2

p. 64: list persons and bodies of major importance (Cited in #6A)

PUBLICATION, DISTRIBUTION, ETC., AREA

AACR 2

7.0B1: *accompanying material* includes publicity material (Cited in *sources of information* section of #6A)

7.4C1: as in 1.4C

1.4C1: place of publication in form on item

7.4D1: omit production agency if named in statement of responsibility (Cited in #6A)

7.4E1. "Add to the name of the publisher, distributor, ... a statement of function as instructed in 1.4E." (Optional addition)

1.4E1. "Add to the name of a publisher, distributor, etc., one of the terms below:

    distributor
    publisher
    ...

unless:

a)   the phrase naming the publisher, distributor, etc., includes words that indicate the function ...

b)   the function ... is clear from the context."

7.4F1: as in 1.4F (Cited in #6A)

1.4F6: copyright date (Cited in #6B)

NBM 2

p. 17: information from publisher's brochures enclosed in brackets (Cited in *sources of information* section of #6B)

p. 19: name of place as given on item (Cited in #6A)

p. 64: list distributor; omit producer named in statement of responsibility (Cited in #6A)

Rule on p. 20 continues:
"*Option.* List a statement of function following the name of the distributor, publisher ..."

PHYSICAL DESCRIPTION AREA — EXTENT OF ITEM

AACR 2

7.5B1: videocassette; *option to drop *video* (Cited in #6A)

Rule continues:
"Add a trade name or other technical specification to the term for a videorecording if the use of the item is conditional upon this information and if it is only available in that particular form. Otherwise, give such data in the note area ..."

7.5B2: playing time (Cited in #6A)

NBM 2

p. 95:
"List the number of ... videocassettes ..."

*"*Option.* If a general material designation is used, the prefix 'video' may be omitted from the specific material designation ..."

"List in its own parentheses after the specific material designation, any technical specification, such as a trade name, which is necessary information for the use of the item. **If the item is available in the media centre in more than one video format the technical specifications are listed in the note area ..."

"List in its own parentheses the total playing time in minutes. ... If no duration is stated on the item, list an approximate time if this can be ascertained readily."

p. 109 (Glossary):
"Cassette — An enclosed container for film or magnetic tape in reel-to-reel format."

---

*Option not applied here or by LC.
**Rule considered but not applied.

Comment

NBM 2 would not include the term *U-matic* in the physical description area because this is a generic term, rather than a trade name used exclusively by a single company. (See NBM 2's rule in the *Note area* section of this chapter.) My own interpretation, however, is to regard *U-matic* as a "technical specification," and thus allowable under 7.5B1 as a qualifier in the extent of item section. Such an interpretation seems to be in keeping with the intent of the rule, since the use of the item is conditional upon this information. While *U-matic* is a common type of format produced by a number of companies, one can certainly not assume that all videorecordings will be of this format. Since this information will indicate the equipment needed to play the videorecording, it is important that it appear prominently in the description, rather than in a note.

In most instances, the Library of Congress will give the technical specifications of format for videorecordings in the notes area rather than in the physical description area. This is because most of the titles cataloged by the Library are available in several formats.

The Library of Congress will express the technical specifications using generic names rather than brand names found on the item. In addition, the Library is abandoning the use of the term *U standard* for *U-matic*. The Library will use *U-matic, Beta, VHS*, etc., rather than *Sony U-matic, Betamax, Victor VHS*, etc., since these formats are compatible with playback equipment from different manufacturers.

Richard Thaxter of the Library of Congress has pointed out that, on the local level, libraries may want the technical specifications statement to follow the *extent of item* statement in order to call greater attention to the format.[5]

PHYSICAL DESCRIPTION AREA—OTHER PHYSICAL DETAILS

AACR 2

7.5C3: sound

7.5C4: color (Cited in #6A)

NBM 2

p. 95:
"List sound and b&w or col."

PHYSICAL DESCRIPTION AREA—DIMENSIONS

AACR 2

7.5D3. "Give the gauge (width) of a videotape in inches."

NBM 2

p. 95:
"*Videotapes*. List width in inches."

Comment

NBM 2 has a general rule (p. 21) which states that "fractions are taken to the next number." From sample card 125 in the chapter on videorecordings, however, it is clear that the width can be recorded as "¾ in."

NOTE AREA

AACR 2

1.7A5. "When appropriate, combine two or more notes to make one note."

7.7B6: statements of responsibility (Cited in #6C)

7.7B7. "*Edition and history*. Make notes relating to ... the history of the ... videorecording.

...

     Based on the novel by Nicolas Mosley"

7.7B10: physical description given if this level of detail is desired (Cited in #6A)

Rule continues:
"g) *Generation of copy*. For videotapes, give the generation of the copy and whether it is a master copy or show copy."

7.7B17: summary (Cited in #6A)

NBM 2

p. 95:
"See page 64 [chapter on motion pictures] for rules covering featured performers and other participants ..."

p. 64: list featured performers or participants (Cited in #6C)

p. 22 (General rules):
"Edition and history"

...

"Additional information about publication, distribution, etc."

NBM 2 (cont'd)

p. 95:
"List the videorecording system, if it has not been listed in the physical description area. The notes 'U standard' or 'Beta' may be used in this area rather than listing a specific system in the extent of item if the format, e.g., Sony U-Matic or Betamax, is one which is compatible with other manufacturers ..."

"*Videotapes* ... List the generation of copy and whether a master or show copy."

p. 64: summary (Cited in #6A)

CHOICE OF ACCESS POINTS

AACR 2

21.1A1: personal author is person chiefly responsible for intellectual content (Cited in #6D)

21.4A. "Enter a work ... by one personal author ... under the heading for that person ..."

21.30G. "**Related works.** Make an added entry under the heading for a work to which the work being catalogued is closely related ... Make such entries in the form of the heading for the person ... under which the related work is, or would be, entered. If the heading is for a person ..., and the title of the related work differs from that of the work being catalogued, add the title of the related work to the heading to form a name-title added entry heading."

NBM 2

p. 18: enter under author, if authorship clearly established (Cited in #6D)

Comment

It might be argued that the extent and nature of collaborative authorship make it difficult to identify any one person who is primarily responsible for the intellectual or artistic content of this work, and that there is a lack of agreement as to which function in the creation of a videorecording is to be considered the most important. However, Bauer's book forms the intellectual content on which the videorecording is based, and while the videorecording is not an exact reproduction of the original work, the same person has been responsible in both cases for deciding on the work's substance and manner of presentation.

NOTES

1.   Library of Congress, Processing Services, *Cataloging Service Bulletin*, no. 13 (Summer 1981), p. 15.

2.   Ibid., p. 16.

3.   *CSB*, no. 12 (Spring 1981), pp. 22-23.

4.   *On-line Audiovisual Catalogers Newsletter*, vol. 1, no. 4 (December 1981), p. 14.

5.   Ibid.

7

GRAPHIC MATERIALS

The category of graphic materials encompasses a wide range of media. Some are specifically instructional in purpose such as flash cards, transparencies, charts, and technical drawings, while others have an aesthetic purpose, such as original works of art and pictures. The category includes media, such as slides, filmstrips, and transparencies, which are intended for projection, as well as those which are opaque, for example, photographs, art originals, and pictures.

It is frequently the case that certain types of graphic items, for example, slides and photographs, are commonly issued as collections or sets. In the following examples, however, the assumption is made that the items to be cataloged are discrete units and as such are described individually.

The Library of Congress intends to issue a detailed manual focusing on the description of original, historical, and archival graphic materials. The manual will be based on chapter 8 of AACR 2.

For a detailed discussion of the cataloging of slides, see Betty Irvine's *Slide Libraries: A Guide for Academic Institutions, Museums, and Special Collections* (Libraries Unlimited, 1979).

7A   BEETLE WALL GAME

DESCRIPTION OF ITEM

Components: 1 poster

Dimensions: 106 centimeters in height; 178 centimeters in width

The poster contains a color photograph of a Volkswagen Beetle. Various parts, such as the steering wheel, gas tank, and sun roof, are identified so that students can compute the linear dimensions.

Upper left hand corner:

> YOU BET YOUR BEETLE (very large print)
> Metric Wall Game (large print)

Lower left hand corner:

> 5705

Lower right hand corner:

> SINGER   SVE/Society For Visual Education, Inc.
> Education Division ...   Chicago, Illinois 60614
>   Copyright c1976 Society for Visual Education, Inc.

CATALOG RECORD

> You bet your Beetle [picture] : metric wall game. — Chicago,
>   Ill. : Society for Visual Education, c1976.
>   1 picture : col. ; 106 x 178 cm.
>   Summary: Picture of Volkswagen provides opportunity for various
> types of linear measurement.
>   "5705"
>
>   I. Society for Visual Education.

SCOPE / CATEGORIZATION

AACR 2

8.0A. "The rules in this chapter cover the description of graphic materials of all kinds, [including] opaque (e.g., two-dimensional art originals and reproductions, charts, photographs, technical drawings) ..., and collections of such graphic materials."

NBM 2

p. 71:
Chapter title: "Pictures"
"*Picture*: a two-dimensional representation generally produced on an opaque backing."

"Pictures ... are included under this heading ..."

Comment

Although labeled 'game' by the publisher, this item would not fit the definition of *game* given in AACR 2's glossary: "A set of materials designed for play according to prescribed rules" (p. 566).

Games are treated in the chapter on three-dimensional materials (chapter 10), which is not suited for description of a two-dimensional object.

SOURCES OF INFORMATION

AACR 2

8.0B1. "The chief source of information for graphic materials is the item itself ..."

NBM 2

p. 71:
"Information for the catalogue record is taken from the following sources in this order:

1. The item itself (Chief source of information)."

TITLE PROPER

AACR 2

8.1B1. "Record the title proper as instructed in 1.1B."

1.1B1. "Transcribe the title proper exactly as to wording, order, and spelling, but not necessarily as to punctuation and capitalization."

NBM 2

p. 18 (General rules):
"The title proper ... is copied exactly from the chief source of information. However, capitalization and punctuation follow prescribed rules."

GENERAL MATERIAL DESIGNATION

AACR 2

8.1C1. (Optional). "Add immediately following the title proper the appropriate general material designation as instructed in 1.1C."

1.1C1. "If general material designations are to be used in cataloguing, ... North American agencies [should use] terms from list 2."

8.1A1. "Enclose the general material designation in square brackets."

(Appendix A—Capitalization):
A.4G. "Lowercase the words making up a general material designation."

1.1C1. (footnote). "... for material treated in chapter 8, use *picture* for any item not subsumed under one of the other terms in list 2 ..."

p. 569 (Glossary):
"**Picture.** A two-dimensional visual representation accessible to the naked eye and generally on an opaque backing. Used when a more specific term (e.g., art original, photograph, study print) is not appropriate."

NBM 2

p. 9 (Chapter on cataloging policy for media centers):
"The North American list of general material designations is used in this book. Those electing [to omit the general material designation or to use] the British list ... or the ISBD list may use the rules on the following pages by disregarding the general material designation or by substituting the appropriate term from the British or ISBD lists."

p. 18 (General rules):
"A general material designation is listed in lower case letters, in the singular, and in its own square brackets immediately following the title proper."

p. 71:
"Pictures ... are ... designated by the term 'picture.' "

Comment

Pictures are not cataloged by the Library of Congress. If the Library ever catalogs this material, the decision on whether to display the general material designation will be decided at that time.

OTHER TITLE INFORMATION

AACR 2

8.1E1. "Record other title information as instructed in 1.1E."

1.1E1. "Transcribe all other title information appearing in the chief source of information according to the instructions in 1.1B."

NBM 2

p. 18 (General rules):
"Other title information ... follows the general material designation and the title proper ... to which it pertains. [It is] listed in the exact wording found in the chief source of information."

PUBLICATION, DISTRIBUTION, ETC., AREA

AACR 2

8.4C1. "Record the place of publication, distribution, etc., as instructed in 1.4C."

1.4C1. "Record the place of publication, etc., in the form ... in which it appears."

*1.4C3. "Add the name of the country, state, province, etc., to the name of the place if it is considered necessary for identification, or if it is considered necessary to distinguish the place from others of the same name."

8.4D1. "Record the name of the publisher, distributor, etc., as instructed in 1.4D."

1.4D2. "Give the name of a publisher, distributor, etc., in the shortest form in which it can be understood and identified internationally."

8.4F1. "Record the date of publication, distribution, etc., as instructed in 1.4F."

1.4F6. "If the dates of publication, distribution, etc., are unknown, give the copyright date ... in its place."

NBM 2

pp. 19, 20 (General rules):
"List the name of the place as it appears on the item and add the name of the province, state, country, etc., if it is necessary for identification."

"List the name of the publisher, producer, distributor, etc., in the shortest form that can be identified internationally."

"If the dates of publication or distribution cannot be ascertained, list the copyright date ..."

Comment

The publisher's order catalog indicates that the Society for Visual Education is a subsidiary of the Singer Company. It is not necessary to give both the abbreviation "SVE" and the full name. The abbreviation alone might not be identifiable; thus "Society for Visual Education" has been transcribed as the name of the publisher.

---

*For LC rule interpretation, see example #4B, p. 81.

PHYSICAL DESCRIPTION AREA—EXTENT OF ITEM

AACR 2

*8.5B1. "Record the number of physical units of a graphic item by giving the number of parts in arabic numerals and one of the following terms as appropriate:

art original	picture
…	…
chart	slide
…	
filmstrip	stereograph
flash card	study print
…	
photograph	technical drawing
	… "

**"*Optionally*, substitute or add a term more specific than those listed above."

NBM 2

*p. 71:
"List the number of … photographs, pictures, … or study prints."[2]

**"*Option*. List a more specific term …"

Comment

The term *picture* is preferred in this instance. AACR 2 does not include a definition for "poster" in its glossary, but NBM 2 defines this term as "A bill or placard intended to be posted" (p. 110). *Chart* would not be an appropriate term here, since it is defined in AACR 2 as "an opaque sheet that exhibits data in graphic or tabular form" (p. 564) and in NBM 2 as "a sheet of information arranged in tabular or graphic form produced on an opaque backing" (p. 109). If none of the above terms were found suitable, and an appropriate term could be determined, the cataloger might make use of the optional rule provided under 8.5B1:

"Optionally, substitute or add a term more specific than those listed above."

---

*The terms listed in this rule citation include only those designations which will be used for the examples in this chapter.
**Option not applied in this example.

PHYSICAL DESCRIPTION AREA—OTHER PHYSICAL DETAILS

AACR 2

8.5C8. "**Pictures.** Give an indication of the colour (col., b&w, etc.)."

NBM 2

p. 71:
"*Pictures, postcards, posters, study prints.* List b&w or col."

PHYSICAL DESCRIPTION AREA—DIMENSIONS

AACR 2

8.5D1. "Give for all graphic materials except filmstrips, filmslips, and stereographs the height and the width in centimetres to the next whole centimetre up."

NBM 2

p. 71:
"*Photographs, pictures, postcards, posters, study prints.* Height x width are listed in centimetres."

Comment

An item of this size would probably be folded when stored. AACR 2 provides the following rule for technical drawings and wall charts (8.5D6): "Give the height and the width when extended and (when appropriate) folded." If one were to "catalog by analogy," this rule might be considered here.

NOTE AREA

AACR 2

8.7B17. "**Summary.** Give a brief objective summary of the content of an item unless another part of the description provides enough information."

8.7B19. "**Numbers.** Give important numbers borne by the item other than ISBNs or ISSNs ..."

NBM 2

p. 22 (General rules):

"Other information which may be given in notes is listed in the following order: ...

Summaries. These are not necessary for media which can be readily examined or adequately described by title and/or series statement....

Numbers associated with item other than ISBNs or ISSNs ..."

CHOICE OF ACCESS POINTS

AACR 2

21.1C. "Enter a work under its title when:

... 3) It emanates from a corporate body but does not fall into one or more of the categories given in 21.1B2 and is not of personal authorship"

NBM 2

The reader would refer to AACR 2.

7B   SUPERMARKET HELPERS

DESCRIPTION OF ITEM

Components: 8 study prints in plastic container

Each study print is 32 centimeters in height, 46 centimeters in width. Each has a color scene on one side, and text on the reverse.

Container:

SUPERMARKET HELPERS
Picture-Story Study Prints - Set SP 123

SVE   Society for Visual Education, Inc.
1345 Diversey Parkway   Chicago, Illinois

Contents
- Stocking shelves
- Packaging Produce
- Serving Produce Customer
- Store Dairy Manager
- Preparing Meat
- Customer Service
- Checking Out an Order
- Unloading Products

Verso of one of the study prints:

CUSTOMER SERVICE

From the SVE Picture-Story Study Print Set

Supermarket Helpers - SP 123

Consultant: Stanley W. McKee
Principal, Lincoln School,
Highland Park, Illinois

Available SVE Picture-Story Study Print Sets:
(8 prints per set)

BASIC SCIENCE
SP 101 Common Insects   ...
SP 102 Spring Wild Flowers   SP 118 Land Forms of Running Water

BASIC SOCIAL STUDIES COMMUNITY HELPERS
SP 119 Police Department Helpers ...
SP 120 Fire Department Helpers   SP 123 Supermarket Helpers

Produced and
Distributed by   SVE   Society for Visual Education Inc.
                                1345 Diversey Parkway   Chicago, Ill. 60614

c MCMLXV, Society for Visual Education, Inc. All Rights Reserved.

CATALOG RECORD

Supermarket helpers [picture]. — Chicago, Ill. : Produced and
distributed by Society for Visual Education, c1965.
8 study prints : col. ; 32 x 46 cm. — (SVE picture-story study
print set ; SP 123. Basic social studies community helpers).
Consultant: Stanley W. McKee.
Text on verso.
Contents: Stocking shelves — Packaging produce — Serving
produce customer — Store dairy manager — Preparing meat —
Customer service — Checking out an order — Unloading products.

I. Society for Visual Education. II. Series.

SCOPE / CATEGORIZATION

AACR 2

8.0A: chapter covers opaque graphic materials (Cited in #7A)

NBM 2

p. 71: "pictures" chapter (Cited in #7A)

Rule also includes:
"... study prints are included under this heading ..."

SOURCES OF INFORMATION

AACR 2

8.0B1: item itself (Cited in #7A)

Rule continues:
"If the item being described consists of two or more separate physical parts (slide set, etc.), treat a container that is the unifying element as the chief source of information if it furnishes a collective title and the items themselves and their labels do not."

NBM 2

p. 71: item itself (Cited in #7A)

p. 17 (General rules):
"If an item consists of more than one part, the chief source of information is as follows:

"1.   The piece that could be considered 'the first part.' In nonbook terms this might be the part which gives meaning to the various parts,[4] e.g., a manual or a container which is the unifying element;[5]"

p. 123 (Appendix A — Notes):
"4.   Authors' interpretation of 'first part' 1.0H (multipart items) applied to nonbook materials."

"5.   'container which is the unifying element.' — 8.0B1."

Comment

On the individual study prints, the title for the set ("Supermarket helpers") appears in much smaller type than the titles for the individual prints. Despite the greater prominence given to the individual titles, the title for the set is selected since it provides a collective title for the unit as a whole. Both codes indicate a clear preference for a title which acts as a unifying element, even if such a title were not to appear on any of the individual parts of a set.

TITLE PROPER

AACR 2

8.1B1: as in 1.1B

1.1B1: transcribed exactly except for punctuation, capitalization (Cited in #7A)

NBM 2

p. 18: exactly from chief source, except for punctuation, capitalization (Cited in #7A)

GENERAL MATERIAL DESIGNATION

AACR 2

8.1C1: follows title proper

1.1C1: North American list

8.1A1: square brackets

A.4G: lowercase

1.1C1: use *picture*

p. 569: definition of *picture*

NBM 2

p. 9: North American list

p. 18: lowercase, singular, brackets; follows title proper (Cited in #7A)

p. 71:
"… study prints are … designated by the term 'picture.' "

STATEMENTS OF RESPONSIBILITY

AACR 2

*8.1F1. "Record statements of responsibility as instructed in 1.1F."

*1.1F1. "Record statements of responsibility appearing prominently in the item in the form in which they appear there."

---

*Rule considered but not applied.

NBM 2

pp. 18, 19 (General rules):
*"The statement(s) of responsibility is listed wherever possible in the wording and order found on the source(s) of information.... Statements of responsibility may include ... any person or corporate body which has contributed to the intellectual or artistic content. Contributors of minor importance may be listed in the notes."

Comment

While AACR 2's 8.1F1 and 1.1F1 prescribe that any statements of responsibility appearing in the chief source be recorded, LC's application of 8.1F1 enables the cataloger to be more selective:

> When deciding whether to give names in the statement of responsibility (7.1F1, 8.1F1) or in a note, generally give the names in the statement of responsibility when the person or body has some degree of overall responsibility; use the note area for others who are responsible for only one segment or one aspect of the work.[1]

PUBLICATION, DISTRIBUTION, ETC., AREA

AACR 2

8.4C1: as in 1.4C

1.4C1: place of publication in form on item

1.4C3: add name of state

8.4D1: as in 1.4D

1.4D2: name in shortest form (Cited in #7A)

1.4D3. "Do not omit from the phrase naming a publisher, distributor, etc.:
a)   words or phrases indicating the function (other than solely publishing) performed by the person or body"

8.4F1: as in 1.4F (Cited in #7A)

1.4F1. "Give dates in Western-style arabic numerals ..."

1.4F6: copyright date (Cited in #7A)

---

*Rule considered but not applied.

NBM 2

pp. 19, 20: name of place as given on item; add state; name of publisher in shortest form; copyright date (Cited in #7A)

PHYSICAL DESCRIPTION AREA—EXTENT OF ITEM

AACR 2

8.5B1: study print (Cited in #7A)

NBM 2

p. 71: study print (Cited in #7A)

p. 110 (Glossary):
"*Study print*—a picture with accompanying text which makes the print significant for study purposes."

PHYSICAL DESCRIPTION AREA—OTHER PHYSICAL DETAILS

AACR 2

8.5C14. "**Study prints.** Give an indication of the colour (b&w or col.)."

NBM 2

p. 71: color (Cited in #7A)

PHYSICAL DESCRIPTION AREA—DIMENSIONS

AACR 2

8.5D1: height x width (Cited in #7A)

NBM 2

p. 71: height x width (Cited in #7A)

*p. 21 (General rules):
"If an item is housed in a container, the type of container may be listed together with its dimensions.[13]"

p. 123 (Appendix A—Notes):
"13.   Measuring the container drawn from [AACR 2] 3.5D5 & 10.5D2. This may be extended to all media if this is useful information."

---

*Rule considered but not applied.

SERIES AREA

AACR 2

8.6B1. "Record each series statement as instructed in 1.6."

1.6B1. "If an item is one of a series, record the title proper of the series as instructed in 1.1B ..."

1.6G1. "Record the numbering of the item within the series in the terms given in the item."

1.6A1. "Precede the numbering within a series or subseries by a semicolon."

1.6H1. "If an item is one of a subseries (a series within a series, whether or not it has a dependent title) and both the series and the subseries are named in the item, give the details of the main series ... first and follow them with the name of the subseries and the details of that subseries."

1.6A1. "Precede the title of a subseries by a full stop."

NBM 2

p. 21 (General rules):
"If applicable, a series statement in parentheses follows the physical description area. The series area in 3rd level cataloguing could include:

title proper of series

...

numbering within series
subseries ..."

Comment

See also LC's guidelines for dealing with series and subseries (*Cataloging Service Bulletin* 11, pp. 10, 11).

NOTE AREA

AACR 2

8.7B6. "**Statements of responsibility**. ... Give statements of responsibility not recorded in the title and statement of responsibility area."

8.7B10. "**Physical description.** Give important physical details that have not been included in the physical description area, especially if these affect the use of the item.

...

Text on verso."

AACR 2 (cont'd)

8.7B18. "**Contents.** Give a list of the individually named parts of a graphic item."

NBM 2

p. 22 (General rules):
"Statements of responsibility. This may include additional information (e.g., performers) not listed in the title and statement of responsibility area ..."

"Additional information concerning the physical description, particularly if such information affects the item's use."

"Contents."

Comment

Note the following LC rule interpretation:

> **7.7B6, 8.7B6.** ... For audiovisual items, generally list persons (other than producers, directors, and writers) who have contributed to the artistic and technical production of a work in a credits note (see 7.1F1/8.1F1).
>
> Give the following persons in the order in which they are listed below. Preface each name or group of names with the appropriate term(s) of function.
> > photographer(s); camera; cameraman/men;
> > cinematographer ... consultant(s); adviser(s)[2]

CHOICE OF ACCESS POINTS

AACR 2

21.1C3: corporate body falls outside 21.1B2—title entry (Cited in #7A)

NBM 2

p. 18 (General rules):
"Authorship is not normally attributed to consultants ..."

The reader would consult AACR 2.

Comment

The consultant is not regarded here as a personal author "chiefly responsible for the creation of the intellectual or artistic content of a work" (AACR 2, rule

21.1A1 — definition of personal authorship). The assumption is made that the consultant's role here is a relatively minor one, and that those responsible for creating the work have not been named.

7C   ARLINGTON CEMETERY PHOTOGRAPH

DESCRIPTION OF ITEM

Components: 1 photograph

Dimensions: 19 centimeters in height; 22⅞ centimeters in width

Black and white; dry mounted; a high-contrast photograph.
Depicts scene in Arlington Cemetery.
No printed information is given anywhere on the item.

CATALOG RECORD

[Arlington Cemetery photograph] [picture].
   — [197-?]
1 photo. : b&w ; 19 x 23 cm.
Title supplied by cataloger.
Dry mounted.
High contrast.

SCOPE / CATEGORIZATION

AACR 2

8.0A: chapter covers photographs (Cited in #7A)

NBM 2

p. 71: "pictures" chapter (Cited in #7A)

Rule also includes:
"... photographs ... are included under this heading ..."

SOURCES OF INFORMATION

AACR 2

8.0B1: item itself (Cited in #7A)

NBM 2

p. 71: item itself (Cited in #7A)

TITLE PROPER

AACR 2

8.1B2. "If a single graphic item lacks a title, supply one as instructed in 1.1B7."

1.1B7. "If no title can be found in any source, devise a brief descriptive title. Enclose such a ... devised title in square brackets.

...

    [Photograph of Theodore Roosevelt]"

NBM 2

p. 17 (General rules):
"Sources of information
5.   Information supplied by the cataloguer. Such information is enclosed in square brackets. Supplied titles should be descriptive, reasonably concise, and if possible begin with a filing word which reflects subject content."

Comment

AACR 2 gives no criteria for the construction of supplied titles. The examples show titles beginning with generic terms. Many catalogers might prefer, however, to begin the title with the subject depicted, rather than with a term such as "photograph of," so that the catalog record will file by a distinctive element. Since the general material designation will indicate the nature of the object, the term "photograph" might be omitted altogether. NBM 2's guidelines, while consistent with AACR 2, provide more specific assistance in this area.

GENERAL MATERIAL DESIGNATION

AACR 2

8.1C1: follows title proper

1.1C1: North American list

8.1A1: square brackets

A.4G: lowercase

1.1C1: use *picture*

p. 569: definition of *picture*

1.0C. "**Punctuation**. ... When adjacent elements within one area are to be enclosed in square brackets, enclose them in one set of square brackets unless one of the elements is a general material designation, which is always enclosed in its own set of brackets."

NBM 2

p. 9: North American list

p. 18: lowercase, singular, brackets; follows title proper (Cited in #7A)

p. 71:
"... photographs ... are ... designated by the term 'picture.' "

PUBLICATION, DISTRIBUTION, ETC., AREA

AACR 2

8.4A2. "**Art originals, unpublished photographs, etc.** For ... unpublished photographs and other unpublished graphic materials, give only the date in this area (see 8.4F2)."

8.4F2. "Record the date of creation of an ... unpublished photograph, or other unpublished graphic item."

1.4F7. "If no date of publication, distribution, etc., copyright date, or date of manufacture can be assigned to an item, give an approximate date of publication.

...

, [197-?]   *Probable decade*

NBM 2

pp. 19, 20: name of place, name of publisher (Cited in #7A)

Rules also include:
*"If no probable place can be listed, give the name of the province, state, country, etc."

*"If the place is unknown, list "S.l." in square brackets."

*"If the publisher, etc., is unknown, list "s.n." in square brackets ..."

"If no date can be found, give an approximate date. (See the *Anglo-American Cataloguing Rules*, 2nd edition, rule 1.4F7.)

---

*Rule considered but not applied.

Comment

AACR 2 regards the inclusion of publication data as inappropriate for unpublished photographs, although no consistent method of treatment for unpublished materials as a whole can be found in the code. Note that the date is the date of creation.

NBM 2 provides its own chapter for locally produced, noncommercial materials, but the rule for transcription of publication data is not appropriate here since this rule is stated only in terms of items which have a statement of responsibility. No direct reference is made to AACR 2's rule that unpublished photographs receive only the date in the imprint. Presumably, NBM 2 intends that the appropriate AACR 2 rule would be applied, but the reader would have to be aware of this special provision for unpublished photographs and art originals in AACR 2. In the separate chapter it has provided for art originals, NBM 2, like AACR 2, requires only the date of creation in the publication, distribution, etc., area. However, this chapter would not be appropriate for this example, since the scope of the chapter includes "original paintings, drawings, architectural renderings, and sculpture"; photographs, on the other hand, are designated "picture."

PHYSICAL DESCRIPTION AREA—EXTENT OF ITEM

AACR 2

8.5B1: photograph (Cited in #7A)

NBM 2

p. 71: photograph (Cited in #7A)

p. 110 (Glossary):
"*Photograph*—An image produced on a photo-sensitized surface by a camera."

PHYSICAL DESCRIPTION AREA—OTHER PHYSICAL DETAILS

AACR 2

8.5C7. "**Photographs** ... Give an indication of the colour (col., b&w, etc.).
...
   3 photos. : negative, b&w"

NBM 2

p. 71:
"*Photographs* ... List b&w or col."

PHYSICAL DESCRIPTION AREA—DIMENSIONS

AACR 2

8.5D1: height x width (Cited in #7A)

NBM 2

p. 71: height x width (Cited in #7A)

p. 21 (General rules):
"Fractions are taken to the next number."

NOTE AREA

AACR 2

8.7B3. **"Source of title proper.** Make notes on the source of the title proper if it is other than the chief source of information."

8.7B10: physical description (Cited in #7B)

NBM 2

p. 22 (General rules):
"Source of title proper"

p. 22: physical description (Cited in #7B)

CHOICE OF ACCESS POINTS

AACR 2

21.1C. "Enter a work under its title when:

1)   the personal authorship is unknown ... or cannot be determined, and the work does not emanate from a corporate body"

NBM 2

The reader would consult AACR 2.

Comment

No information is available on the authorship of the item; thus this work is considered to be of unknown authorship and title main entry is given. AACR 2 offers an explicit general rule covering the condition of unknown authorship. In NBM 2, the basic rule for unknown authorship must be drawn from AACR 2.

While the photographer of this item is unknown, the work is almost certainly the artistic effort of one person, who, if identified, would be regarded as the principal creator. Both codes recognize photographers as the authors of the works they create.

7D   HEBREW EYE CHART

DESCRIPTION OF ITEM

Components: 1 black and white chart

Dimensions: 57½ centimeters in height; 36¼ centimeters in width

Hebrew letters in chart designed for testing vision.

Only bibliographic data is the following, in lower left hand corner (very small print):

c Copyright 1971 Barsky & Assoc.

CATALOG RECORD

[Hebrew eye chart] [chart]. — [United States? : s.n.],
c1971.
1 chart : b&w ; 58 x 37 cm.
Title supplied by cataloger.
"Copyright 1971 Barsky & Assoc."
Summary: Hebrew letters in chart designed for testing vision.

SCOPE / CATEGORIZATION

AACR 2

8.0A: chapter covers charts (Cited in #7A)

NBM 2

p. 25:
Chapter title: "Charts"
"*Chart*: a sheet of information arranged in tabular or graphic form produced on an opaque backing."

"Charts ... are included under this heading ..."

SOURCES OF INFORMATION

AACR 2

8.0B1: item itself (Cited in #7A)

NBM 2

p. 17 (General rules):
"Cataloguing information ... should be taken from the following sources in the order indicated:

1.   The material itself ..."

TITLE PROPER

AACR 2

8.1B2: as in 1.1B7

1.1B7: supplied title in brackets (Cited in #7C)

NBM 2

p. 17: supplied title in brackets (Cited in #7C)

GENERAL MATERIAL DESIGNATION

AACR 2

8.1C1: follows title proper

1.1C1: North American list

8.1A1: square brackets

A.4G: lowercase

1.0C: punctuation (Cited in #7C)

p. 564 (Glossary):
"**Chart.** 1. An opaque sheet that exhibits data in graphic or tabular form, e.g., a wall chart."

NBM 2

p. 9: North American list

p. 18: lowercase, singular, brackets; follows title proper (Cited in #7A)

p. 25:
"Charts ... are ... designated by the term 'chart.' "

Comment

The Library of Congress does not catalog charts, but the general material designation will be displayed if the Library ever does catalog the material.

PUBLICATION, DISTRIBUTION, ETC., AREA

AACR 2

8.4C1: as in 1.4C (Cited in #7A)

1.4C6. "If no probable place* can be given, give the name of the country, state, province, etc. If, in such a case, the country, state, province, etc., is not certain, give it with a question mark."

**"If no place or probable place can be given, give the abbreviation *s.l.* (sine loco), or its equivalent in nonroman scripts."

8.4D1: as in 1.4D (Cited in #7A)

1.4D6. "If the name of the publisher, distributor, etc., is unknown, give the abbreviation *s.n.* (sine nomine) or its equivalent in nonroman scripts."

8.4F1: record date as in 1.4F

1.4F6: copyright date (Cited in #7A)

NBM 2

pp. 19, 20: **"S.l." for place unknown; "s.n." for publisher unknown; copyright date (Cited in #7A, amplified by #7C)

Comment

Note the following LC interpretations:

1.4B. ... If the item does not name a publisher and in the absence of evidence to the contrary, assume that the copyright holder named in the copyright statement is the publisher if it is a corporate body known as a publishing entity. Consider that other corporate bodies ... are the publishers only if the particular cases make the inference very plausible. ***In case of any doubt, do not consider the copyright holder as publisher.[3]

1.4C6. If the place of publication, etc., is not named in the item, give it in its well-established English form if there is one. If the place being supplied is only probable rather than certain, give it with a question mark.
    If no probable place can be given, give the name of the country (in its well-established English form if there is one) ...[4]

PHYSICAL DESCRIPTION AREA—EXTENT OF ITEM

AACR 2

8.5B1: chart (Cited in #7A)

---

*i.e., "place" in terms of a city.

**Rule considered but not applied.

***No information about the nature of the company of Barsky & Assoc. was available.

NBM 2

p. 25:
"List the number of charts ..."

PHYSICAL DESCRIPTION AREA—OTHER PHYSICAL DETAILS

AACR 2

8.5C8: color; no specific rule for charts (Cited in #7A)

NBM 2

p. 25:
"List b&w or col."

Comment

In AACR 2, rule 8.5C lists 18 of the 19 terms used as specific material designations, and for each of these terms prescribes the data to be included as "other physical details." The one specific material designation which is not included in 8.5C is the term "chart." Presumably, "picture" and "wall chart" would be the appropriate terms to use as models.

PHYSICAL DESCRIPTION AREA—DIMENSIONS

AACR 2

8.5D1: height x width (Cited in #7A)

NBM 2

p. 25:
"Height x width are listed in centimetres."

NOTE AREA

AACR 2

8.7B3: source of title proper (Cited in #7C)

8.7B9. **"Publication, distribution, etc.** Make notes on publication, distribution, etc., details that are not included in the publication, etc., area and are considered to be important."

8.7B17: summary (Cited in #7A)

NBM 2

p. 22: source of title proper (Cited in #7C)

p. 22 (General rules):
"Additional information about publication, distribution, etc."

p. 22: summary (Cited in #7A)

CHOICE OF ACCESS POINTS

AACR 2

21.1C1: authorship unknown; title entry (Cited in #7C)

NBM 2

The reader would consult AACR 2.

7E   MUSIKANTEN

DESCRIPTION OF ITEM

Components: 1 original painting. Oil on canvas, colored, wood frame.
On frame: "Musikanten"
Size when framed: 36 x 26 centimeters (height x width)
Unframed: 30 x 20 centimeters

Depicts young musicians performing on a street corner.
Painted by Margo Treue in Bad Godesburg, Germany in 1960.
Donated by the artist in 1961.

CATALOG RECORD

Treue, Margo.
Musikanten [art original]. — [1960]
1 art original : oil on canvas ; 30 x 20 cm.
Title from frame.
Painted by Margo Treue.
Donated by the artist in 1961.
Size when framed 36 x 26 cm.

I. Title.

Difference in NBM 2 version (note area):

'Title from frame' note would be omitted.

SCOPE / CATEGORIZATION

AACR 2

8.0A: chapter covers two-dimensional art originals (Cited in #7A)

NBM 2

p. 23:
Chapter title: "Art originals[15]"

"*Art original*: an original two- or three-dimensional work of art."

"Original paintings ... are included under this heading ..."

p. 123 (Appendix A—Notes):
"15. Two-dimensional works of art are discussed in AACR/2, chapter 8 and three-dimensional works of art in chapter 10. Therefore, the rules here are drawn from both chapters."

Comment

AACR 2 assigns two-dimensional art originals to the chapter on graphics, i.e., two-dimensional materials. NBM 2, which for the most part has divided up its chapters according to the North American list of general material designations, has put together a separate chapter for art originals both two- and three-dimensional, with rules drawn from AACR 2's chapters 8 and 10.

SOURCES OF INFORMATION

AACR 2

8.0B1: item itself (Cited in #7A)

Rule continues:
"If the information is not available from the chief source, take it from the following sources ...

container (box, frame, etc.)"

NBM 2

p. 23:
"Sources of information[16]
Information for the catalogue record is taken from the following sources in this order:

1. The item itself;
2. Frame or mount; ..."

p. 124 (Appendix A—Notes):
"16.   8.0B1 excludes the frame from being a chief source of information; 10.0B1 allows the item, accompanying material, and container to be chief sources. Because the title for most paintings, etc., is found on the mount or frame, the authors advocate the application of 10.0B1 to all art originals, and therefore, have not indicated the chief source of information."

Comment

Note that NBM 2, drawing from chapter 10 of AACR 2, allows the frame ("container") to serve as chief source. For this reason, the source of the title will not be given in a note in the NBM 2 record.

TITLE PROPER

AACR 2

8.1B1: as in 1.1B

1.1B1: transcribed exactly except for punctuation, capitalization (Cited in #7A)

NBM 2

p. 18: exactly from chief source, except for punctuation, capitalization (Cited in #7A)

GENERAL MATERIAL DESIGNATION

AACR 2

8.1C1: follows title proper

1.1C1: North American list

8.1A1: square brackets

A.4G: lowercase (Cited in #7A)

p. 563 (Glossary):
"Art original. The original two- or three-dimensional work of art (other than an art print (q.v.) or a photograph) created by the artist, e.g., a painting, a drawing, or sculpture, as contrasted with a reproduction of it."

NBM 2

p. 9: North American list

p. 18: lowercase, singular, brackets; follows title proper (Cited in #7A)

p. 23:
"Original paintings ... are ... designated by the term 'art original.' "

Comment

The Library of Congress does not catalog art originals. If it ever does catalog this material, it will decide whether to display the general material designation at that time.

STATEMENTS OF RESPONSIBILITY

AACR 2

8.1F1: as in 1.1F (Cited in #7B)

1.1F2. "If no statement of responsibility appears prominently in the item, neither construct one nor extract one from the content of the item.
Do not include statements of responsibility that do not appear prominently in the item in the title and statement of responsibility area. If such a statement is necessary, give it in a note."

NBM 2

The reader would consult AACR 2.

PUBLICATION, DISTRIBUTION, ETC., AREA

AACR 2

8.4A2: date only for unpublished graphic materials (Cited in #7C)

Rule also includes:
"For art originals, ... give only the date in this area (see 8.4F2)."

8.4F2: date of creation for unpublished graphic (Cited in #7C)

Rule also includes:
"Record the date of creation of an art original ..."

NBM 2

p. 23:
"Publication, distribution, etc. area
List only the date of creation."

PHYSICAL DESCRIPTION AREA—EXTENT OF ITEM

AACR 2

8.5B1: art original (Cited in #7A)

NBM 2

p. 23:
"List the number of art originals."

*"*Option.* If the general material designation 'art original' is used, a specific term may be listed ..."

PHYSICAL DESCRIPTION AREA—OTHER PHYSICAL DETAILS

AACR 2

8.5C1. **"Art originals.** Give the medium (chalk, oil, pastel, etc.) and the base (board, canvas, fabric, etc.).

   1 art original : oil on canvas"

NBM 2

p. 23:
"List materials used, e.g., oil on canvas."

PHYSICAL DESCRIPTION AREA—DIMENSIONS

AACR 2

8.5D1: height x width (Cited in #7A)

Rule continues:
"For additional instructions on the dimensions of art works, ... see 8.5D4-8.5D6."

8.5D4. **"Art originals** ... Give the height and the width of the item, excluding any frame or mount. (See also 8.7B10.)"

---

*Option not applied in this example.

NBM 2

p. 23:
"For two-dimensional items, height x width of the item itself excluding mount or frame are listed in centimetres."

NOTE AREA

AACR 2

8.7B3: source of title proper (Cited in #7C)

8.7B6: statements of responsibility (Cited in #7B)

Rule continues:
"**Donor, source, etc., and previous owner(s).** Make notes on the donor or source of a graphic item ... Add the year ... of accession to the name of the donor or source ..."

8.7B10: physical description (Cited in #7B)

Includes example:
"Size when framed: 40 x 35 cm."

NBM 2

p. 22: statements of responsibility (Cited in #7B)

Rule also includes:
"This may include ... statements of responsibility not taken from the chief source of information ..."

p. 22: physical description (Cited in #7B)

CHOICE OF ACCESS POINTS

AACR 2

21.1A1. "A personal author is the person chiefly responsible for the creation of the intellectual or artistic content of a work. For example, ... artists and photographers are the authors of the works they create."

21.4A. "Enter a work ... by one personal author ... under the heading for that person whether named in the work or not."

NBM 2

p. 18 (General rules):
"A work for which authorship can be clearly established is entered under author." (Quotes AACR 2's definition of authorship.)

7F   SUMMY'S GREGORIAN NOTATION

DESCRIPTION OF ITEM

Components: 44 black and white flash cards; 18.8 centimeters high; 15.2 wide

1 study pamphlet (12 p.) in envelope

Container:

SUMMY'S
GREGORIAN NOTATION
FLASH CARDS
and
STUDY PAMPHLET

Prepared by
School Sisters of St. Francis

Alverno College of Music
Milwaukee, Wis.

Contents: Forty-four Gregorian Notation
Flash Cards with Study Pamphlet

CLAYTON F. SUMMY CO.
Milwaukee   CHICAGO   Peoria

Each card contains notation from Gregorian chants on one side, with an identification of the notation on the reverse side.

Verso on one of the cards:

SCANDICUS FLEXUS
[Instructions on count and melody for this notation]

CLAYTON F. SUMMY CO.
Milwaukee   CHICAGO   Peoria
copyright 1946 by Clayton F. Summy Co.

CATALOG RECORD

Summy's Gregorian notation flash cards and study pamphlet [flash
card] / prepared by School Sisters of St. Francis, Alverno
College of Music, Milwaukee, Wis. — Milwaukee ; Chicago :
C. F. Summy Co., c1946.
44 flash cards : b&w ; 19 x 16 cm. + 1 pamphlet.
Text on verso.
Designed to aid the teaching of the Gregorian chant.

I. School Sisters of St. Francis. II. Clayton F. Summy Co.

Difference in NBM 2 version: option to substitute *card* for *flash card*:

44 cards : b&w ; 19 x 16 cm. + 1
pamphlet.

SCOPE / CATEGORIZATION

AACR 2

8.0A: chapter covers opaque graphic materials (Cited in #7A)

NBM 2

p. 34:
Chapter title: "Flash cards"
"*Flash card*: a card printed with words, numerals, or pictures, designed for
rapid identification."

Comment

Since the flash cards contain musical notation, one might briefly consider
AACR 2's chapter 5, which covers the description of published music. However,
the cards do not comprise a musical work, but rather serve as an instructional
device the format of which is best described through rules in AACR 2's chapter 8.
NBM 2 describes the *content* of flash cards in terms too specific to include
musical notation, but if the *purpose* of the item is kept in mind, there would
appear to be little doubt that the categorization of "flash card" would apply in
this case.

SOURCES OF INFORMATION

AACR 2

8.0B1: item itself; container as unifying element (Cited in #7A, amplified by #7B)

NBM 2

p. 17: material itself (Cited in #7D)

p. 34:
"The container is preferred to the accompanying data."

TITLE PROPER

AACR 2

8.1B1: as in 1.1B

1.1B1: transcribed exactly except for punctuation, capitalization (Cited in #7A)

1.1B2. "If the title proper includes a statement of responsibility or the name of a publisher, distributor, etc., and the statement or name is an integral part of the title proper (i.e., connected by a case ending or other grammatical construction), transcribe it as such."

NBM 2

p. 18: exactly from chief source, except for punctuation, capitalization (Cited in #7A)

Rule also includes:
"The following will provide guidance for the cataloguing of many nonbook items. When these brief rules will not suffice, see the *Anglo-American Cataloguing Rules*, 2nd edition, rule 1.1."

GENERAL MATERIAL DESIGNATION

AACR 2

8.1C1: follows title proper

1.1C1: North American list

8.1A1: square brackets

A.4G: lowercase

p. 566 (Glossary):
"**Flash card.** A card or other opaque material printed with words, numerals, or pictures and designed for rapid display."

NBM 2

p. 9: North American list

p. 18: lowercase, singular, brackets; follows title proper (Cited in #7A)

Comment

The Library of Congress does not catalog flash cards, but the general material designation will be displayed if the Library ever does catalog the material.

STATEMENTS OF RESPONSIBILITY

AACR 2

8.1F1: as in 1.1F1

1.1F1: record in form appearing on item (Cited in #7B)

1.1F13. "When a name associated with responsibility for the item is transcribed as part of the title proper (see 1.1B2) ... do not make any further statement relating to that name unless such a statement is required for clarity, or unless a separate statement of responsibility including or consisting of that name appears in the chief source of information."

NBM 2

pp. 18, 19: record wording and order found on source (Cited in #7B)

PUBLICATION, DISTRIBUTION, ETC., AREA

AACR 2

8.4C1: as in 1.4C

1.4C1: place of publication in form on item

1.4C3: add name of state (Cited in #7A)

1.4C5. "If a publisher, distributor, etc., has offices in more than one place and these are named in the item, always give the first named place, and the first of

AACR 2 (cont'd)

any subsequently named places that is ... given prominence by the layout of the source of information. Omit all other places."

8.4D1: as in 1.4D

1.4D2: name in shortest form

8.4F1: as in 1.4F

1.4F6: copyright date (Cited in #7A)

NBM 2

pp. 19, 20: name of place as given on item; add state; name of publisher in shortest form; copyright date (Cited in #7A)

Rules also include:
"When more than one place appears on the item, list in the following order:

the first named place, and

the most prominently named place, if different from the first named place ..."

PHYSICAL DESCRIPTION AREA—EXTENT OF ITEM

AACR 2

8.5B1: flash card (Cited in #7A)

NBM 2

p. 34:
"List the number of flash cards."

"*Option*. If the general material designation 'flash card' is used, the word 'card(s)' may be substituted for 'flash card(s)' ..."

p. 20 (General rules):
"*Option*.[10] If the general material designation and the specific material designation are the same, the specific material designation can be omitted ..."

p. 123 (Appendix A—Notes):
"10.   The only chapter in AACR/2 which does not allow the omission of the specific material designation or a prefix when a general material designation is used is Chapter 8, Graphics. This seems inconsistent and so this provision has been extended to all media. In actual fact, the only media from Chapter 8 to which this will apply are flash cards and filmstrips."

Comment

Note the option in NBM 2 to drop the term "flash" from the specific material designation "flash card" if a general material designation is used. This provision, in NBM 2's view, is a more consistent application of similar rules found in other chapters of AACR 2, and thus is typical of suggestions made by NBM 2 which deviate from rules in AACR 2.

PHYSICAL DESCRIPTION AREA—OTHER PHYSICAL DETAILS

AACR 2

8.5C5. "**Flash cards.** Give an indication of colour (col. or b&w)."

NBM 2

p. 34:
"List b&w or col."

PHYSICAL DESCRIPTION AREA—DIMENSIONS

AACR 2

8.5D1: height x width (Cited in #7A)

NBM 2

p. 34:
"Height x width are listed in centimetres."

PHYSICAL DESCRIPTION AREA—ACCOMPANYING MATERIALS

AACR 2

8.5E1. "Record the name, and *optionally*,* the physical description, of any accompanying material as instructed in 1.5E."

1.5E1. "There are four ways of recording information about accompanying material:

   a)   record the details ... in a separate entry
or   b)   record the details ... in a multilevel description ...
or   c)   record the details ... in a note ...
or   d)   record the name of accompanying material at the end of the physical description"

---

*Option not applied in this example.

AACR 2 (cont'd)

8.5A1. "**Punctuation.** ... "Precede a statement of accompanying material by a plus sign"

NBM 2

p. 21 (General rules):
"If an item contains two or more media, one of which is clearly predominant, it is catalogued by the dominant medium and the subordinate accompanying material may be listed after the dimensions."

"*Punctuation.* The statement of accompanying material is preceded by a space-plus sign-space (+)."

NOTE AREA

AACR 2

8.7B10: physical description (Cited in #7B)

Includes example:
"Text on verso"

8.7B17: summary (Cited in #7A)

NBM 2

p. 22: physical description (Cited in #7B)

p. 22: summary (Cited in #7A)

CHOICE OF ACCESS POINTS

AACR 2

21.1C3: corporate body falls outside 21.1B2—title entry (Cited in #7A)

NBM 2

The reader would consult AACR 2.

7G ADMINISTRATIVE SERVICES BUILDING

DESCRIPTION OF ITEM

Components: 3 blueprints

Dimensions: (height x width):
43.4 x 66.0 centimeters — sheet size
40.6 x 61.0 centimeters — within border
22 x 17 centimeters — size when folded

First sheet, bottom right hand corner:

UNIVERSITY OF MICHIGAN ENGINEERING SERVICES			
SCALE As noted	ADMINISTRATIVE SERVICES BLDG. IMPROVE VENTILATION OF MECH. ROOM 1018M & ELECT. ROOM 1018B		ORDER NO. 6263
DATE 11/15/79			SHEET NO. 1 of 3
DRAWN P.W./J.O.			FILE C
CHECKED ✓	BLDG NO. 815	INQUIRY NO. 7471	ISSUED TO 2,3,4,6,7,8,24,50	DRAWING NO. 570

Upper right hand corner has title:

Duct work changes

The information on the bottom right hand corner is essentially the same for sheets two and three. The three sheets contain drawings of proposed duct work changes. The drawings are in various scales.

CATALOG RECORD

University of Michigan. Engineering Services.
Administrative Services Bldg. [technical drawing] : improve venti-
lation of mech. room 1018M & elect. room 1018B / University of
Michigan Engineering Services ; drawn [by] P.W., J.O. — 1979.
3 technical drawings : blueprint ; 44 x 66 cm. folded to 22 x
17 cm.
Title in upper right corner: Duct work changes.
Scales vary.
Drawing no. 570.

I. Title. II. Title: Duct work changes

Differences in NBM 2 version:

3 mechanical drawings : blueprint ; 41 x 61 cm. folded to 22 x
17 cm.

SCOPE / CATEGORIZATION

AACR 2

8.0A: chapter covers technical drawings (Cited in #7A)

NBM 2

p. 91:
Chapter title: "Technical Drawings[60]"
"*Technical drawing*: a plan, elevation, cross section, detail, diagram,
perspective, etc., made for use in an engineering, architectural, or other technical
context."

p. 125 (Appendix A—Notes):
"60. The rules for technical drawings in AACR/2, Chapter 8 do not seem
complete enough to satisfy the needs of engineering libraries. Therefore, the
authors have expanded this section. Of our source documents, only NBMCR
[*Non-Book Materials Cataloguing Rules*, issued by the (British) Library
Association] dealt with technical drawings, and we found it to be only partially
helpful. Most of the ideas for this section have come from the staff of media
centres which contain technical drawings and from professional engineers who
use them. The authors have attempted to fit these ideas into an AACR/2
framework."

SOURCES OF INFORMATION

AACR 2

8.0B1: item itself (Cited in #7A)

Rule continues:
"In describing a collection of graphic materials as a unit, treat the whole collection as the chief source."

NBM 2

p. 91:
"Information for the catalogue record is taken from the following sources in this order:

1.   The item itself (Chief source of information). If there is more than one title on the item, preference should be given to information in the title block;"

Comment

Note that NBM 2 gives more specific guidance in choosing between conflicting titles.

TITLE PROPER

AACR 2

8.1B1: as in 1.1B

1.1B1: transcribed exactly except for punctuation, capitalization (Cited in #7A)

p. 550 (Appendix B — Abbreviations):
B.4. "Use the following categories of abbreviations in the title and statement of responsibility area ...

a)   those found in the prescribed sources of information for the particular area ..."

NBM 2

p. 18: exactly from chief source, except for punctuation, capitalization (Cited in #7A)

GENERAL MATERIAL DESIGNATION

AACR 2

8.1C1: follows title proper

1.1C1: North American list

8.1A1: square brackets

A.4G: lowercase

p. 571 (Glossary):
"**Technical drawing.** A cross section, detail, diagram, elevation, perspective, plan, working plan, etc., made for use in an engineering or other technical context."

NBM 2

p. 9: North American list

p. 18: lowercase, singular, brackets; follows title proper (Cited in #7A)

Comment

The Library of Congress does not catalog technical drawings. If it ever does catalog this material, it will decide whether to display the general material designation at that time.

OTHER TITLE INFORMATION

AACR 2

8.1E1: as in 1.1E

1.1E1: transcribe as in 1.1B (Cited in #7A)

NBM 2

p. 18: exact wording found in source (Cited in #7A)

STATEMENTS OF RESPONSIBILITY

AACR 2

8.1F1: as in 1.1F

1.1F1: record in form appearing on item (Cited in #7B)

1.1F3. "If a statement of responsibility precedes the title proper in the chief source of information, transpose it to its required position ..."

1.1F6. "If there is more than one statement of responsibility, record them in the order indicated by their sequence on, or by the layout of, the chief source of information."

1.1F8. "Add an explanatory word ... to the statement of responsibility if the relationship between the title and the person(s) ... named in the statement is not clear."

NBM 2

pp. 18, 19: record wording and order found on source (Cited in #7B)

Rule continues:
"A word ... may be added in square brackets in order to clarify the type of responsibility."

PUBLICATION, DISTRIBUTION, ETC., AREA

AACR 2

8.4A2: date only for unpublished graphic materials

8.4F2: date of creation (Cited in #7C)

NBM 2

p. 91:
"There are few technical drawings marketed by commercial producers. Most drawings are produced by the firm or individual responsible for their creation. While the firm or individual may sell the drawings in some instances, they do not constitute a publisher/distributor. The rules for Locally-Produced, Non-Commercial Materials on page 99 should be used for this area, when appropriate."

"*Date.* List date of the latest revision."

p. 99 (Chapter on locally produced, noncommercial materials):
"If the 'author' is also responsible for the manufacture of the item and is named in the statement of responsibility, the name, together with the place, is not repeated in the publication/distribution area."

Comment

Since this item has been issued to eight recipients, the question could be raised as to whether it should be regarded as "unpublished" in AACR 2's terms.

PHYSICAL DESCRIPTION AREA—EXTENT OF ITEM

AACR 2

8.5B1: technical drawing (Cited in #7A)

NBM 2

p. 91:
"List the number of technical drawings using a specific term, such as structural sketch, mechanical drawing."

Comment

Since each sheet contains more than one drawing, the question arises as to whether, in AACR 2's "extent of item" statement, one is describing the number of physical parts, i.e., sheets of paper, or the number of drawings. Rule 8.5B1 is stated in terms of "physical units," but some ambiguity results in using the term "drawings" to describe physical units. A similar ambiguity exists in the rules for description of maps. See example #4C, "Osaka."

PHYSICAL DESCRIPTION AREA—OTHER PHYSICAL DETAILS

AACR 2

8.5C15. "**Technical drawings.** Give the method of reproduction if any (blueprint, photocopy, etc.)"

NBM 2

p. 91:
"List the method of reproduction or the material of the drawing, whichever term or phrase indicates whether a drawing can be reproduced. For example, the terms 'mylar,' 'tracing paper,' and 'white linen' indicate reproducible drawings, while "whiteprints,' 'blueprints,' and 'blue linen' are not reproduced easily."

PHYSICAL DESCRIPTION AREA—DIMENSIONS

AACR 2

8.5D1: height x width (Cited in #7A)

Rule continues:
"For additional instructions on the dimensions of ... technical drawings, ... see 8.5D4-8.5D6."

8.5D6. "**Technical drawings and wall charts.** Give the height and the width when extended and (when appropriate) folded."

NBM 2

p. 91:
"List height x width of the drawing measured from the inside border. If the drawing is folded, list these dimensions also."

Comment

Note that NBM 2's rules specify measurement from the inside border, and thus differ from AACR 2.

NOTE AREA

AACR 2

8.7B4. **"Variations in title.** Make notes on titles borne by the item other than the title proper."

8.7B10: physical description (Cited in #7B)

Includes example:
"Scales vary."

8.7B19: numbers (Cited in #7A)

NBM 2

p. 22 (General rules):
"Variations in title"

p. 91:
"List the scale in the terms used on the drawing(s). If the scales in a set vary, use the term 'scales vary' or list the range of scales."

p. 22: numbers (Cited in #7A)

Comment

Note the following LC rule interpretation:

7.7B4, 8.7B4. ... When considering 7.7B4 and 8.7B4 for a variation in title, decide first whether an added title entry is needed under the variant title. Decide this primary issue by consulting 21.2. If the variation in title is as great as the differences in titles described in 21.2 [any change in first five words, etc.], make the added entry and justify the added entry by means of a note formulated under 7.7B4 or 8.7B4.[5]

CHOICE OF ACCESS POINTS

AACR 2

21.1B2. "Enter a work emanating from one or more corporate bodies under the heading for the appropriate corporate body if it falls into one or more of the following categories:

a)   those of an administrative nature dealing with the corporate body itself

...

or   its resources ...”

21.1B4. "If a work falls into one or more of the categories given in 21.1B2 and if a subordinate unit of a corporate body is responsible for it, apply the following provisions:

a)   if the responsibility of the named subordinate unit is stated prominently, enter the work under the heading for the subordinate unit.”

NBM 2

The reader would consult AACR 2.

Comment

The assumption made here is that this is a work of an administrative nature, dealing with the corporate body itself and possibly with its resources. Rule 21.1B2 applies even though the work does not deal with the particular subordinate unit which is responsible. My experience in teaching AACR 2 has shown that the intended meaning of this rule is often misunderstood. Frances Hinton, in a commentary on a similar example, explains:

> The usual reaction is that the intent of 21.1B2 must have been that the "appropriate corporate body" is the body dealt with, not one of its subordinate units, and that therefore, this work should be entered under title according to the provision of 21.1C. This is pure speculation, for the rule seems clear and its application to this work correct.[6]

FORM OF HEADING

AACR 2

24.13. "Enter a subordinate or related body as a subheading of the name of the body to which it is subordinate or related if its name belongs to one or more of the following types.

...

TYPE 3. A name that has been, or is likely to be, used by another higher body for one of its subordinate or related bodies.”

For the University of Michigan's name:

24.1. "Enter a corporate body directly under the name by which it is predominantly identified ..."

NBM 2

Outside the scope of this code. The reader would consult AACR 2.

7H   MEET THE NEWBERY AUTHOR

DESCRIPTION OF ITEM

Components: 1 filmstrip; 35 millimeters

1 tape cassette; 1 7/8 ips, mono., 2-track; 3 7/8 x 2 1/2 inches; tape width 1/8 inch, in cardboard container

---

Filmstrip contains following:

(Numbered) Frames 1-11	colored illustrations
12:	Miller-Brody Productions Presents MEET THE NEWBERY AUTHOR copyright MCMLXXIV
13:	SCOTT O'DELL
14-81	colored photographs and illustrations
82	Acknowledgements Script: Ronald Kidd Photography: Ronald Perkins

---

Tape cassette label:

MEET THE NEWBERY AUTHOR

Scott O'Dell   Time:
                          13:15

MNA 1004-C

(P) MCMLXXIV by Miller-Brody Productions, Inc.

(C) MCMLXXIV by Miller-Brody Productions, Inc.

Cardboard box:

MEET THE NEWBERY AUTHOR

[ ] MNA 1001 Eleanor Estes   [x] MNA 1004 Scott O'Dell
[ ] MNA 1002 Lloyd Alexander   [ ] MNA 1005 Madeleine L'Engle
[ ] MNA Jean Craighead George   [ ] MNA 1006 Marguerite Henry

Miller-Brody Productions, Inc. New York, N.Y. 10017

Content:

Author Scott O'Dell tells about his life and works.

CATALOG RECORD

Scott O'Dell [filmstrip] / script: Ronald Kidd ; photography: Ronald
Perkins. — New York, N.Y. : Miller-Brody, c1974.
1 filmstrip (82 fr.) : col. ; 35 mm. + 1 sound cassette (14 min. : 1⅞
ips, 2 track, mono.). — (Meet the Newbery author ; MNA 1004)
Summary: Author Scott O'Dell tells about his life and
works.

I. Kidd, Ronald. II. Perkins, Ronald. III. Miller-Brody
Productions. IV. Series.

Differences in NBM 2 version (Option to omit specific material designation):

82 fr. : col. ; 35 mm. + 1 sound cassette (14 min. : 1⅞ ips, 2 track,
mono.). — (Meet the Newbery author ; MNA 1004)

SCOPE / CATEGORIZATION

AACR 2

8.0A. "The rules in this chapter cover the description of graphic materials ...
intended to be projected or viewed (e.g., filmstrips, radiographs, slides) ..."

1.10. "Items made up of several types of material"

1.10B. "If an item has one predominant component, describe it in terms of
that component and give details of the subsidiary component(s) as accompanying
material following the physical description (see 1.5E) or in a note (see 1.7B11)."

NBM 2

p. 30:
Chapter title: "Filmstrips"
"*Filmstrip*: A roll of film containing a succession of images designed to be viewed one frame at a time."

"Filmstrips ... are included under this heading ..."

p. 40 (Chapter on kits):
"If one part of the item is clearly dominant, the item is not catalogued as a kit, but rather as the dominant medium, with the other media listed as accompanying material ..."

Comment

The assumption made here is that the visual component of this item is more important than the aural one. Opinions will differ on this matter, however, and the argument could be made that the item should be cataloged as a kit, or even as a sound recording. AACR 2 leaves the decision up to the cataloger.

AECT 4 provides the following guidance:

> A *filmstrip* is a roll of film, usually 35 millimeters wide, on which there is a succession of still pictures intended for projection one at a time.... In a *sound filmstrip* the sound track is usually recorded separately on a disc, or on a tape in cassette or reel format. Sound and frames are synchronized, with or without audible signals, for use in manual or automatic advance projectors (p. 69).

> A filmstrip with a synchronized audiorecording and an accompanying teacher's guide with script, though issued as a unit, is not cataloged as a kit but as a filmstrip, which is the dominant medium (p. 111).

SOURCES OF INFORMATION

AACR 2

8.0B1: item itself; container (Cited in #7A, amplified by #7E)

p. 30:
"Information for the catalogue record is taken from the following sources in this order:

1. The item itself (chief source of information). Preference should be given to the information on the title frames rather than the leader frames.[22] Title frames immediately precede the main body of the filmstrip while the leader frames are separated from the body of the filmstrip by a length of blank film;

NBM 2 (cont'd)

2. Container;
..."

p. 124 (Appendix A—Notes):
"22. Preference given to title frames drawn from NBM/1."

Comment

Note that NBM 2 indicates a preferred order for data found on the filmstrip.

TITLE PROPER

AACR 2

8.1B1: as in 1.1B

1.1B1: transcribed exactly except for punctuation, capitalization (Cited in #7A)

NBM 2

p. 18: exactly from chief source, except for punctuation, capitalization (Cited in #7A)

GENERAL MATERIAL DESIGNATION

AACR 2

8.1C1: follows title proper

1.1C1: North American list

8.1A1: square brackets

A.4G: lowercase

p. 566 (Glossary):
"**Filmstrip.** A length of film containing a succession of images intended for projection one at a time, with or without recorded sound."

NBM 2

p. 9: North American list

p. 18: lowercase, singular, brackets; follows title proper (Cited in #7A)

p. 30:
"Filmstrips ... are ... designated by the term 'filmstrip.' "

Comment

The Library of Congress will display the general material designation for filmstrips.

STATEMENTS OF RESPONSIBILITY

AACR 2

8.1F1: as in 1.1F

1.1F1: record in form appearing on item (Cited in #7B)

NBM 2

pp. 18, 19: exact wording found in source (Cited in #7B)

PUBLICATION, DISTRIBUTION, ETC., AREA

AACR 2

8.4C1: as in 1.4C

1.4C1: place of publication in form on item

1.4C3: add name of state

8.4D1: as in 1.4D

1.4D2: name of publisher in shortest form

8.4F1: as in 1.4F1

1.4F6: copyright date (Cited in #7A)

NBM 2

pp. 18, 19: name of place as given on item; add state; name of publisher in shortest form; copyright date (Cited in #7A)

PHYSICAL DESCRIPTION AREA—EXTENT OF ITEM

AACR 2

8.5B1: filmstrip (Cited in #7A)

AACR 2 (cont'd)

8.5B2. "Add to the designation for a ... filmstrip ... the number of frames ..."

NBM 2

p. 30:
"List the number of filmstrips ... and in parentheses the number of frames. The last numbered frame ... is recorded.[23]"

p. 124 (Appendix A — Notes):
"23. Last numbered frame taken from 2.5B2, [revised chapter 12 of AACR] rule 228D1, & ISBD (NBM) 5.1.11."

p. 30:
"*Option.* If a general material designation is used, the term '1 filmstrip' may be omitted ..."

pp. 20; 123: rationale for option to omit specific material designation (Cited in #7F)

Comment

NBM 2 allows an option, not permitted in AACR 2, for omitting the specific material designation if the general material designation has been used. As in many other instances, NBM 2 has included a rule which is at once a departure from AACR 2 and an attempt to provide a logical extension and more consistent application of AACR 2's own rules. At the same time, NBM 2 provides more specific guidance in determining the number of frames for filmstrips. The instruction to give the last numbered frame is based on the method of recording the pagination of books.

PHYSICAL DESCRIPTION AREA—OTHER PHYSICAL DETAILS

AACR 2

8.5C4. "**Filmstrips and filmslips.** Give an indication of sound if the sound is integral. If the sound is not integral, describe the accompanying sound as accompanying material (see 8.5E). Give an indication of the colour (col. or b&w)."

NBM 2

p. 30:
"If the sound is integral, list it."

"List b&w or col."

PHYSICAL DESCRIPTION AREA — DIMENSIONS

AACR 2

8.5D2. **"Filmstrips and filmslips.** Give the gauge (width) of the film in millimetres."

NBM 2

p. 30:
"Width is listed in millimetres."

PHYSICAL DESCRIPTION AREA — ACCOMPANYING MATERIALS

AACR 2

8.5E1: as in 1.5E

1.5E1: four ways of recording accompanying material (Cited in #7F)

Rule 1.5E1 continues:
"*Optional addition.* If ... further physical description is desired, add a statement of the extent, other physical details, and dimensions of the accompanying material as appropriate. Formulate such additional descriptions in accordance with the rules for the material or type of publication to which the accompanying material belongs."

8.5A1: punctuation, plus sign (Cited in #7F)

Rule 8.5A1 continues:
"Enclose physical details of accompanying material in parentheses."

(Chapter on sound recordings):
6.5B2. "Add to the [specific material] designation the stated total playing time of the sound recording in minutes (to the next minute up) ..."

6.5C3. "Give the playing speed of a tape in inches per second (ips)."

6.5C6. "For tape ... cassettes, ... give the number of tracks, unless the number of tracks is standard for that item.²"

footnote:
"2. The standard number of tracks for a cartridge is 8, for a cassette 4."

6.5C7. **"Number of sound channels.** Give one of the following terms as appropriate:

mono.
...   "

AACR 2 (cont'd)

*6.5D5. "Give the dimensions of the cassette if they are other than the standard dimensions (3⅞ x 2½ in.) in inches, and the width of the tape if other than the standard width (⅛ in.) in fractions of an inch."

NBM 2

p. 21: give subordinate accompanying material after dimensions (Cited in #7F)

p. 81 (Chapter on sound recordings):
"List in parentheses after the specific material designation the total playing time stated on the item ..."

"*Tapes*. List playing speed in inches per second (ips)."

"List the number of tracks only if it is not standard for the item."

"List mono., stereo ..."

*"*Cassettes*. List the dimensions in inches only if they are other than 3⅞ x 2½ in."

*"List the width of the tape in fractions of an inch only if it is other than ⅛ in."

Comment

Note that in both codes, the reader would consult the chapter on sound recordings for the detailed description of the accompanying material.

SERIES AREA

AACR 2

8.6B1: as in 1.6

1.6B1: title proper as in 1.1B (Cited in #7B)

1.6B2. "If variant forms of the title of the series ... appear, choose the title given in the chief source of information as the title proper of the series. **Give the variant form(s) in the note area if it is of value in identifying the item."

---

*Rule must be considered, to determine that no dimensions are given.
**Rule considered but not applied.

*1.1B2: title includes name of publisher (Cited in *title proper* section of #7F)

1.6G1: numbering (Cited in #7B)

NBM 2

p. 21: title proper; numbering (Cited in #7B)

Comment

The title proper of the series, as given in the chief source, includes the name of the producer ("presenter"). A Library of Congress rule interpretation will not regard such "credits" as part of the title proper. This rule interpretation applies to chapter seven ("Motion Pictures and Videorecordings"), but would seem equally appropriate in this case:

> **7.1B1.** ... When credits for performer, author, director, producer, "presenter," etc., precede or follow the title in the chief source, in general do not consider them as part of the title proper, even though the language used integrates the credits with the title. (In the examples below the underlined words are to be considered the title proper.)

> Twentieth Century Fox presents *Star wars*

> Steve McQueen in *Bullit*[7]

NOTE AREA

AACR 2

8.7B17: summary (Cited in #7A)

NBM 2

p. 22: summary (Cited in #7A)

CHOICE OF ACCESS POINTS

AACR 2

21.1C3: corporate body falls outside 21.1B2 — title entry (Cited in #7A)

NBM 2

The reader would consult AACR 2.

---

*Rule considered but not applied.

Comment

If the item being cataloged is the visual component, which contains only photographs, the only author under consideration is the photographer. While personal authorship in AACR 2 and NBM 2 is defined in terms of "the person chiefly responsible for the creation of the intellectual or artistic content of a work" (21.1A1), the decision as to what constitutes "chiefly responsible" is left with the cataloger. In this example, we are not likely to consider the photographer, credited at the end of the filmstrip in small print, as *chiefly* responsible. AECT 4 cautions that: "care should be exercised in determining if authors, consultants, etc., cited ... are the real creators of the filmstrip. For example, the author ... of the text that appears as captions on the filmstrip frames need not be the primary creator of the work" (p. 70).

71   OHIO, INDIANA, AND MICHIGAN

DESCRIPTION OF ITEM

Components: 1 slide, 2 x 2 inches, black and white

The slide is a reproduction of a map published in the early 1800s.
The original map is colored, and bears the title: "Ohio, Indiana, and Michigan." No statement of scale appears on the original map itself, but a scale of 1:1,570,000 has been computed by comparing the map with another map of known scale.

CATALOG RECORD

Ohio, Indiana, and Michigan [slide]. —
Scale ca. 1:1,570,000. — [United States? : s.n., 197-?]
1 slide : b&w.
Reproduction of colored map of early 1800s.

SCOPE / CATEGORIZATION

AACR 2

(Introductory chapter):
0.24. *"... the starting point for description is the physical form of the item in hand, not the original or any previous form in which the work has been published."

---

*This citation does not reflect the order in which these sentences appear.

"It is a cardinal principle of the use of Part I that the description of a physical item should be based in the first instance on the chapter dealing with the class of materials to which that item belongs.... There will be need in many instances to consult the chapter dealing with the original form of the item, especially when constructing notes."

(General rules for description):
1.11A. "In describing a facsimile, photocopy, or other reproduction of printed ... maps, ... give all the data relating to the facsimile, etc., in all areas except the note area.... If a facsimile, etc., is in a form of library material different from that of the original (e.g., a manuscript reproduced as a book), use the chapter on the form of the facsimile, etc., in determining the sources of information (e.g., for a manuscript reproduced as a book, use chapter 2). In addition to instructions given in the relevant chapters, follow the instructions in this rule."

8.0A: chapter covers slides (Cited in #7A, amplified by #7H)

NBM 2

p. 77:
Chapter title: "Slides"
"*Slide*: a small unit of transparent material containing an image, mounted in rigid format and designed for use in a slide viewer or projector."

"Slides ... are included under this heading ..."

Comment

This item is a map reproduced as a slide. According to AACR 2, the starting point for the description of such an item is the format of the reproduction, that is, the physical item in hand; therefore, cataloging of this item is based on chapter 8 (graphic materials) with chapter 3 (cartographic materials) used in conjunction. The user of NBM 2 must keep in mind the "cardinal principle" expressed in AACR 2's rule 0.24, since this principle is not mentioned in NBM 2. The rules for reproductions, contained in the general chapter on description in AACR 2 (1.11), state the same principle from a different perspective.

In the categorization of cartographic materials, two kinds of distinctions can be observed:

1) a cartographic item whose original form is a category of material dealt with in one of the chapters in Part One (e.g., a photograph, or three-dimensional artefact). Such items are governed by the rules for cartographic materials in Chapter 3.

2) a cartographic item (as is the case here) whose original form has been *reproduced* in a format dealt with in one of the chapters in Part One — for example, a map reproduced in microform. Such an item is governed by the rules for the format in which the map has been reproduced.

SOURCES OF INFORMATION

AACR 2

8.0B1: item itself (Cited in #7A)

NBM 2

p. 77:
"Information for the catalogue record should be taken from the following sources in this order:

1. The item itself. (Chief source of information). Preference is given to information on the slide rather than the mount;[54]"

p. 125 (Appendix A—Notes):
"54. Authors' interpretation of 8.0B1."

TITLE PROPER

AACR 2

8.1B1: as in 1.1B

1.1B1: transcribed exactly except for punctuation, capitalization (Cited in #7A)

NBM 2

p. 18: exactly from chief source, except for punctuation, capitalization (Cited in #7A)

GENERAL MATERIAL DESIGNATION

AACR 2

8.1C1: follows title proper

1.1C1: North American list

8.1A1: square brackets

A.4G: lowercase

p. 570 (Glossary):
"**Slide.** Transparent material on which there is a two-dimensional image, usually held in a mount, and designed for use in a projector or viewer."

NBM 2

p. 9: North American list

p. 18: lowercase, singular, brackets; follows title proper (Cited in #7A)

p. 77:
"Slides ... are ... designated by the term 'slide.' "

Comment

The Library of Congress will display the general material designation for slides.

MATHEMATICAL DATA AREA

AACR 2

(Chapter on cartographic materials):
3.3B1. "Give the scale of a cartographic item as a representative fraction expressed as a ratio (1:   ). Precede the ratio by the word *scale.*"

"If no statement of scale is found on the item, ... compute a representative fraction ... by comparison with a map of known scale. Give the scale preceded by *ca.*"

NBM 2

p. 48 (Chapter on maps):
"Mathematical data area
Scale. List the term 'Scale' and a representative fraction expressed as a ratio, e.g., Scale 1:1,000,000."

"If no scale is found, use a ... comparison with the scale of a similar map to determine one. Such a representative fraction is preceded by the term 'ca.' "

Comment

Since the chapter for cartographic materials is being used here in conjunction with the chapter for graphic materials, the mathematical data area can be included and a statement of scale indicated. However, the question can be raised as to whether the statement of scale would be appropriate, since the scale applies to the original and not to the reduced reproduction.

PUBLICATION, DISTRIBUTION, ETC., AREA

AACR 2

8.4C1: as in 1.4C (Cited in #7A)

1.4C6: name of country (Cited in #7D)

8.4D1: as in 1.4D (Cited in #7A)

1.4D6: publisher unknown (Cited in #7D)

8.4F1: as in 1.4F (Cited in #7A)

1.4F7: approximate date (Cited in #7C)

NBM 2

pp. 19, 20: name of country; publisher unknown; approximate date (Cited in #7C)

Comment

If the slide were known to have been issued in only one copy, and were thus to be considered as "unpublished," only the date would be given, according to the rule for unpublished graphic materials (8.4A2, as cited in example #7C).

PHYSICAL DESCRIPTION AREA—EXTENT OF ITEM

AACR 2

1.11D. "Give the physical description of the facsimile, etc., in the physical description area. Give the physical description of the original in the note area (see 1.11F)."

8.5B1: slide (Cited in #7A)

NBM 2

p. 77:
"List the number of slides."

PHYSICAL DESCRIPTION AREA—OTHER PHYSICAL DETAILS

AACR 2

8.5C12. "**Slides** ... Give an indication of the colour (col., b&w, etc.)."

NBM 2

p. 77:
"List b&w or col."

PHYSICAL DESCRIPTION AREA—DIMENSIONS

AACR 2

8.5D1. "For additional instructions on the dimensions of ... slides ... see 8.5D4-8.5D6."

8.5D5. "Give the height and the width only if the dimensions are other than 5 x 5 cm. (2 x 2 in.)."

NBM 2

p. 77:
"Height x width in centimetres are listed only if they are other than 5 x 5 cm."

NOTE AREA

AACR 2

*1.7A4. "In describing an item that is a reproduction of another (e.g., ... a set of maps reproduced as slides) give the notes relating to the reproduction and then the notes relating to the original. Combine the notes relating to the original in one note, giving the details in the order of the areas to which they relate."

8.7B17: summary (Cited in #7A)

NBM 2

p. 22: summary (Cited in #7A)

CHOICE OF ACCESS POINTS

AACR 2

21.1C1: authorship unknown; title entry (Cited in #7C)

NBM 2

The reader would consult AACR 2.

---

*Altered rule appears in AACR 2 revisions.

7J   WINNIE THE POOH AND THE HONEY TREE

DESCRIPTION OF ITEM

Components: 3 colored "Talking View-Master" reels (stereograph reels with attached sound component)

1 booklet (15p.) in cardboard box, 20.6 x 21 centimeters

Reel front:

1
Walt Disney Presents
WINNIE THE POOH
AND THE HONEY TREE

gaf® VIEW-MASTER   ®GAF Corporation
Stereo Reel   New York, N.Y., U.S.A.

Made in U.S.A.

©MCMLXIV Walt Disney Productions

On container:

Package Design c 1973

CATALOG RECORD

Winnie the Pooh and the honey tree [slide]. — New York, N.Y. : GAF Corp., c1964.

3 stereograph reels (View-Master) (7 double fr. each) : col. + 1 booklet.

Based on the story by A. A. Milne.

Text on mounts.

Stereograph reels contain attached sound component.

Summary: Pooh's love of honey gets him into trouble.

I. Milne, A. A. Winnie the Pooh. II. Walt Disney Productions.

Differences in NBM 2 version:

3 stereograph reels (7 double fr. each) : sd. (GAF Talking View-Master Reels), col. + 1 booklet.

SCOPE / CATEGORIZATION

AACR 2

8.0A: chapter covers slides (Cited in #7H)

NBM 2

p. 77: "slides" chapter (Cited in #7I)

Rule also includes:
"... stereographs are included under this heading ..."

SOURCES OF INFORMATION

AACR 2

8.0B1: item itself (Cited in #7A)

NBM 2

p. 77: item itself (Cited in #7I)

TITLE PROPER

AACR 2

8.1B1: as in 1.1B

1.1B1: transcribed exactly except for punctuation, capitalization (Cited in #7A)

*1.1B2: title includes statement of responsibility (Cited in #7F)

NBM 2

p. 18: exactly from chief source, except for punctuation, capitalization (Cited in #7A)

GENERAL MATERIAL DESIGNATION

AACR 2

8.1C1: follows title proper

---

*Rule considered but not applied.

AACR 2 (cont'd)

1.1C1: North American list

8.1A1: square brackets

A.4G: lowercase (Cited in #7A)

p. 570: definition of slide (Cited in #7I)

NBM 2

p. 9: North American list

p. 18: lowercase, singular, brackets; follows title proper (Cited in #7A)

p. 77:
"... stereographs are ... designated by the term 'slide.' "

PUBLICATION, DISTRIBUTION, ETC., AREA

AACR 2

8.4C1: as in 1.4C

1.4C1: place in form appearing on item

8.4D1: as in 1.4D

1.4D2: name in short form

8.4F1: date as in 1.4F

1.4F6: copyright date (Cited in #7A)

NBM 2

pp. 19, 20: name of place appearing on item; name of publisher in shortest form; copyright date (Cited in #7A)

Comment

The date given is the one appearing on the chief source.

PHYSICAL DESCRIPTION AREA—EXTENT OF ITEM

AACR 2

8.5B1: stereograph (Cited in #7A)

Rule continues:
"Add the trade name or other technical specification to the term for a stereograph."

"Add to ... stereograph the [word] ... *reel* when appropriate.

...

 3 stereograph reels (Viewmaster)"

8.5B2. "Add to the designation for a ... stereograph the number of frames or pairs of frames, the latter designated *double frames.*

...

 1 stereograph reel (Viewmaster) (7 double fr.)"

8.5B5. "If the parts of a multipart ... stereograph ... have the same number of components (frames, sheets, etc.) ..., use the form *3 filmstrips (50 fr. each)* ...

 4 filmstrips (50 double fr. each)"

NBM 2

p. 77:
"*Stereographs.* List the number of stereographs. If the stereograph is circular, use the term 'stereograph reel.' The trade name or other technical specification and the number of double frames are added, each in its own parentheses."

Comment

The term "Talking Viewmaster Reels" can be considered both as a trade name and as a sound statement. In this example, the term is recorded in the "other physical details" section as a sound statement in the NBM 2 record, since NBM 2 provides a rule for an integral sound component of a stereograph. AACR 2 makes no such provision, at least not explicitly, and so the term is added as a trade name after the extent of item.

PHYSICAL DESCRIPTION AREA—OTHER PHYSICAL DETAILS

AACR 2

*By analogy:
 8.5C12: rules for slides (Cited in #7I)

 Rule also includes:
 "**Slides.** Give an indication of sound if the sound is integral. Add the name

---

*This analogy was considered but not applied.

AACR 2 (cont'd)

of the system (e.g., 3M Talking Slide) after the indication of sound.

> 12 slides : sd. (3M Talking Slide), col."

8.5C13. "**Stereographs.** Give an indication of the colour (col., b&w, etc.).

> 1 stereograph reel (Viewmaster) (7 double fr.) : col."

NBM 2

p. 77:
"If the sound is integral, list it.[55] Name the sound system in parentheses ..."

"List b&w or col."

p. 125 (Appendix A—Notes):
"55. AACR/2 gives directions for sound slides only (8.5C12). This has been extended to stereographs because there seems to be no reason why a producer could not market sound stereographs."

Comment

This format, a stereograph with attached sound, has not been provided for in AACR 2. As the rules stand, integral sound can be indicated for slides, but not for stereographs, which can be described only in terms of color. Presumably, this particular format had not been anticipated by the writers of the code. If one catalogs by analogy, one could borrow from the rules appropriate for slides with an integral sound component (8.5C12). NBM 2 has already included such an analogy in its rules, out of the recognition that rule 8.5C12 is capable of a broader application.

AECT 4 makes no mention of sound stereographs in its rules, but includes an example of such a format in its model cards. In this case, however, the audio-component is described as accompanying material:

> "21 stereoscope slides: col.; in 3 circular cardboard reels, 9 cm. & 1 audiodisc, 8 cm.; attached to reel."   (p. 191)

PHYSICAL DESCRIPTION AREA—DIMENSIONS

AACR 2

8.5D3. "**Stereographs.** Do not give any dimensions."

NBM 2

p. 77:
"*Stereographs.* Dimensions are not listed."

Comment

No dimensions for stereographs are given in AACR 2, presumably on the assumption that the size and shape of this medium are uniform. This is an erroneous assumption, however, since there are stereographs which are rectangular in shape and of varying dimensions. The code would do better to require that dimensions be given if they are other than the standard for the medium, as is done, for example, in the case of slides (8.5D5). AECT 4, on the other hand, appears to make no exception for stereographs in its rules for the statement of dimensions.

PHYSICAL DESCRIPTION AREA—ACCOMPANYING MATERIALS

AACR 2

8.5E1: as in 1.5E

1.5E1: four ways of recording accompanying material

8.5A1: punctuation (Cited in #7F)

NBM 2

p. 21: give subordinate accompanying material after dimensions (Cited in #7F)

NOTE AREA

AACR 2

8.7B7. **"Edition and history.** Make notes relating to the edition being described or to the history of the item.

...

Based on the fairy tale by H. C. Andersen."

8.7B10: physical description (Cited in #7B)

8.7B17: summary (Cited in #7A)

NBM 2

p. 22 (General rules):
"Edition and history"

p. 22: physical description (Cited in #7B)

p. 22: summary (Cited in #7A)

CHOICE OF ACCESS POINTS

AACR 2

21.9. "Enter a work that is a modification of another under the heading appropriate to the new work if the modification has substantially changed the nature and content of the original or if the medium of expression has been changed."

"For specific applications of this general rule, see 21.10-21.23."

21.10. "Enter a paraphrase, rewriting ... under the heading for the adapter. If the name of the adapter is unknown, enter under title. Make a name-title added entry for the original work."

21.30G. "Make an added entry under the heading for a work to which the work being catalogued is closely related (see 21.8-21.28 for guidance in specific cases).
Make such entries in the form of the heading for the person ... or the title under which the related work is, or would be, entered. If the heading is for a person ..., and the title of the related work differs from that of the work being catalogued, add the title of the related work to the heading to form a name-title added entry heading."

NBM 2

The reader would consult AACR 2.

FORM OF HEADING

AACR 2

22.3A. "If the forms of a name vary in fullness, choose the form most commonly found."

22.16A. "If part or all of a name is represented by initials and the full form is known, add the spelled out form in parentheses if necessary to distinguish between names that are otherwise identical."

*"*Optionally*, make the above additions to other names containing initials."

NBM 2

Outside the scope of this code. The reader would consult AACR 2.

---

*Option not applied.

Comment

Note the following LC rule interpretation:

Even though for headings established after December 1980, the Library of Congress practice is to add full forms within parentheses whenever the information is known (as opposed to adding it only in cases of conflict), this will not be applied to headings established before January 1981. Thus the heading "Eddison, C. D." should be accepted as an AACR 2 one, even though the heading would be "Eddison, C. D. (Carlton Daniel)" if he were a new author.[8]

NOTES

1.   Library of Congress, Processing Services, *Cataloging Service Bulletin*, no. 13 (Summer 1981), p. 15.

2.   Ibid., p. 16.

3.   *CSB*, no. 12 (Spring 1981), p. 7.

4.   *CSB*, no. 13 (Summer 1981), p. 9.

5.   Ibid., p. 16.

6.   Frances Hinton, "Part II: Choice of Access Points," in *Examples for Applying the Anglo-American Cataloguing Rules, Second Edition* (Chicago: American Library Association, 1980), p. 23.

7.   *CSB*, no. 13 (Summer 1981), p. 15.

8.   *CSB*, no. 11 (Winter 1981), p. 26.

8

THREE-DIMENSIONAL ARTEFACTS
AND REALIA

Three-dimensional artefacts and realia is a comprehensive category that includes various instructional media (e.g., models, dioramas, games), naturally occurring objects (e.g., microscope specimens, rocks), works of art (e.g., sculptures, mobiles), and innumerable types of artefacts (e.g., clothing, furniture, machines) which were not originally intended for communication but can serve as an object of study or appreciation.

In AACR, these materials were excluded entirely. In AACR 2, a method for description is given which is consistent with the description of other library materials. Although such materials may have a most "unbook-like" appearance, their description as prescribed by AACR 2 and ISBD guidelines presents relatively few problems.

Since many objects in this category are not "published" in the usual sense of the word, provision is made to omit the publication data for naturally occurring objects and for artefacts not intended primarily for communication.

8A   MONOPOLY GAME

DESCRIPTION OF ITEM

> Components: 1 playing board (49 centimeters square)
> 2 dice
> 8 tokens (figures to mark a player's move)
> 32 plastic houses
> 12 plastic hotels
> Title deed cards
> "Chance" cards
> "Community chest" cards
> Play money
> Instructions
>
> All of above in container.
> Dimensions of container: 25½ x 50 x 3½ centimeters (height x width x depth)

Container, front:

MONOPOLY
Parker Brothers Real Estate Trading Game

_____

Container, side:

MONOPOLY	Parker Brothers
A Parker Game No. 9	Real Estate
2 to 8 Players	Trading Game
Ages 8 to adult	

c1935, 1961, 1975 Parker Brothers Div. of General Mills Fun Group, Inc.
Salem, Mass. 01970 Made in U.S.A.

_____

Instruction booklet:

c1935, 1936, 1947, 1951, 1952, 1954, 1961, 1973

Object ... The object of the game is to become the wealthiest player through buying, renting and selling property.

_____

CATALOG RECORD

Monopoly [game] : Parker Brothers real estate trading
game. — Salem, Mass. : Parker, c1975.
1 game (1 players' manual, 1 board, cards, 2 dice, 8 tokens, 44
plastic markers, play money) : col. ; in box, 26 x 50 x 4 cm. — (A
Parker game ; no. 9).
Ages 8 to adult.
For 2 to 8 players.
"The object of the game is to become the wealthiest player through
buying, renting and selling property."

I. Parker Brothers.

_____

SCOPE / CATEGORIZATION

AACR 2

10.0A. "The rules in this chapter cover the description of three-dimensional artefacts of all kinds (other than those covered in previous chapters), including models, dioramas, games (including puzzles and simulations) ..."

NBM 2

p. 36:
Chapter title: "Games"
"*Game*: a set of materials designed for play according to prescribed rules."

SOURCES OF INFORMATION

AACR 2

10.0B1. "The chief source of information for the materials covered in this chapter is the object itself together with any accompanying textual material and container issued by the 'publisher' or manufacturer of the item. Prefer information found on the object itself (including any permanently affixed labels) to information found in accompanying textual material or on a container."

NBM 2

p. 17 (General rules):
"If an item consists of more than one part, the chief source of information is as follows:

1.   The piece that could be considered 'the first part.' In nonbook terms this might be the part which gives meaning to the various parts,[4] e.g., a manual or a container which is the unifying element;[5] ..."

"The chief source of information is identified in most of the sections of this book dealing with a specific medium. It is from this source that the title and statements of responsibility are taken. If the title must be taken from another part of the item, ... the source of the title is given in the note area. Dioramas, games, microscope slides, models, and realia are exceptions to this because the item, accompanying materials, and container are all considered chief sources of information."

p. 123 (Appendix A—Notes):
"4.   Authors' interpretation of 'first part' 1.0H (multipart items) applied to nonbook materials."

"5.   'container which is the unifying element'—8.0B1."

TITLE PROPER

AACR 2

10.1B1. "Record the title proper as instructed in 1.1B."

1.1B1. "Transcribe the title proper exactly as to wording, order and spelling, but not necessarily as to punctuation and capitalization."

NBM 2

p. 18 (General rules):
"The title proper ... is copied exactly from the chief source of information. However, capitalization and punctuation follow prescribed rules."

GENERAL MATERIAL DESIGNATION

AACR 2

10.1C1. (Optional). "Add immediately following the title proper the appropriate general material designation as instructed in 1.1C."

1.1C1. "If general material designations are to be used in cataloguing, ... North American agencies [should use] terms from list 2."

10.1A1. "Enclose the general material designation in square brackets."

(Appendix A — Capitalization):
A.4G. "Lowercase the words making up a general material designation."

p. 566 (Glossary):
"**Game.** A set of materials designed for play according to prescribed rules."

NBM 2

p. 9 (Chapter on cataloging policy for media centers):
"The North American list of general material designations is used in this book. Those electing [to omit the general material designation or to use] the British list ... or the ISBD list may use the rules on the following pages by disregarding the general material designation or by substituting the appropriate term from the British or ISBD lists."

p. 18 (General rules):
"A general material designation is listed in lower case letters, in the singular, and in its own square brackets immediately following the title proper."

Comment

The Library of Congress does not catalog games, but the general material designation will be displayed if the Library ever does catalog the material.

OTHER TITLE INFORMATION

AACR 2

10.1E1. "Record other title information as instructed in 1.1E."

AACR 2 (cont'd)

1.1E1. "Transcribe all other title information appearing in the chief source of information according to the instructions in 1.1B."

1.1E4. "If the other title information includes ... the name of a publisher, distributor, etc., and the ... name is an integral part of the other title information, transcribe it as such."

NBM 2

p. 18 (General rules):
"TITLE AND STATEMENT OF RESPONSIBILITY AREA
The following will provide guidance for the cataloguing of many nonbook items. When these brief rules will not suffice, see the *Anglo-American Cataloguing Rules*, 2nd edition, rule 1.1."

"Other title information ... follows the general material designation and the title proper ... to which it pertains. [It is] listed in the exact wording found in the chief source of information."

PUBLICATION, DISTRIBUTION, ETC., AREA

AACR 2

10.4C1. "Record the place of publication, distribution, etc., as instructed in 1.4C."

1.4C1. "Record the place of publication, etc., in the form ... in which it appears."

*1.4C3. "Add the name of the country, state, province, etc., to the name of the place if it is considered necessary for identification, or if it is considered necessary to distinguish the place from others of the same name."

10.4D1. "Record the name of the publisher, distributor, etc., as instructed in 1.4D."

1.4D4. "If the name of the publisher, distributor, etc., appears in a recognizable form in the title and statement of responsibility area, give it in the publication, distribution, etc., area in a shortened form."

10.4F1. "Record the date of publication, distribution, etc., as instructed in 1.4F."

1.4F6. "If the dates of publication, distribution, etc., are unknown, give the copyright date ... in its place."

---

*For LC rule interpretation, see example #4B, p. 81.

NBM 2

pp. 19, 20 (General rules):
"List the name of the place as it appears on the item and add the name of the province, state, country, etc., if it is necessary for identification."

"A publisher, etc., who has appeared in the title and statement of responsibility area is listed in an abbreviated form."

"If the dates of publication or distribution cannot be ascertained, list the copyright date."

PHYSICAL DESCRIPTION AREA—EXTENT OF ITEM

AACR 2

10.5B1. "Record the number of physical units of a three-dimensional artefact or object by giving the number of parts in arabic numerals and one of the terms listed below, as appropriate. If none of these terms is appropriate, give the specific name of the item or the names of the parts of the item as concisely as possible.

diorama	microscope slide
exhibit	mock up
game	model "

*"*Optionally*, if general material designations are used and the general material designation consists of one of the above listed terms, drop that term and give the number of pieces alone (see 10.5B2)."

10.5B2. "Add to the designation, when appropriate, the number and the name(s) of the pieces.
1 game (2 players' manuals, board, cards, role cards, 2 dice)"

**"If the pieces cannot be named concisely or cannot be ascertained, add the term *various pieces*, and *optionally* give the details of the pieces in a note (see 10.7B10)."

NBM 2

p. 36:
"List the number of games in the item and add, if appropriate, in parentheses, the number and names of the pieces. **When the number and/or type of pieces cannot be ascertained easily, the term 'various pieces' is used."

---

*This option was not applied here.
**Rule considered but not applied.

NBM 2 (cont'd)

*"*Option*. If the general material designation 'game' is used, the term '1 game' may be omitted ..."

Comment

Whether the extent will be described in terms of the components of the game or as "various pieces" will depend on one's definition of a "concise" description.

The Library of Congress will not apply the option in 10.5B1 of AACR 2.

PHYSICAL DESCRIPTION AREA — OTHER PHYSICAL DETAILS

AACR 2

10.5C1. "**Material.** If the material(s) cannot be stated concisely, either omit them or give them in a note."

10.5C2. "**Colour.** When appropriate, give the abbreviation *col.* for multicoloured objects, ... or give the abbreviation *b&w*."

NBM 2

p. 36:
"List ... col. or b&w, if such information is useful."

PHYSICAL DESCRIPTION AREA — DIMENSIONS

AACR 2

10.5D1. **"*Give the dimensions of the object, when appropriate, in centimetres, to the next whole centimetre up.... If multiple dimensions are given, record them as height x width x depth ..."

10.5D2. "If the object is in a container, name the container and give its dimensions either after the dimensions of the object or as the only dimensions."

NBM 2

p. 36:
"List the type of packaging and its dimensions in centimetres."

p. 21 (General rules):
"[T]hree-dimensional materials [are measured] height x width x depth. Fractions are taken to the next number."

---

*Option not applied.
**Rule considered but not applied.

SERIES AREA

AACR 2

10.6B1. "Record each series statement as instructed in 1.6."

1.6B1. "If an item is one of a series, record the title proper of the series as instructed in 1.1B ..."

1.6G1. "Record the numbering of the item within the series in the terms given in the item."

NBM 2

p. 21 (General rules):
"If applicable, a series statement in parentheses follows the physical description area. The series area in 3rd level cataloguing could include:

title proper of series

...

numbering within series"

NOTE AREA

AACR 2

10.7B14. "**Audience.** Make a brief note of the intended audience for, or intellectual level of, an item if this information is stated in the item."

10.7B17. "**Summary.** Give a brief objective summary of the content of an item unless another part of the description gives enough information."

NBM 2

p. 22:
"Audience level as stated on the item is listed.* Such information may not be desirable in a public catalogue, particularly for juvenile and youth collections."

"Summaries. *These are not necessary for media which can be readily examined or adequately described by title and/or series statement ..."

---

*Rule considered but not applied.

CHOICE OF ACCESS POINTS

AACR 2

21.1C. "Enter a work under its title when:

... 3) it emanates from a corporate body but does not fall into one or more of the categories given in 21.1B2 and is not of personal authorship"

NBM 2

The reader would consult AACR 2.

8B   ART NOUVEAU

DESCRIPTION OF ITEM

Components: 1 two-sided jigsaw puzzle, colored, cardboard, in box,
30 x 20.3 x 4.9 centimeters (height x width x depth)

Box, side:

JP 23-400

ART NOUVEAU
Two-Sided Puzzle
15" x 22". Over 500 pieces
The Puzzle Factory 363 E. 76th St. New York, N.Y. 10021

Opposite side of box:

JP 23-400

THEATRE
Two-Sided Puzzle
15" x 22". Over 500 Pieces
The Puzzle Factory 363 E. 76th St. New York, N.Y. 10021

One side of the box shows a representation of the assembled puzzle "Theatre." This is a reproduction of a poster advertising a theatre performance. The other side of the box shows a representation of the assembled puzzle "Art nouveau." This is a reproduction of two posters of the turn of the century.

CATALOG RECORD

Art nouveau : two-sided puzzle ; Theatre : two-sided puzzle [game]. —
New York, N.Y. : Puzzle Factory, [197?].
1 jigsaw puzzle (ca. 500 pieces) : cardboard, col. ; in box,
30 x 21 x 5 cm.
When assembled, the puzzles are 15 x 22 inches, and depict two
posters of the turn of the century.
"JP 23-400"

I. Title: Theatre. II. Puzzle Factory.

SCOPE / CATEGORIZATION

AACR 2

10.0A: chapter covers puzzles (Cited in #8A)

NBM 2

p. 36: "games" chapter (Cited in #8A)

SOURCES OF INFORMATION

AACR 2

10.0B1: chief source is item itself, container (Cited in #8A)

NBM 2

p. 17: chief source is item itself, container (Cited in #8A)

TITLE PROPER

AACR 2

10.1B1: as in 1.1B

1.1B1: transcribed exactly except for punctuation, capitalization (Cited in #8A)

10.1G1. "If an item lacks a collective title, record the titles of the individual works as instructed in 1.1B."

1.1G2. "If, in an item lacking a collective title, no one part predominates, record the titles of the individually titled parts in the order in which they are named in the chief source of information, or in the order in which they appear in

AACR 2 (cont'd)

the item if there is no single chief source of information. Separate the titles of the parts by semicolons if the parts are all by the same person(s) or body (bodies), even if the titles are linked by a connecting word of phrase. *If the individual parts are by different persons or bodies, or in case of doubt, follow the title of each part by its ... other title information, ... and a full stop followed by two spaces."

NBM 2

p. 18: exactly from chief source, except for punctuation, capitalization (Cited in #8A)

p. 19 (General rules):
"Items without a collective title may be described in one of the following ways:

...

2. If no work is predominant, list the titles ... in the order in which they appear in the chief source of information."

"*Punctuation*. If the works are all by the same author(s), the individual titles are separated by space-semicolon-space (;). *If the works are by different authors, the title and statement of responsibility area for each work is separated from the one previously listed by a period and 2 spaces (.)."

**"3. Make a separate description[8] for each part that has a distinctive title, and link the descriptions with a 'with' note ..."

p. 123 (Appendix A—Notes):
"8.   3.1G1 & 3.1G4, 6.1G1 & 6.1G4, 7.1G1 & 7.1G4, 11.1G1 & 11.1G4 allow this method. 8.1G1 & 10.1G1 do not. This seems inconsistent and therefore has been made a general rule in this book."

Comment

In applying AACR 2's rule 1.1G2, it is necessary to decide whether the individual parts are by different persons or bodies. While the two posters are not by the same artist, the two titles being cataloged both are issued by the same corporate body, The Puzzle Factory, which has provided these titles as names for the two sides of the puzzle. Neither title is the original title given by the two artists to their posters.

---

*Rule considered but not applied.
**Option not applied in this example.

Note that NBM 2 allows an option to provide separate bibliographic records for each title. This is a departure from AACR 2, and is drawn from similar rules in the chapters for sound recordings, motion pictures and videorecordings, cartographic materials, and microforms. For similar examples of works without collective titles, see the Osaka example, #4C, and the Devienne example, #5F. Since there is no discernible order to the two titles, either title could appear first.

GENERAL MATERIAL DESIGNATION

AACR 2

10.1C1: follows title proper

1.1C1: North American list

10.1A1: square brackets

A.4G: lowercase

p. 566: definition of game (Cited in #8A)

NBM 2

p. 9: North American list

p. 18: lowercase, singular, brackets; follows title proper (Cited in #8A)

p. 19 (General rules):
"The general material designation is listed immediately after the last of a group of titles by one author."

OTHER TITLE INFORMATION

AACR 2

10.1E1: as in 1.1E

1.1E1: transcribe as in 1.1B (Cited in #8A)

NBM 2

p. 18: exact wording found in source (Cited in #8A)

Comment

The definition of "other title information" in AACR 2 would support the inclusion of "two-sided jigsaw puzzle" in the title area, rather than in a note: **"Other title information.** Any title borne by an item other than the title proper ...;

also any phrase appearing in conjunction with the title proper ... indicative of the character, contents, etc., of the item ..." (p. 568, Glossary).

PUBLICATION, DISTRIBUTION, ETC., AREA

AACR 2

10.4C1: as in 1.4C

1.4C1: place in form on item

1.4C3: add name of state

10.4D1: as in 1.4D (Cited in #8A)

1.4D2. "Give the name of a publisher, distributor, etc., in the shortest form in which it can be understood and identified internationally."

10.4F1: as in 1.4F (Cited in #8A)

1.4F7. "If no date of publication, distribution, etc., copyright date, or date of manufacture can be assigned to an item, give an approximate date of publication."

NBM 2

pp. 19, 20: name of place as given on item; add state; name of publisher in shortest form; date (Cited in #8A)

p. 20, rule continues:
"If no date can be found, give an approximate date. (See the *Anglo-American Cataloguing Rules*, 2nd edition, rule 1.4F7.)"

PHYSICAL DESCRIPTION AREA—EXTENT OF ITEM

AACR 2

10.5B1: specific name of item

10.5B2: number of pieces (Cited in #8A)

NBM 2

p. 36: game; number of pieces (Cited in #8A)

p. 20 (General rules):
"If the components are too numerous to count, an approximate figure may be listed, e.g., 1 filmstrip (ca. 90 fr.) ..."

Comment

AACR 2's chapter 10 does not make an explicit provision for stating an approximate number of pieces. Some other chapters, however, include rules for stating an approximate number for component parts; for example, the chapter on graphic materials, in rule 8.5B2: "If the frames [of a filmstrip, filmslip, or stereograph] are unnumbered and are too numerous to count, give an approximate figure." Similar rules are provided for books, pamphlets, and printed sheets (2.5B7), and for motion pictures and videorecordings (rule 7.5B2), which would support the extension of these provisions by analogy, to chapter 10. Note that NBM 2 (p. 20) gives a general rule which is applicable to all materials.

NBM 2 permits the more specific term "jigsaw puzzle" to be used in place of the general term "game," but the reader would have to refer to AACR 2 for this instruction.

AECT 4 defines *puzzle* as "a work which presents a problem that requires solution, and tests problem-solving skills" (p. 219).

PHYSICAL DESCRIPTION AREA — OTHER PHYSICAL DETAILS

AACR 2

10.5C1: material

10.5C2: color (Cited in #8A)

NBM 2

p. 36: color (Cited in #8A)

Rule also includes:
"List the material from which the item was made ..."

PHYSICAL DESCRIPTION AREA — DIMENSIONS

AACR 2

10.5D1: height x width x depth

10.5D2: container (Cited in #8A)

NBM 2

p. 36: height x width x depth; packaging (Cited in #8A)

NOTE AREA

AACR 2

1.7A5. "When appropriate, combine two or more notes to make one note."

10.7B1. "**Nature of the item.** Give the nature of the item unless it is apparent from the rest of the description."

10.7B10. "**Physical description.** Give important physical details that have not been included in the physical description area, especially if these affect the use of the item."

10.7B17: summary (Cited in #8A)

10.7B19. "**Numbers.** Give important numbers borne by the item other than ISBNs or ISSNs ..."

NBM 2

p. 22 (General rules):
"Nature, scope, or artistic form"

"Additional information concerning the physical description, particularly if such information affects the use of the item ..."

p. 22: summary (Cited in #8A)

"Numbers associated with the item other than ISBNs or ISSNs ..."

CHOICE OF ACCESS POINTS

AACR 2

21.1C3: corporate body falls outside 21.1B2 — title entry (Cited in #8A)

NBM 2

The reader would consult AACR 2.

8C   KIDNEY MODEL

DESCRIPTION OF ITEM

Components: 1 model of a kidney; red and yellow; plastic

The model is made of two separate pieces, which open to show a cross section of a kidney. It stands 14 centimeters high and 9 centimeters wide.

Printed on the model is "Merck and Co., Inc., c1961." A reference source indicates that this company is located in Rahway, N.J.

CATALOG RECORD

[Kidney] [model]. — [Rahway, N.J.] : Merck, c1961.
   1 model (2 pieces) : plastic, red and yellow ; 14 x
9 cm.
      Title supplied by cataloger.
      Model opens for viewing cross section of kidney.

SCOPE / CATEGORIZATION

AACR 2

10.0A: chapter covers models (Cited in #8A)

NBM 2

p. 62:
Chapter title: "Models"
"*Model*: a three-dimensional representation of an object, either exact or to scale; a mock-up."

SOURCES OF INFORMATION

AACR 2

10.0B1: object itself (Cited in #8A)

NBM 2

p. 17: item itself (Cited in #8A)

Comment

This item undoubtedly was housed in some sort of container at the time of its issuance. Since the container has been discarded, and was not available at the time of cataloging, the description is on the basis of the item itself as the sole source of information.

TITLE PROPER

AACR 2

10.1B1: as in 1.1B (Cited in #8A)

1.1B7. "If no title can be found in any source, devise a brief descriptive title. Enclose such a ... devised title in square brackets."

NBM 2

p. 17 (General rules):
"SOURCES OF INFORMATION
5. Information supplied by the cataloguer. Such information is enclosed in square brackets. Supplied titles should be descriptive, reasonably concise, and if possible begin with a filing word which reflects subject content."

GENERAL MATERIAL DESIGNATION

AACR 2

10.1C1: follows title proper

1.1C1: North American list

10.1A1: square brackets

A.4G: lowercase (Cited in #8A)

p. 568 (Glossary):
"Model. A three-dimensional representation of a real thing, either of the exact size of the original or to scale."

1.0C. **"Punctuation.** ... When adjacent elements within one area are to be enclosed in square brackets, enclose them in one set of square brackets unless one of the elements is a general material designation, which is always enclosed in its own set of brackets."

NBM 2

p. 9: North American list

p. 18: lowercase, singular, brackets; follows title proper (Cited in #8A)

Comment

The Library of Congress does not catalog models, but the general material designation will be displayed if the Library ever does catalog the material.

PUBLICATION, DISTRIBUTION, ETC., AREA

AACR 2

10.0B2. **"Prescribed sources of information.** ... Enclose information taken from outside the prescribed source(s) in square brackets."

" AREA	PRESCRIBED SOURCES OF INFORMATION
...	...
Publication, distribution, etc.	Chief source of information"

10.4C1: as in 1.4C

1.4C1: place in form on item

1.4C3: add name of state

10.4D1: as in 1.4D (Cited in #8A)

1.4D2: name of publisher in shortest form (Cited in #8B)

10.4F1: as in 1.4F

1.4F6: copyright date (Cited in #8A)

NBM 2

pp. 19, 20: name of place as given on item; add state; name of publisher in shortest form; copyright date (Cited in #8A)

p. 17 (General rules):
"5. Information supplied by the cataloguer. Such information is enclosed in square brackets."

Comment

This item will be considered as an "artefact intended primarily for communication" since its basic purpose is educational. (See discussion in example #8D.)

PHYSICAL DESCRIPTION AREA—EXTENT OF ITEM

AACR 2

10.5B1: model

10.5B2: number of pieces

(Cited in #8A)

NBM 2

p. 62:
"List the number of models in the item and add, if appropriate, in parentheses the number of pieces."

*"*Option*. If the general material designation 'model' is used, the term '1 model' may be omitted ..."

PHYSICAL DESCRIPTION AREA—OTHER PHYSICAL DETAILS

AACR 2

10.5C1. "When appropriate, give the material(s) of which the object is made."

10.5C2. "... name the colour(s) of the object if it is in one or two colours ..."

NBM 2

p. 62:
"List the material from which the item was made.... If the item is in one or two colours, state these colours."

PHYSICAL DESCRIPTION AREA—DIMENSIONS

AACR 2

10.5D1: height x width in centimeters (Cited in #8A)

NBM 2

p. 62:
"List the dimensions in centimetres with, if necessary, **a word or phrase identifying the dimension."

p. 21: fractions (Cited in #8A)

---

*Option not applied.
**Rule considered but not applied.

NOTE AREA

AACR 2

10.7B3. **"Source of title proper.** Make notes on the source of the title proper if it is other than the chief source of information."

10.7B10: physical description (Cited in #8B)

NBM 2

p. 22 (General rules):
"Source of title proper"

p. 22: physical description (Cited in #8B)

CHOICE OF ACCESS POINTS

AACR 2

21.1C3: corporate body falls outside 21.1B2—title entry (Cited in #8A)

NBM 2

The reader would consult AACR 2.

8D   WITCH PUPPET

DESCRIPTION OF ITEM

Components: 1 hand puppet; various colors; 50 centimeters high.

The puppet, depicting a witch, was designed and made by Ruthette Mills, a Michigan artisan. The item was acquired at an art fair in 1979. Ms. Mills lives in McMillan, Michigan.

CATALOG RECORD

Mills, Ruthette.
[Witch puppet] [realia]. — [1979? (McMillan, Mich. : Ruthette Mills)]
1 hand puppet : cloth, col. ; 50 cm. high.
Title supplied by cataloger.
Designed and made by Ruthette Mills.

SCOPE / CATEGORIZATION

AACR 2

10.0A: chapter covers three-dimensional artefacts (Cited in #8A)

NBM 2

p. 75:
Chapter title: "Realia"
"*Realia*: actual objects; artifacts, samples, specimens."

Comment

While some may find it difficult to accept the term "realia" for an object of this kind, and while "actual objects" or "real things as they are" may be difficult to reconcile in a metaphysical sense (is not a book or a map "real"?), a quick perusal of the other available categories reveals that this is the only possible place in the codes for three-dimensional artefacts; that is, "three-dimensional" in the sense that all three dimensions are needed to convey the artistic or intellectual message of the medium.

AECT 4 defines *realia* as: "... real things as they are, without alteration. Realia include both natural objects and those produced by human workmanship" (p. 178).

Since this item was produced in multiple copies, albeit by hand, and made available for purchase, it was not considered appropriate to use NBM 2's chapter for "locally-produced non-commercial materials" (p. 99).

SOURCES OF INFORMATION

AACR 2

10.0B1: item itself (Cited in #8A)

NBM 2

p. 17: item itself (Cited in #8A)

TITLE PROPER

AACR 2

10.1B1: as in 1.1B (Cited in #8A)

1.1B7: supplied title (Cited in #8C)

NBM 2

p. 17: supplied title (Cited in #8C)

GENERAL MATERIAL DESIGNATION

AACR 2

10.1C1: follows title proper

1.1C1: North American list

10.1A1: square brackets

A.4G: lowercase

p. 569 (Glossary):
"**Realia.** Actual objects (artefacts, specimens) as opposed to replicas."

1.0C: punctuation (Cited in #8C)

NBM 2

p. 9: North American list

p. 18: lowercase, singular, brackets; follows title proper (Cited in #8A)

Comment

The Library of Congress does not catalog realia, but the general material designation will be displayed if the Library ever does catalog the material.

STATEMENTS OF RESPONSIBILITY

AACR 2

10.1F1. "Record statements relating to persons or bodies responsible for the creation of the item ... as instructed in 1.1F."

1.1F2. "If no statement of responsibility appears prominently in the item, neither construct one nor extract one from the content of the item.... If such a statement is necessary, give it in a note."

NBM 2

The reader would refer to AACR 2.

PUBLICATION, DISTRIBUTION, ETC., AREA

AACR 2

10.4C2. "In the case of ... artefacts not intended primarily for communication, do not record any place of publication, etc."

10.4D2. "In the case of ... artefacts not intended primarily for communication, do not record any name of publisher, distributor, etc."

10.4F2. "In the case of artefacts not intended primarily for communication, give the date of manufacture as the first element of this area."

1.4F7: approximate date (Cited in #8B)

10.4G1. "If the name of the publisher, distributor, etc., is unknown or not applicable (see 10.4C2 and 10.4D2), give the place and the name of the manufacturer, if known, as instructed in 1.4G."

1.4G1. "If the name of the publisher is unknown, give the place and name of the manufacturer if they are found in the item.

[S.l. : s.n.], 1970 (London : High Fidelity Sound Studios)"

1.4G2. "In recording the place and name of the manufacturer, follow the instructions in 1.4B-1.4D."

10.4A1. "Enclose the details of manufacture (place, name, date) in parentheses."

NBM 2

p. 75:
"List the place, publisher/producer/distributor and date for items which have been packaged or mounted by an outside agency ..."

"List only meaningful dates for all other realia ..."

p. 20 (General rules):
"*Option.* If the information is considered important, the place, name of manufacturer, and/or date of manufacture may be added in parentheses at the end of the publication, distribution, etc., area."

Comment

There will undoubtedly be some differences of opinion as to whether this item is to be considered as an artefact "not intended primarily for communication." My own experience in teaching the AACR 2 code has shown that the phrase can convey a variety of meanings. The examples given to illustrate the rules in question include an "English Victorian costume" and a "United States silver dollar." The puppet would appear to be in a similar category, but some might view it as having an artistic message. The assumption made here, however, will be that the object is "not intended primarily for communication."

NBM 2 has avoided this phrase, and instead bases its rules for inclusion of publication data on whether the items "have been packaged or mounted by an outside agency." Thus NBM 2's criterion for inclusion of publication data rests upon whether the item can be considered as "published" in the sense of being made presentable for distribution.

The place and name of the "manufacturer" have been given in accordance with 10.4G1. This rule refers the reader to 1.4G, which states, "If the name of the publisher is unknown, give the place and name of the manufacturer if they are found in the item." I am assuming here, however, that the place and name of the manufacturer need not be stated on the item itself in order for 10.4G1 to be applied. This assumption is based on the fact that 10.4G1 makes no specific mention of such a requirement, while in every other chapter in which an analogous rule appears (2.4G, 3.4G, 5.4G, 6.4G, 7.4G, and 8.4G) it is specifically stated that the information must appear on the item itself. I am assuming that NBM 2 wishes to be consistent with AACR 2's rules for recording the place and name of manufacture.

PHYSICAL DESCRIPTION AREA—EXTENT OF ITEM

AACR 2

10.5B1: specific name of item (Cited in #8A)

NBM 2

p. 75:
"List the number and the specific names of the item(s)."

PHYSICAL DESCRIPTION AREA—OTHER PHYSICAL DETAILS

AACR 2

10.5C1: material (Cited in #8C)

10.5C2: color (Cited in #8A)

NBM 2

p. 75:
"If appropriate, list material from which the object was made, the colour ..."

PHYSICAL DESCRIPTION AREA — DIMENSIONS

AACR 2

10.5D1: in centimeters (Cited in #8A)

Rule also includes:
"If necessary, add a word to indicate which dimension is being given."

NBM 2

p. 75:
"If appropriate, list dimensions in centimetres with a word or phrase identifying the dimension."

NOTE AREA

AACR 2

10.7B3: source of title proper (Cited in #8C)

10.7B6. "**Statements of responsibility.** ... Give statements of responsibility not recorded in the title and statement of responsibility area."

NBM 2

p. 22: source of title proper (Cited in #8C)

p. 22 (General rules):
"Statements of responsibility. This may include ... statements of responsibility not taken from the chief source of information ..."

CHOICE OF ACCESS POINTS

AACR 2

21.0B. "[In determining access points,] use information ... appearing outside the item only when the statements appearing in the chief source of information are ambiguous or insufficient."

21.1A1. "A personal author is the person chiefly responsible for the creation of the intellectual or artistic content of a work."

21.4A. "Enter a work ... by one personal author ... under the heading for that person whether named in the work or not."

NBM 2

p. 18 (General rules):
"A work for which authorship can be clearly established is entered under author." (Quotes AACR 2's definition of authorship.)

Comment

For certain types of materials—books, maps, music scores, for example—AACR 2 has explicitly indicated which persons are to be regarded as authors, or which categories of creative activity are to be regarded as authorship functions. No such explicit indication is given for the example shown here; however, since whatever creative responsibility is involved rests with a single individual, "authorship" of the work can be ascribed to this person.

8E PARASITIC FUNGI

DESCRIPTION OF ITEM

Components: 1 set of 25 slides, glass, stained, in plastic case.

Dimensions: Slides—3 x 8 centimeters (length x width)
Container—3 x 9.2 x 7.5 centimeters (height x width x depth)

Label on container:

Berott Bio Slides
Set 4
Parasitic fungi

Label on each slide:

Berott Bio Slides
Slide no. _____
[Name of species]
Green Lake, Wis.

CATALOG RECORD

Parasitic fungi [microscope slide]. — Green Lake, Wis. : [s.n., 197-?].
25 microscope slides : stained ; 3 x 8 cm. in case, 3 x 10 x 8 cm. — (Berott bio slides ; set 4)

I. Series.

SCOPE / CATEGORIZATION

AACR 2

10.0A. "[This chapter] also covers the description of naturally occurring objects, including microscope specimens ... and other specimens mounted for viewing."

AACR 2 (cont'd)

(Chapter on graphic materials):
8.0A. "The rules in this chapter cover the description of graphic materials of all kinds.... For microscope slides, see chapter 10."

NBM 2

p. 60:
Chapter title: "Microscope slides"
"*Microscope slide*: a specialized slide produced specifically for use with a microscope or microprojector."

Comment

Note that AACR 2 categorizes microscope slides in terms of the *content* of the slides, i.e., the natural specimen to be viewed. In AECT 4, microscope slides were assigned to the category of slides, or the *medium* of the mount which makes the viewing possible. A third possibility, as shown in NBM 2, is to assign this format to its own special category.

SOURCES OF INFORMATION

AACR 2

10.0B1: chief sources include object itself, container (Cited in #8A)

NBM 2

p. 17: chief sources include item itself, container (Cited in #8A)

TITLE PROPER

AACR 2

10.1B1: as in 1.1B

1.1B1: transcribed exactly except for punctuation, capitalization (Cited in #8A)

NBM 2

p. 18: exactly from chief source, except for punctuation, capitalization (Cited in #8A)

GENERAL MATERIAL DESIGNATION

AACR 2

10.1C1: follows title proper

1.1C1: North American list

10.1A1: square brackets

A.4G: lowercase (Cited in #8A)

p. 567 (Glossary):
"**Microscope slide.** A slide designed for holding a minute object to be viewed through a microscope or by a microprojector."

NBM 2

p. 9: North American list

p. 18: lowercase, singular, brackets; follows title proper (Cited in #8A)

Comment

The Library of Congress does not catalog microscope slides, but the general material designation will be displayed if the Library ever does catalog the material.

PUBLICATION, DISTRIBUTION, ETC., AREA

AACR 2

10.4C1: as in 1.4C

1.4C1: place in form on item (Cited in #8A)

*10.4C2. "In the case of naturally occurring objects (other than those mounted for viewing or packaged for presentation) ... do not record any place of publication, etc."

10.4D1: as in 1.4D (Cited in #8A)

*10.4D2. "In the case of naturally occurring objects (other than those mounted for viewing or packaged for presentation) ... do not record any name of publisher, distributor, etc."

---

*Rule must be considered, to determine that publication data are required.

AACR 2 (cont'd)

1.4D6. "If the name of the publisher, distributor, etc., is unknown, give the abbreviation *s.n.* (sine nomine) ..."

10.4F1: as in 1.4F (Cited in #8A)

*10.4F2. "In the case of naturally occurring objects (other than those mounted for viewing or packaged for presentation), do not give a date."

1.4F7: approximate date (Cited in #8B)

1.0C. "When adjacent elements within one area are to be enclosed in square brackets, enclose them in one set of square brackets ..."

NBM 2

p. 19: place as given on item (Cited in #8A)

p. 20 (General rules):
"If the publisher, etc., is unknown, list 's.n.' in square brackets ..."

p. 20: approximate date (Cited in #8B)

PHYSICAL DESCRIPTION AREA—EXTENT OF ITEM

AACR 2

10.5B1: microscope slide (Cited in #8A)

NBM 2

p. 60:
"List the number of microscope slides."

**"*Option.* If the general material designation 'microscope slide' is used, the term 'slide(s)' may be substituted for 'microscope slide(s)' ..."

PHYSICAL DESCRIPTION AREA—OTHER PHYSICAL DETAILS

AACR 2

10.5C1. ***"Give the material of which a microscope slide is made if it is other than glass."

---

*Rule must be considered, to determine that publication data are required.

**Option not applied in this example.

***Rule must be considered, to determine that no statement is made.

10.5C2: color (Cited in #8A)

Rule continues:
"If a microscope slide is stained, state this."

NBM 2

p. 60:
*"If the microscope slide is made of material other than glass, list this material."

"If a microscope slide is stained, list this."

PHYSICAL DESCRIPTION AREA—DIMENSIONS

AACR 2

10.5D1: centimeters

10.5D2: container (Cited in #8A)

10.5D1 also includes: "for microscope slides, length x width"

NBM 2

p. 60:
"List length x width in centimetres. When an item is packaged, the type of package and its dimensions in centimetres are given."

p. 21: fractions (Cited in #8A)

SERIES AREA

AACR 2

10.6B1: as in 1.6

1.6B1: title proper as in 1.1B

1.6G1: numbering (Cited in #8A)

NBM 2

p. 21: title proper, numbering (Cited in #8A)

---

*Rule must be considered, to determine that no statement is made.

NOTE AREA

Comment

While no notes have been given for this example, the reader should bear in mind that NBM 2 makes the following specific provisions in its rules for notes:

p. 60:
Type of stain and the particular aspect of the slide the stain highlights is noted, if applicable.

Method of preparation, e.g., sectioning, orientation, material in which specimen is embedded, spread, smear, whole mount, etc., is noted.

CHOICE OF ACCESS POINTS

AACR 2

21.1C3: corporate body falls outside 21.1B2—title entry (Cited in #8A)

NBM 2

The reader would consult AACR 2.

8F   ULMUS AMERICANA

DESCRIPTION OF ITEM

Components: 1 plant specimen, mounted on sheet.
Dimensions: plant—25 centimeters tall
sheet—40 x 27 centimeters (height x width)

The specimen has been dried, for preservation. The colors are green, brown, and white.

Label on sheet in lower right hand corner:

Department of Botany, The University of Michigan
Ulmus americana L.
American elm

Collected and mounted by Rachel Valerie Pleasants
Corner of Ann St. and Ingalls St.
Ann Arbor, Michigan. May 20, 1969

CATALOG RECORD

Ulmus americana L. [realia] = American elm / collected and
mounted by Rachel Valerie Pleasants. — [Ann Arbor, Mich.] :
Dept. of Botany, University of Michigan, [1969?].
1 plant specimen ; 25 cm. high.
Collected in Ann Arbor, Mich., May 20, 1969.
Dried; mounted on sheet 40 x 27 cm.

I. Pleasants, Rachel Valerie.

———————————

Differences in NBM 2 version (physical description and note areas):

1 plant specimen ; dried ; 25 cm. high.
...
Mounted on sheet 40 x 27 cm.

———————————

SCOPE / CATEGORIZATION

AACR 2

10.0A: chapter covers specimens mounted for viewing (Cited in #8E)

NBM 2

p. 75: "realia" chapter (Cited in #8D)

SOURCES OF INFORMATION

AACR 2

10.0B1: item itself (Cited in #8A)

NBM 2

p. 17: item itself (Cited in #8A)

TITLE PROPER

AACR 2

10.1B1: as in 1.1B

1.1B1: transcribed exactly except for punctuation, capitalization (Cited in #8A)

NBM 2

p. 18: exactly from chief source, except for punctuation, capitalization (Cited in #8A)

GENERAL MATERIAL DESIGNATION

AACR 2

10.1C1: follows title proper

1.1C1: North American list

10.1A1: square brackets

A.4G: lowercase (Cited in #8A)

p. 569: definition of realia (Cited in #8D)

NBM 2

p. 9: North American list

p. 18: lowercase, singular, brackets; follows title proper (Cited in #8A)

PARALLEL TITLES

AACR 2

10.1D1. "Record parallel titles as instructed in 1.1D."

1.1D1. "Record parallel titles in the order indicated by their sequence on, or by the layout of, the chief source of information."

1.1D2. "In preparing a second-level description ..., give the first parallel title."

10.1A1. "**Punctuation.** ... Precede each parallel title by an equals sign."

p. 568 (Glossary):
"**Parallel title.** The title proper in another language and/or script."

NBM 2

p. 18 (General rules):
"Parallel titles are listed after the general material designation.... [They are] listed in the exact wording found in the chief source of information."

"*Punctuation.* A parallel title is separated from the title proper by a space-equal sign-space (=) ..."

STATEMENTS OF RESPONSIBILITY

AACR 2

10.1F1. "Record statements relating to persons or bodies responsible for the creation of the item, or for its display or selection, as instructed in 1.1F."

NBM 2

p. 18 (General rules):
"The statement(s) of responsibility is listed wherever possible in the wording and order found on the source(s) of information."

PUBLICATION, DISTRIBUTION, ETC., AREA

AACR 2

10.4C1: as in 1.4C

1.4C1: place in form on item (Cited in #8A)

10.4C2: no place would be given if object were not mounted for viewing (Cited in #8E)

10.4D1: as in 1.4D (Cited in #8A)

10.4D2: no publisher would be given if object were not mounted for viewing (Cited in #8E)

10.4F1: as in 1.4F (Cited in #8A)

10.4F2: no date would be given if object were not mounted for viewing (Cited in #8E)

1.4F7: approximate date (Cited in #8B)

NBM 2

p. 75: place, publisher, date given for items mounted by outside agency (Cited in #8D)

p. 20: approximate date (Cited in #8B)

Comment

Note that if a naturally occurring object has been packaged or mounted, it is regarded as "published" in that publication data are considered appropriate for inclusion. The date and place on this item refer to the place and date of collection; hence the "publication" date required by AACR 2 and NBM 2 has been conjectured and bracketed, and the place has also been bracketed. In contrast, AECT 4 allows the date and place of collection to be included in its publication area.

PHYSICAL DESCRIPTION AREA — EXTENT OF ITEM

AACR 2

10.5B1: specific name of item (Cited in #8A)

NBM 2

p. 75: specific name of item (Cited in #8D)

PHYSICAL DESCRIPTION AREA — OTHER PHYSICAL DETAILS

AACR 2

10.5C1: material would be given if appropriate (Cited in #8C)

10.5C2: color would be given if appropriate (Cited in #8A)

NBM 2

p. 75: material and color, if appropriate (Cited in #8D)

Rule also includes:
"If appropriate, list ... the method of preservation.[53]"

p. 125 (Appendix A — Notes):
"53. 'method of preservation' [in sample card 87] 'dried' likened to process in 8.5C2 and method of reproduction in 8.5C3 & 8.5C15."

p. 76 (Excerpt from sample card 87):
"5 sea-horses : dried; 6 cm. or smaller in vial, 8 cm. high."

Comment

Note that NBM 2 allows the preservation method to be included among the other physical details. This is drawn from rules in AACR 2's chapter for graphic materials, which allows the cataloger to indicate the process for art prints (8.5C2), and the method of reproduction for art reproductions (8.5C3) and for technical drawings (8.5C15).

PHYSICAL DESCRIPTION AREA—DIMENSIONS

AACR 2

10.5D1: centimeters; indicate dimensions given (Cited in #8A, amplified by #8D)

NBM 2

p. 75: centimeters; identify dimensions (Cited in #8D)

NOTE AREA

AACR 2

10.7B7. **"Edition and history.** Make notes relating to the edition being described or to the history of the item."

10.7B10: physical description (Cited in #8B)

NBM 2

p. 22 (General rules):
"Edition and history"

p. 22: physical description (Cited in #8B)

CHOICE OF ACCESS POINTS

AACR 2

21.1C3: corporate body falls outside 21.1B2—title entry (Cited in #8A)

Or possibly:
21.1C. "Enter a work under its title when:

1) the personal authorship is unknown ..., diffuse ..., or cannot be determined, and the work does not emanate from a corporate body"

NBM 2

The reader would consult AACR 2.

Comment

Since this is a naturally occurring object, "authorship" responsibility cannot be attributed, and AACR 2's rule dealing with "unknown" authorship might be considered. Another approach might be to view the "packaged" item as being issued by a corporate body, but not falling into any of the categories in 21.1B2. An added entry could be made, in any case, for the corporate body.

9

MICROFORMS

No part of AACR 2 has sparked more controversy than the chapter on microforms. In AACR, microform reproductions were described in terms of the original text, and data pertaining to the microform were given in a note. AACR 2 proposed a radical change in the bibliographic description of reproductions issued in microform when it prescribed that the starting point for the description be the microform reproduction rather than the original.

Widespread dissatisfaction with AACR 2's treatment of microforms became apparent from the outset of the publication of the rules. Those objecting to this approach argued that, to the user, the information pertaining to the original was of greater importance. Also frequently stressed were the economic implications of preparing new records for "copies" issued in microform. There was far less agreement, however, on an alternative solution. As a result, the Library of Congress announced the adoption of a policy in which works issued in microform reproductions would be described in terms of the original, with details of the microform given in a note. This "policy" was issued as a rule interpretation. As such it has been adopted as a standard by major U.S. libraries and bibliographic utilities. Since this approach has not been submitted as a rule revision to the Joint Steering Committee for Revision of AACR 2 for a vote, other countries are applying the chapter on microforms as written. A recent article outlining the major arguments in the microform controversy is Janet Swan Hill's "Descriptions of Reproductions of Previously Existing Works: Another View," in *Microform Review* 11 (Winter 1982).

EXPLANATION OF EXAMPLES

The following examples will show the application of the AACR 2 approach. Catalog records reflecting the LC policy are also included, but are not documented with rule citations, since at this point the LC policy does not contain detailed instructions for application. The practical effect of the LC policy is to apply the chapter appropriate for the original work (e.g., chapter 2 for books, chapter 5 for music) for the description and to use the microforms chapter as a guideline for composing a note containing the microform description.

The reader should note that if the microform reproduction is to be described in terms of the original, and if the original is not in hand, some of the data needed for description of the original may be unavailable. This is particularly likely in the recording of dimensions. For this reason, no dimensions statement is included in the following records reflecting LC policy.

Regardless of whether the microform reproduction is described in terms of the original or in terms of the reproduction, the cataloger will need to be familiar with the chapter on microforms as well as the chapter pertaining to the original form of the work. In either case, both aspects of the work – the original and the reproduction – will be described in the catalog record, the major difference being which aspect of the work appears in the body of the record and which is described in a note.

The statement below gives the Library of Congress policy for the cataloging of microreproductions.

1) *Materials covered.* This policy applies to reproductions in micro- and macroform of previously existing materials. Specifically the policy applies to micro- and macroreproductions of

> books,pamphlets, and printed sheets
> cartographic materials
> manuscripts
> music
> graphic materials in macroform
> serials

It applies to reproductions of dissertations issued by University Microfilms International and "on demand" reproductions of books by the same company.

It is the intent of this policy to apply AACR 2 in determining the choice and form of access points but to emphasize in the bibliographic description data relating to the original item, giving data relating to the reproduction in a secondary position. As a result, rule 1.11 and chapter 11 of AACR 2 will not be applied to these materials except to provide directions for the formulation of the note describing the micro- or macroform characteristics of the reproduction. (Items that are microreproductions of material prepared or assembled specifically for bringing out an original edition in microform will be cataloged as instructed in chapter 11 of AACR 2.)

2) *Bibliographic description*

a) *General.* Apply chapter 2 to books (including dissertations cataloged as books), pamphlets, and sheets; chapter 3 to cartographic materials; chapter 4 to manuscripts (including dissertations not cataloged as books); chapter 5 to music; relevant portions of chapter 8 to graphic materials in macroform; and chapter 12 to serials. Transcribe the bibliographic data appropriate to the work being reproduced in the following areas:

> title and statement of responsibility
> edition
> material (or type of publication) specific details for cartographic materials and serials
> publication, distribution, etc.
> physical description
> series

Record in the note area all details relating to the reproduction and its publication/availability. Introduce the note with the word that is the specific material designation appropriate to the item.

b) *Microreproductions.* Add the general material designation "[microform]" in the title and statement of responsibility area according to 1.1C2. Record in the note area the bibliographic details relating to the reproduction required by 11.4, in the order and form provided by this rule, followed by the details required by 11.5-7. If a note of the 11.7B10 type is necessary, transcribe it before any series statement required by 11.6.

Microfilm. Ann Arbor, Mich. : University Microfilms, 1981. 1 microfilm reel ; 16 mm. High reduction.
Microfilm. Washington : Library of Congress, 1981. 1 microfilm reel ; 5 in., 35 cm.[1]

9A   BELLOMY REPORT

DESCRIPTION OF ITEM

Components: 2 microfiche, 102 frames, black and white, negative, in envelope.

Dimensions of fiche: 10.4 x 14.8 centimeters (height x width)

Original document includes charts, and is numbered ii-v, 1-95 p.

Abstract: "The feasibility of undertaking a major university-wide library systems development program for the University of California libraries was studied ..."

Envelope:

Educational Resources Information Center
U.S. Office of Education
ERIC
REPORTS

Prepared by ERIC Document Reproduction Service
Operated by
Leasco Information Products, Inc.
4827 Rugby Avenue, Bethesda, Maryland 20014

Top margin of fiche (eye readable):

ED 063 001   FINAL REPORT OF THE FINDINGS OF THE FEASIBILITY PHASE. FRED L. BELLOMY. CALIFORNIA UNIV., SANTA BARBARA. LIBRARY SYSTEMS DEVELOPMENT PROGRAM. 2 APR 71. 101P.

First frame of fiche:

DOCUMENT RESUME

ED 063 001   LI 003 682

AUTHOR   Bellomy, Fred L.
TITLE   Final Report of the Findings of the Feasibility Phase
INSTITUTION   California University, Santa Barbara. Library Systems Development Program.
REPORT NO.   LSD 71-23A
PUB. DATE   2 April 1971
NOTE   101 p.; (50 References)

Second frame of fiche:

Library Systems Development Program
LSD 71-23A

FINAL REPORT OF THE FINDINGS
OF THE
FEASIBILITY PHASE
issued by
Fred L. Bellomy
on behalf of the
UC LIBRARIES
2 April 1971

Santa Barbara, California 93106

After last frame:

END

DEPT. OF HEALTH
EDUCATION AND
WELFARE
U.S. OFFICE OF
EDUCATION
ERIC
DATE FILMED
8 19 72

CATALOG RECORD

University of California, Santa Barbara.
  Library Systems Development Program.
  Final report of the findings of the feasibility phase [microform] /
issued by Fred L. Bellomy on behalf of the UC Libraries. — Bethesda,
Md. : ERIC, 1972.
  2 microfiches (102 fr.) : negative, charts ; 11 x 15 cm.
  "ED 063 001."
  "LI 003 682."
  Microreproduction of original: Santa Barbara, Calif. : Library
Systems Development Program, California University, Santa
Barbara, 1971. v, 95 p. : charts. Includes bibliography. "LSD
71-23A."

  I. Bellomy, Fred L. II. Title.

LC VERSION

University of California, Santa Barbara.
  Library Systems Development Program.
  Final report of the findings of the feasibility phase [microform] /
issued by Fred L. Bellomy on behalf of the UC Libraries. — Santa
Barbara, Calif.: Library Systems Development Program, California
University, Santa Barbara, 1971.
  v, 95 p. : charts.
  "LSD 71-23A."
  "ED 063 001."
  "LI 003 682."
  Includes bibliography.
  Microfiche. Bethesda, Md. : ERIC, 1972. 2 microfiches (102
fr.) : negative, charts ; 11 x 15 cm.

  I. Bellomy, Fred L. II. Title.

SCOPE / CATEGORIZATION

AACR 2

(Introductory chapter):
0.24. "It is a cardinal principle of the use of Part I that the description of a
physical item should be based in the first instance on the chapter dealing with the
class of materials to which that item belongs. For example, a printed monograph
in microform should be described as a microform (using the rules in chapter 11).
There will be need in many instances to consult the chapter dealing with the
original form of the item, especially when constructing notes. So, using the same
example, the chapter dealing with printed books (chapter 2) will be used to
supplement chapter 11. In short, the starting point for description is the physical

form of the item in hand, not the original or any previous form in which the work has been published."

(General rules for description):
1.11A. "In describing a facsimile, photocopy, or other reproduction of printed texts, ... give all the data relating to the facsimile, etc., in all areas except the note area.... If a facsimile, etc., is in a form of library material different from that of the original (e.g., a manuscript reproduced as a book), use the chapter on the form of the facsimile, etc., in determining the sources of information (e.g., for a manuscript reproduced as a book, use chapter 2). In addition to instructions given in the relevant chapters, follow the instructions in this rule."

11.0A. "The rules in this chapter cover the description of all kinds of material in microform. Microforms include microfilms, microfiches ..."

NBM 2

p. 54:
Chapter title: "Microforms"
"*Microform*: a miniature reproduction of printed or other graphic matter which cannot be utilized without magnification."

"Microfilms, microfiches ... are included under this heading ..."

Comment

All elements of description, with the exception of some of the notes, are in reference to the microform reproduction. The "cardinal" principle outlined in rule 0.24 must be kept in mind throughout the chapter. There is no further explicit mention of this principle in the chapter on microforms.

SOURCES OF INFORMATION

AACR 2

11.0B1. "The chief source of information for microfiches ... is the title frame. *If there is no such information or if the information is insufficient, treat the eye-readable data printed at the top of the fiche ... as the chief source of information. If information normally presented on the title frame or title card is presented on successive frames ..., treat these frames ... as the chief source of information.

If information is not available from the chief source, take it from the following sources (in this order of preference):

    the rest of the item ...

    container ..."

---

*Rule included here to indicate preferred order for chief sources. Altered rule in AACR 2 revisions gives additional detail.

NBM 2

p. 54:
"Information for the catalogue record is taken from the following sources in this order:

1. The item itself (Chief source of information). ... In *microfiches* preference is given to information on the title frame(s), secondarily to the eye-readable data on the top of the item, and thirdly from the rest of the item.

2. Container;"

Comment

AACR 2's rules do not explicitly state whether the title frame to be used as the chief source must be the title frame specific to the microform itself, or the title page of the original. In this cataloger's judgment, the second frame, which reproduces the title page of the original, is used as the chief source, and the first title frame is considered as analogous in function to a "preliminary" page of a printed book, or a "bibliographic data sheet" or "documentation page" of a technical report.

Those arguing in favor of the first title frame as the chief source might point to AACR 2's general principle of describing the physical format of the item in hand. This principle, however, can result in the recording of data not originally intended to serve the purpose for which it is being used here. For example, the author's name on the first frame is given in inverted form, probably because the name is presented more as a heading than as a formal "statement of responsibility."

TITLE PROPER

AACR 2

11.1B1. "Record the title proper as instructed in 1.1B."

1.1B1. "Transcribe the title proper exactly as to wording, order and spelling, but not necessarily as to punctuation and capitalization."

NBM 2

p. 18 (General rules):
"The title proper ... is copied exactly from the chief source of information. However, capitalization and punctuation follow prescribed rules."

GENERAL MATERIAL DESIGNATION

AACR 2

11.1C1. (Optional). "Add immediately following the title proper the appropriate general material designation as instructed in 1.1C."

1.1C1. "If general material designations are to be used in cataloguing, ... North American agencies [should use] terms from list 2."

11.1A1. "Enclose the general material designation in square brackets."

(Appendix A — Capitalization):
A.4G. "Lowercase the words making up a general material designation."

p. 567 (Glossary):
"**Microform.** A generic term for any medium, transparent or opaque, bearing microimages."

NBM 2

p. 9 (Chapter on cataloging policy for media centers):
"The North American list of general material designations is used in this book. Those electing [to omit the general material designation or to use] the British list ... or the ISBD list may use the rules on the following pages by disregarding the general material designation or by substituting the appropriate term from the British or ISBD lists."

p. 18 (General rules):
"A general material designation is listed in lower case letters, in the singular, and in its own square brackets immediately following the title proper."

p. 54:
"Microfilms, microfiches ... are ... designated by the term 'microform.' "

Comment

The Library of Congress will display the general material designation for microforms.

STATEMENTS OF RESPONSIBILITY

AACR 2

11.1F1. "Record statements of responsibility as instructed in 1.1F."

1.1F1. "Record statements of responsibility appearing prominently in the item in the form in which they appear there."

NBM 2

p. 18 (General rules):
"The statement(s) of responsibility is listed wherever possible in the wording and order found on the source(s) of information."

PUBLICATION, DISTRIBUTION, ETC., AREA

AACR 2

1.11C. "If the facsimile, etc., has the ... publication details ... of the original as well as those of the facsimile, etc., give those of the facsimile, etc., in the ... publication, distribution, etc., ... [area]. Give the details of the original in the note area (see 1.11F)."

11.4C1. "Record the place of publication, distribution, etc., as instructed in 1.4C."

1.4C1. "Record the place of publication, etc., in the form ... in which it appears."

*1.4C3. "Add the name of the country, state, province, etc., to the name of the place if it is considered necessary for identification, or if it is considered necessary to distinguish the place from others of the same name."

11.4D1. "Record the name of the publisher, distributor, etc., as instructed in 1.4D."

1.4D2. "Give the name of a publisher, distributor, etc., in the shortest form in which it can be understood and identified internationally."

11.4F1. "Record the date of publication, distribution, etc., of a microform as instructed in 1.4F."

1.4F1. "If there is no edition statement, give the date of the first edition."

NBM 2

pp. 19, 20 (General rules):
"List the name of the place as it appears on the item and add the name of the province, state, country, etc., if it is necessary for identification."

"List the name of the publisher, producer, distributor, etc., in the shortest form that can be identified internationally."

"List the publication date of the item being catalogued."

---

*For LC rule interpretation, see example #4B, p. 81.

PHYSICAL DESCRIPTION AREA—EXTENT OF ITEM

AACR 2

1.11D. "Give the physical description of the facsimile, etc., in the physical description area. Give the physical description of the original in the note area (see 1.11F)."

*11.5B1. "Record the number of physical units of a microform item by giving the number of parts in arabic numerals and one of the following terms as appropriate:

...

microfiche   microfilm ..."

**"*Optionally*, if the general material designation *microform* is used, drop the prefix *micro* from these terms."

"Add the number of frames of a microfiche if it can be easily ascertained. Make the addition in parentheses.

1 microfiche (120 frames)"

Note, Errata and Corrigenda:
"11.5B1. 6th example. For (120 frames) *read* (120 fr.)"

p. 567 (Glossary):
"**Microfiche.** A sheet of film bearing a number of microimages in a two-dimensional array."

NBM 2

*p. 54:
"List the number of ... microfiches, microfilms ..."

**"*Option.* If a general material designation is used, the prefix 'micro' may be omitted from the specific material designation ..."

"*Microfiches.* List the number of frames in parentheses, if this can be ascertained easily."

p. 109 (Glossary):
"*Microfiche*—A microfilm on a flat sheet of film."

Comment

The Library of Congress will not apply the option in AACR 2's rule 11.5B1.

---

*The terms listed in this rule citation include only those designations which will be used for the examples in this chapter.
**Option not applied.

PHYSICAL DESCRIPTION AREA — OTHER PHYSICAL DETAILS

AACR 2

11.5C1. "If a microform is negative, indicate this."

11.5C2. "If a microform contains, or consists of, illustrations, indicate this as instructed in 1.5C."

1.5C1. "Give physical data (other than extent or dimensions) about an item as instructed in the following chapters."

(Chapter on books, pamphlets, and printed sheets):
2.5C1. "Describe an illustrated printed monograph as *ill.* unless the illustrations are all of one or more of the particular types mentioned in the next paragraph."

2.5C2. "If the illustrations are of one or more of the following types, and are considered to be important, designate them by the appropriate term or abbreviation (in this order): charts, ... maps, music ..."

NBM 2

p. 54:
"If appropriate, list negative; positive is not recorded."

"List col.; b&w is not given, this being the norm for microforms."

"List illustrations; the manner of listing illustrations is similar to that for books."

Comment

It is relatively easy to distinguish the reproduction from the original in terms of title, statement of responsibility, publication, and physical format. On the other hand, the illustrations could be considered as belonging to the content of the original as well as to the reproduction. The question could thus be raised, in AACR 2's rules 1.11D and 11.5C2, as to whether the illustration statement should be recorded in the physical description for the microform, or for the original. Since the description applies to both, it was decided here to record the illustration statement in both areas.

PHYSICAL DESCRIPTION AREA — DIMENSIONS

AACR 2

11.5D1. "Give the dimensions of a microform as set out in the following rules. Record a fraction of a centimetre or inch as the next whole centimetre or inch up."

11.5D3. **"Microfiches.** Give the height x width of a microfiche in centimetres."

NBM 2

p. 54:
"Aperture cards, microfiches ... Height x width are listed in centimetres."

p. 21 (General rules):
"Fractions are taken to the next number."

NOTE AREA

AACR 2

*1.7A4. **"Notes relating to items reproduced.** In describing an item that is a reproduction of another (e.g., a text reproduced in microform ...) give the notes relating to the reproduction and then the notes relating to the original. Combine the notes relating to the original in one note, giving the details in the order of the areas to which they relate."

*11.7B. **"Notes.** Make notes as set out in the following subrules and in the order given there."

11.7B19. **"Numbers.** Give important numbers borne by the item other than ISBNs or ISSNs ..."

*11.7B22. **"Notes relating to original.** Give information on the original of a microform item."

NBM 2

p. 55:
"Original format. If the microform was published originally in another format, the bibliographic details of this publication are noted."

p. 22 (General rules):
"Numbers associated with item other than ISBNs or ISSNs ..."

CHOICE OF ACCESS POINTS

AACR 2

**21.1B2. "Enter a work emanating from one or more corporate bodies under the heading for the appropriate corporate body if it falls into one or more of the following categories:

a) those of an administrative nature dealing with the corporate body itself

or   its internal policies, procedures, and/or operations"

---

*Altered rules appearing in AACR 2 revisions.

**For LC rule interpretation and discussion, see #6C.

NBM 2

p. 18 (General rules):
"1. A reproduction of a work originally produced in another medium is entered in the same manner as the original work."

The reader would consult AACR 2.

FORM OF HEADING

AACR 2

24.13. "Enter a subordinate or related body as a subheading of the name of the body to which it is subordinate or related if its name belongs to one or more of the following types....

"TYPE 3. A name that has been, or is likely to be, used by another higher body for one of its subordinate or related bodies."

NBM 2

Outside the scope of this code. The reader would consult AACR 2.

9B   JACKSON DISSERTATION

DESCRIPTION OF ITEM

Components: 1 roll of microfilm, black and white, 198 frames, 16 mm gauge

The original text has leaves numbered ii-x, 1-192.

First frame of film:

DOCTORAL DISSERTATION SERIES
PUBLICATION: 5050

AUTHOR: Jay Mervin Jackson, Ph.D., 1953.
University of Michigan
TITLE: ANALYSIS OF INTERPERSONAL
RELATIONS IN A FORMAL ORGANIZATION

University Microfilms, Ann Arbor, Michigan, 1953.

Second frame:

ANALYSIS OF INTERPERSONAL RELATIONS
IN A FORMAL ORGANIZATION
by
Jay M. Jackson

(Example continues on next page)

A dissertation submitted in partial fulfillment
of the requirements for the degree of
Doctor of Philosophy in the
University of Michigan
1953

CATALOG RECORD

Jackson, Jay M. (Jay Mervin)
Analysis of interpersonal relations in a formal organization [micro-
form] / by Jay M. Jackson. — Ann Arbor, Mich. : University
Microfilms, 1953.
1 microfilm reel ; 16 mm. — (Doctoral dissertation series ; publi-
cation 5050)
Microreproduction of typescript (photocopy): 1953. x, 192 leaves.
Thesis (Ph.D.) — University of Michigan, 1953.

I. Title. II. Series.

LC VERSION

Jackson, Jay M. (Jay Mervin)
Analysis of interpersonal relations in a formal organization [micro-
form] / by Jay M. Jackson. — 1953.
x, 192 leaves.
Thesis (Ph. D.) — University of Michigan, 1953.
Microfilm. Ann Arbor, Mich. : University Microfilms,
1953. 1 microfilm reel ; 16 mm. (Doctoral dissertation series ; publication 5050)

I. Title. II. Series: Doctoral dissertation series ; publication
5050.

SCOPE / CATEGORIZATION

AACR 2

0.24: cardinal principle

1.11A: describe reproduction

11.0A: chapter covers microfilms (Cited in #9A)

(Chapter on manuscripts):
4.0A. "The rules in this chapter cover the description of manuscript
(including typescript) texts of all kinds, including manuscript books, dissertations.... For reproductions of manuscript texts published in multiple copies, see
chapter 2, or chapter 11, as appropriate."

NBM 2

p. 54: "microforms"; chapter includes microfilms (Cited in #9A)

Comment

Note that AACR 2's chapter 4 refers the reader to chapter 11 if the reproduction of the manuscript has been "published in multiple copies." This raises the theoretical question as to what constitutes "publication" for an item, and subsequently, the manner in which the code deals with various kinds of "unpublished" items. It also raises the practical question of when a microform item is to be considered as a "copy" of the original, and on the other hand, when it is appropriate to prepare separate records for the "published" item and for the original.

SOURCES OF INFORMATION

AACR 2

11.0B1. "The chief source of information for microfilms is the title frame (i.e., a frame, usually at the beginning of the item, bearing the full title, and, normally, publication details of the item)."

NBM 2

p. 54: item itself (Cited in #9A)

Rule also includes:
"In *microfilms* preference is given to the information on the title frame(s). *If the information from this source is inadequate or nonexistent, data is drawn from the rest of the item including a container which is an integral part of the item."

Comment

Note that, for the chief source of information, AACR 2 prefers the frame "usually at the beginning of the item." I am assuming that this can include the frame reproducing the title page of the original.

TITLE PROPER

AACR 2

11.1B1: as in 1.1B

1.1B1: wording, order, spelling transcribed exactly except for punctuation, capitalization (Cited in #9A)

---

*Last sentence of rule included to indicate preferred order for chief source.

NBM 2

p. 18: exactly from chief source except for capitalization, punctuation (Cited in #9A)

GENERAL MATERIAL DESIGNATION

AACR 2

11.1C1: follows title proper

1.1C1: North American list

11.1A1: square brackets

A.4G: lowercase

p. 567: definition of microform (Cited in #9A)

NBM 2

p. 9: North American list

p. 18: lower case, singular, square brackets; follows title proper

p. 54: microform (Cited in #9A)

STATEMENTS OF RESPONSIBILITY

AACR 2

11.1F1: as in 1.1F

1.1F1: in form appearing on item (Cited in #9A)

1.1F7. "Include titles and abbreviations of titles of ... address, honour, and distinction ... with the names of persons in statements of responsibility if:
a) such a title is necessary grammatically
    ...
b) the omission would leave only the person's given name or surname
    ...
c) the title is necessary to identify the person
    ...
Omit all other titles, etc., from the names of persons in statements of responsibility. Do not use the mark of omission."

NBM 2

p. 18: in wording and order on source (Cited in #9A)

PUBLICATION, DISTRIBUTION, ETC., AREA

AACR 2

1.11C: describe reproduction

11.4C1: as in 1.4C

1.4C1: place of publication in form on item

1.4C3: add name of state

11.4D1: name of publisher

1.4D2: name in shortest form

11.4F1: as in 1.4F

1.4F1: date of first edition (Cited in #9A)

NBM 2

pp. 19, 20: name of place as appears on item; add state; name of publisher in shortest form; publication date (Cited in #9A)

PHYSICAL DESCRIPTION AREA—EXTENT OF ITEM

AACR 2

1.11D: describe reproduction

11.5B1: microfilm (Cited in #9A)

Rule 11.5B1 continues:
"Add to *microfilm* one of the terms *cartridge, cassette,* or *reel,* as appropriate."

p. 567 (Glossary):
"**Microfilm.** A length of film bearing a number of microimages in linear array."

NBM 2

p. 54: microfilm (Cited in #9A)

p. 109 (Glossary):
"*Microfilm*—A microform on a roll of film."

p. 54; rule continues:
"If appropriate, add the [term] ... 'reel.' "

PHYSICAL DESCRIPTION AREA — OTHER PHYSICAL DETAILS

AACR 2

*11.5C1: indicate if negative (Cited in #9A)

NBM 2

*p. 54: indicate if negative (Cited in #9A)

PHYSICAL DESCRIPTION AREA — DIMENSIONS

AACR 2

11.5D1: as in following rules (Cited in #9A)

11.5D4. "**Microfilms.** *If the diameter of a microfilm reel is other than three inches, give the diameter in inches. Give the width of a microfilm in millimetres."

NBM 2

p. 54:
*"*Microfilms.* If the reel is other than 3 inches in diameter, list this fact in inches ..."

"List the width of the film in millimetres."

SERIES AREA

AACR 2

11.6B1. "Record each series statement relating to a microform as instructed in 1.6."

1.6B1. "If an item is one of a series, record the title proper of the series as instructed in 1.1B ..."

1.6G1. "Record the numbering of the item within the series in the terms given in the item."

NBM 2

p. 21 (General rules):
"If applicable, a series statement in parentheses follows the physical description area. The series area in 3rd level cataloguing could include:
title proper of series

...

numbering within series ..."

---

*Rule must be considered, to determine that no statement is given.

NOTE AREA

AACR 2

1.7A4, 11.7B22: notes relating to original (Cited in #9A)

(Chapter on manuscripts):
4.4. "Date area"

4.4B. "Date of the manuscript"

4.4B1. "Give the date or inclusive dates of the manuscript ..."

4.5B1. "**Single manuscripts.** Record sequences of leaves or pages, whether numbered or not, as instructed in 2.5B."

(Chapter on books, pamphlets, and printed sheets):
2.5B1. "Record the number of pages or leaves in a publication in accordance with the terminology suggested by the volume. That is, ... describe a volume with leaves printed on one side only in terms of leaves ..."

2.5B2. "Record the number of ... leaves ... in terms of the numbered or lettered sequences in the volume. Record the last numbered ... leaf ... in each sequence and follow it with the appropriate term or abbreviation."

(Chapter on manuscripts):
4.7B13. "If a manuscript is a dissertation, give this as instructed in 2.7B13."

(Chapter on books, pamphlets, and printed sheets):
2.7B13. "If the item being described is a dissertation or thesis presented in partial fulfillment of the requirements for an academic degree, give the designation of the thesis (using the English word *thesis*) followed by a brief statement of the degree for which the author was a candidate (e.g., M.A. or Ph.D. ...), the name of the institution or faculty to which the thesis was presented, and the year in which the degree was granted.
Thesis (Ph.D.)—University of Toronto, 1974"

NBM 2

p. 55: bibliographic details of original (Cited in #9A)

Comment

In order to describe the original document, the cataloger must consult the chapter on manuscripts. Note that the publication data for manuscripts can be given only in terms of the date. In LC practice, there is a space between "Ph." and "D." in the thesis note.

CHOICE OF ACCESS POINTS

AACR 2

21.4A. "Enter a work ... by one personal author (or any reprint, reissue, etc., of such a work) under the heading for that person ..."

NBM 2

p. 18: entry of reproduction same as original (Cited in #9A)

p. 18 (General rules):
"2. A work for which authorship can be clearly established is entered under author."

FORM OF HEADING

AACR 2

22.1A. "Choose, as the basis of the heading for a person, the name by which he or she is commonly known."

22.1B. "Determine the name by which a person is commonly known from the chief sources of information ... of works by that person issued in his or her language."

22.16A. "If part or all of a name is represented by initials and the full form is known, add the spelled out form in parentheses if necessary to distinguish between names that are otherwise identical."

"If the initials occur in the inverted part of the name (forenames, etc.) ... add the full form of the inverted part ... at the end of the name."

"*Optionally*, make the above additions to other names containing initials."

NBM 2

The reader would refer to AACR 2.

Comment

Note the following LC rule interpretation for 22.16A:

Apply the optional provision. This means adding the fuller forms in parentheses whenever they are available from the item being cataloged."[2]

9C   MALTA LIBRARY ASSOCIATION YEAR BOOK

DESCRIPTION OF ITEM

Components: 1 microfiche, black and white, negative, in envelope.

Dimensions of fiche: 10.4 x 14.8 centimeters (height x width)

This is the first issue of the serial.

Envelope:

Educational Resources Information Center
U.S. Office of Education
ERIC
REPORTS

Prepared by ERIC Document Reproduction Service

Operated by
Leasco Information Products, Inc.
4827 Rugby Avenue, Bethesda, Maryland 20014

Top margin of fiche (eye-readable):

ED 062 997   MALTA LIBRARY ASSOCIATION YEAR BOOK 1971.
CARMEL G. BONAVIA ED. ET AL., MALTA LIBRARY
ASSOCIATION, VALLETTA. 71. 49P.

First frame of fiche:

DOCUMENT RESUME

ED 062 997   LI 003 678

AUTHOR	Bonavia, Carmel G. Ed., and others
TITLE	Malta Library Association Year Book 1971.
INSTITUTION	Malta Library Association Valletta.
PUB DATE	71
NOTE	49p.; (22 References)
AVAILABLE FROM	Malta Library Association Year Book 1971, Malta Library Association, 226 So. Paul Street, Valletta, Malta ($1.50)

Second frame of fiche:

MALTA LIBRARY
ASSOCIATION
YEAR BOOK
1971

(Example continues on page 323)

Edited by Carmel G. Bonavia
Carmel G. Bonavia
Anthony Sapienza
Lillian Sciberras
and Paul Xuereb
Valletta
Malta Library Association
1971

After the last frame:

END

Dept. of Health
Education and
Welfare
U.S. Office of
Education
ERIC
Date filmed
8 19 72

CATALOG RECORD

Malta Library Association.
   Malta Library Association year book [microform]. — 1971-
— Bethesda, Md. : ERIC, 1972-
      microfiches : negative ; 11 x 15 cm.
   Microreproduction of original published: Valletta, Malta : Malta
Library Association, 1971-

LC VERSION

Malta Library Association.
   Malta Library Association year book [microform]. — 1971-
— Valletta, Malta : The Association, 1971-
      v.
   Microfiche. Bethesda, Md. : ERIC, 1972.   microfiches : nega-
tive ; 11 x 15 cm.

SCOPE / CATEGORIZATION

AACR 2

0.24: cardinal principle

1.11A: describe reproduction

AACR 2 (cont'd)

11.0A: chapter covers microfiches (Cited in #9A)

(Chapter on serials):
12.0A. "The rules in this chapter cover the description of serial publications of all kinds and in all media."

p. 570 (Glossary):
"**Serial.** A publication in any medium issued in successive parts bearing numerical or chronological designations and intended to be continued indefinitely."

NBM 2

p. 54: "microforms" chapter; includes microfiche (Cited in #9A)

Comment

As a serial publication which has been reproduced as a microform, this item is cataloged using AACR 2's chapter on serial publications to describe the serial aspects of the item, in conjunction with the chapter on microforms to describe the physical format. NBM 2 includes a few references to serial publications, but the reader would have to consult AACR 2 for full detail of the description of serials.

SOURCES OF INFORMATION

AACR 2

(Chapter on serials):
12.0B2. "**Sources of information. Nonprinted serials**
Follow the instructions given at the beginning of the relevant chapter in Part I ..."

11.0B1: title frame (Cited in #9A)

NBM 2

p. 54: title frame (Cited in #9A)

TITLE PROPER

AACR 2

11.1B1: as in 1.1B

1.1B1: transcribed exactly except for punctuation, capitalization (Cited in #9A)

(Chapter on serials):
12.1B1. "Record the title proper as instructed in 1.1B."

12.1B2. "In case of doubt about whether a corporate body's name ... is part of the title proper, treat the name as such only if it is consistently so presented in various locations in the serial (cover, caption, masthead, editorial pages, etc.) ..."

12.1B6. "If the title proper includes a date or numbering that varies from issue to issue, omit this date or numbering and *replace it by the mark of omission, unless it occurs at the beginning of the title proper ..."

NBM 2

p. 18: exactly from chief source except for capitalization, punctuation (Cited in #9A)

Comment

Note that "1971" is not recorded as part of the title proper, according to rule 12.1B6. This will mean that the item will not have to be recataloged with each new issue (rule 21.2C: "If the title proper of a serial changes, make a separate main entry for each title.").

The Library of Congress has decided to apply 12.1B6 as follows:

If a date or numbering occurs at the end of the title proper, do not transcribe it as part of the title proper. However, use ellipses to show this omission in the following two cases only:

1) there is a linking word between the designation and the preceding part of the title proper;

   source: Sport in 1981
   transcription: Sport in ...

2) case endings of one or more words in the chronological designation link these words with antecedents within the preceding part of the title proper.[3]

GENERAL MATERIAL DESIGNATION

AACR 2

11.1C1: follows title proper

1.1C1: North American list

---

*This part of rule considered but not applied.

AACR 2 (cont'd)

11.1A1: square brackets

A.4G: lowercase

p. 567: definition of microform (Cited in #9A)

NBM 2

p. 9: North American list

p. 18: lowercase, singular, square brackets; follows title proper

p. 54: microform (Cited in #9A)

STATEMENTS OF RESPONSIBILITY

AACR 2

(Chapter on serials):
12.1F2. "If a statement of responsibility has appeared, in full or abbreviated form, as part of the title proper ..., do not give a further statement of responsibility unless such a statement appears separately in the chief source of information."

12.1F3. "Do not record as statements of responsibility statements relating to personal editors of serials. If a statement relating to an editor is considered necessary by the cataloguing agency, give it in a note (see 12.7B6)."

NBM 2

The reader would consult AACR 2.

NUMERIC AND/OR ALPHABETIC, CHRONOLOGICAL, OR OTHER DESIGNATION AREA

AACR 2

11.3B. "Record the numeric and/or chronological or other designation of a ... serial reproduced in microform as instructed in 12.3."

12.3C1. "If the first issue of a serial is identified by a chronological designation, record it in the terms used in the item."

12.3A1. "**Punctuation.** ... Follow the ... date of the first issue of a serial by a hyphen."

NBM 2

p. 19 (General rules):
"Mathematical Data or Material Specific Details Area
This area is used only with cartographic materials and serials in the sections on globes, maps, and microforms."

p. 54:
"Material specific details area
Do not use this area unless:

...

2. A serial has been reproduced in microform. In this case, list numeric and/or chronological data, such as volume or issue number(s), date(s) of issue."

PUBLICATION, DISTRIBUTION, ETC., AREA

AACR 2

1.11C: describe reproduction

11.4C1: as in 1.4C

1.4C1: place of publication in form on item

1.4C3: add name of state

11.4D1: name of publisher

1.4D2: name in shortest form

11.4F1: as in 1.4F

1.4F1: date of first edition (Cited in #9A)

(Chapter on serials):
12.4C1. "Record the place of publication, distribution, etc., as instructed in 1.4C."

12.4D1. "Record the name of the publisher, distributor, etc., as instructed in 1.4D."

12.4F1. "Record the date of publication of the first issue as instructed in 1.4F. Follow the date with a hyphen and four spaces."

NBM 2

pp. 19, 20: name of place as given on item; add state; name of publisher in shortest form; publication date (Cited in #9A)

PHYSICAL DESCRIPTION AREA—EXTENT OF ITEM

AACR 2

(Chapter on serials):
12.5B1. "For a serial that is still in progress, give the relevant specific material designation (taken from rule 5B in the chapter dealing with the type of material to which the serial belongs, e.g., 11.5B for microform serials) preceded by three spaces."

1.11D: describe reproduction

11.5B1: microfiche

p. 567: definition of microfiche (Cited in #9A)

NBM 2

p. 54: microfiche

p. 109: definition (Cited in #9A)

PHYSICAL DESCRIPTION AREA—OTHER PHYSICAL DETAILS

AACR 2

(Chapter on serials):
12.5C1. "Give the other physical details appropriate to the item being described as instructed in rule 5C in the chapter dealing with the type of material to which the serial belongs (e.g., 2.5C for printed serials)."

11.5C1: indicate if negative (Cited in #9A)

NBM 2

p. 54: indicate if negative (Cited in #9A)

PHYSICAL DESCRIPTION AREA—DIMENSIONS

AACR 2

12.5D1. "Give the dimensions of the serial as instructed in rule .5D in the chapter dealing with the type of material to which the serial belongs ..."

11.5D1: as in following rules; fractions to next whole centimeter

11.5D3: height x width in centimeters (Cited in #9A)

NBM 2

p. 54: height x width in centimeters

p. 21: fractions to next number (Cited in #9A)

NOTE AREA

AACR 2

1.7A4, 11.7B22: notes relating to original (Cited in #9A)

(Chapter on serials):
*12.7B1. "**Frequency.** Make notes on the frequency of the serial unless it is apparent from the content of the title ..."

*12.7B6. "**Statements of responsibility.** ... Give the name of any editor considered to be an important means of identifying the serial (e.g., if a particular person edited the serial for all or most of its existence; if the person's name is likely to be better known than the title of the serial)."

NBM 2

p. 55: bibliographic details of original (Cited in #9A)

CHOICE OF ACCESS POINTS

AACR 2

21.1B2a: deals with corporate body itself (Cited in #9A)

NBM 2

p. 22: entry of reproduction same as original (Cited in #9A)

The reader would consult AACR 2.

9D   BAYNES SOUND

DESCRIPTION OF ITEM

Components: 1 reproduction of a map; microfiche; black and white; low reduction.
Dimensions of fiche: 10.4 x 14.8 cm.

———————————

Envelope:

MICROCHART NAVIGATION SYSTEMS
SAN RAFAEL, CA 94901

———————————

---

*Rule must be considered, to determine that no statement of frequency is made.

Top margin of fiche (eye-readable):

FILMED 3-12-75
MICROCHART NAVIGATION SYSTEMS
1500 WESTLAKE N. SEATTLE, WASH. 98109
... filmed by special permission of the Canadian Hydrographic Service
dated January 15, 1974

Lower left of map:

BRITISH COLUMBIA - VANCOUVER ISLAND
BAYNES SOUND
(very large print)
AND APPROACHES
Surveyed by the Canadian Hydrographic Service, 1969-1971
Scale 1:40,000 (Lat. 49° 30')
Projection: Mercator

Lower border:

Previous Editions 1973
New Edition Oct. 4, 1974
Corrections from Canadian
Notices to Mariners to: 1975
PUBLISHED BY THE CANADIAN HYDROGRAPHIC SERVICE
DEPARTMENT OF THE ENVIRONMENT, OTTAWA
c Her Majesty the Queen in Right of Canada 1974
Printed by Surveys and Mapping Service, Department of Energy,
Mines and Resources
British Columbia - Vancouver Island
BAYNES SOUND AND APPROACHES

CATALOG RECORD

Canadian Hydrographic Service.
Baynes Sound and approaches [microform] : British Columbia-
Vancouver Island / surveyed by the Canadian Hydrographic Ser-
vice. — Scale 1:40,000 ; Mercator proj. — Seattle, Wash. : Microchart
Navigation Systems, 1975.
1 microfiche : 1 map ; 11 x 15 cm.
Low reduction.
Microreproduction of hydrographic chart. New edition Oct. 4,
1974. Ottawa : Canadian Hydrographic Service, c1974.

I. Title. II. Title: British Columbia-Vancouver
Island.

LC VERSION

Canadian Hydrographic Service.
Baynes Sound and approaches [microform] : British Columbia-Vancouver Island / surveyed by the Canadian Hydrographic Service. — New ed. Oct. 4, 1974. — Scale 1:40,000 ; Mercator proj. — Ottawa : The Service, c1974.
1 map.
Microfiche. Seattle, Wash. : Microchart Navigation Systems, 1975.
1 microfiche : 1 map ; 11 x 15 cm. Low reduction.

I. Title. II. Title: British Columbia-Vancouver Island.

SCOPE / CATEGORIZATION

AACR 2

0.24: cardinal principle

1.11A: describe reproduction

11.0A: chapter covers microfiche (Cited in #9A)

NBM 2

p. 54: "microforms" chapter: includes microfiche (Cited in #9A)

Comment

Since this map has been reproduced as a microfiche, the starting point for description in AACR 2 is the chapter on microforms, with the chapter on cartographic materials to be used in conjunction, as appropriate. See the discussion in the *Scope / categorization* section of example #7I in the chapter on graphic materials; the latter example is of a map reproduced as a slide.

SOURCES OF INFORMATION

AACR 2

11.0B1: title frame (Cited in #9A)

NBM 2

p. 54: title frame (Cited in #9A)

TITLE PROPER

AACR 2

11.1B1: as in 1.1B

1.1B1: transcribed exactly except for punctuation, capitalization (Cited in #9A)

(Chapter on cartographic materials):
3.1B3. "If the chief source of information bears more than one title, [and if] both or all of the titles are in the same language and script, choose the title proper on the basis of the sequence or layout of the titles. If these are insufficient to enable the choice to be made or are ambiguous, choose the most comprehensive title."

NBM 2

p. 18: exactly from chief source except for capitalization, punctuation (Cited in #9A)

p. 48 (Chapter on maps):
"Information for the catalogue record is taken from the following sources in this order:[40]

1. The item itself (Chief source of information). If two or more titles are given on the face of the map, preference is given in the following order:

a) The most appropriate title,

b) The title within the border of the map,

c) The title in the margin;"

p. 125 (Appendix A — Notes):
"40. Drawn from NBM/1 & [AECT 4]."

Comment

AACR 2's guidelines in chapter 3 for the selection of titles appearing on a map indicate that the selection is to be made on the basis of sequence or layout. In this case, the title "British Columbia - Vancouver Island" appears first in the sequence, but "Baynes Sound" is by far the more prominent in terms of typography. In addition, it is the latter title which indicates the specific geographic area covered by the map.

In NBM 2, criteria for selecting a title are contained in the rules for chief source of information.

GENERAL MATERIAL DESIGNATION

AACR 2

11.1C1: follows title proper

1.1C1: North American list

11.1A1: square brackets

A.4G: lowercase

p. 567: definition of microform (Cited in #9A)

NBM 2

p. 9: North American list

p. 18: lowercase, singular, square brackets; follows title proper

p. 54: microform (Cited in #9A)

p. 18 (General rules):
"Select the general material designation for the format, not for the content. For example, a map on a transparency is designated 'transparency' rather than 'map.' "

OTHER TITLE INFORMATION

AACR 2

11.1E1. "Record other title information as instructed in 1.1E."

1.1E1. "Transcribe all other title information appearing in the chief source of information according to the instructions in 1.1B."

NBM 2

p. 18 (General rules):
"Other title information ... follows the general material designation and the title proper ... to which it pertains. [It is] listed in the exact wording found in the chief source of information."

STATEMENTS OF RESPONSIBILITY

AACR 2

11.1F1: as in 1.1F

1.1F1: in form appearing on item (Cited in #9A)

NBM 2

p. 18: wording and order on source (Cited in #9A)

EDITION AREA

AACR 2

1.11C. "If the facsimile, etc., has the edition statement ... of the original as well as [that] for the facsimile, etc., give [that] of the facsimile, etc., in the edition [area]. Give the details of the original in the note area ..."

*11.2B1. "Transcribe a statement relating to an edition of a microform that contains differences from other editions, or that is a named reissue of that microform, as instructed in 1.2B."

NBM 2

*p. 19 (General rules):
"The edition statement is listed as it appears on the item ..."

The reader would consult AACR 2.

Comment

AACR 2's rule 1.11C states that the edition statement for the original is included in a note if there is also an edition statement for the reproduction; however, if the only edition statement present pertains to the original, the course of action remains less certain. The date of the edition statement (1974) does not accord with the date of publication for the reproduction (1975); thus rule 1.4F1 would suggest that the edition statement here be relegated to a note: 1.4F1. "Give the date of publication, distribution, etc., of the edition named in the edition area."

MATHEMATICAL DATA AREA

AACR 2

11.3A. "Record the mathematical data of a cartographic item in microform as instructed in 3.3"

(Chapter on cartographic materials):
3.3B1. "Give the scale of a cartographic item as a representative fraction expressed as a ratio (1:). Precede the ratio by the word *scale*."

3.3C1. "Give the statement of projection if it is found on the item.... Use standard abbreviations (see Appendix B) ...

Conic equidistant proj."

3.3A1. "**Punctuation.** ... Precede the projection statement by a semicolon."

---

*Rule considered but not applied.

NBM 2

p. 19: area used only with cartographic materials and serials (Cited in #9C)

p. 48 (Chapter on maps):
"*Scale.* List the term 'Scale' and a representative fration expressed as a ratio, e.g., Scale 1:1,000,000."

"*Projection.* List projection if it is found in the first three sources of information."

"*Punctuation.* ... [Scale information is separated] from projection by a space-semicolon-space ..."

Comment

Rule 11.3A makes it clear that Area Three can be applied, and a statement of scale indicated. As with example #7I (map reproduced as a slide) in the chapter on graphic materials, one must ask whether a statement of the scale of the original is appropriate when the object being described is a reproduction.

PUBLICATION, DISTRIBUTION, ETC., AREA

AACR 2

1.11C: describe reproduction

11.4C1: as in 1.4C

1.4C1: place of publication in form on item

1.4C3: add name of state

11.4D1: name of publisher

1.4D2: name in shortest form

11.4F1: as in 1.4F

1.4F1: date of first edition (Cited in #9A)

NBM 2

pp. 19, 20: name of place as given on item; add state; name of publisher in shortest form; publication date (Cited in #9A)

PHYSICAL DESCRIPTION AREA—EXTENT OF ITEM

AACR 2

1.11D: describe reproduction

11.5B1: microfiche—number of frames

p. 567: definition of microfiche (Cited in #9A)

NBM 2

p. 54: microfiche—number of frames

p. 109: definition (Cited in #9A)

Comment

Opinions may differ as to whether it is appropriate to add (*1 frame*) to the statement of extent.

PHYSICAL DESCRIPTION AREA—OTHER PHYSICAL DETAILS

AACR 2

11.5C1: indicate if negative

11.5C2: illustrations as in 1.5C

1.5C1: physical data as in following chapters

2.5C1: illustrations

2.5C2: indicate illustrations of particular types—maps (Cited in #9A)

2.5C4. "Specify the number of illustrations if their number can be easily ascertained ...

   ...

  : ill., 3 forms, 1 map"

NBM 2

p. 54: indicate if negative; list illustrations (Cited in #9A)

Comment

AACR 2 fails to provide adequate instruction for description of "other physical details" of microforms. In providing an "illustration" statement for this item, one must keep in mind that the entire item consists of a map, which is one of the types of illustrations listed in AACR 2's rule 2.5C1 in the chapter on books. Rule 11.5C2 directs the reader to rule 1.5C1, which in turn directs one to the appropriate rule from whichever of the chapters in Part One best suits the item. Although this item is a map, none of the rules in 3.5C is suited, and instead rule 2.5C1, which provides for the description of illustrations in books, seems most appropriate. The solution arrived at here, "1 map," serves both as a statement of other physical details, for the microform reproduction, and as a "substitute statement of extent" for the *content* of the original.

PHYSICAL DESCRIPTION AREA—DIMENSIONS

AACR 2

11.5D1: as in following rules

11.5D3: height x width in centimeters (Cited in #9A)

NBM 2

p. 54: height x width in centimeters

p. 21: fractions to next number (Cited in #9A)

NOTE AREA

AACR 2

11.7B10. "**Physical description.** Make the following physical description notes:
Reduction ratio. Give the reduction ratio if it is outside the 16x-30x range. Use one of the following terms:
    Low reduction   *For less than 16x*"

1.7A4, 11.7B22: notes relating to original (Cited in #9A)

NBM 2

p. 54:
"*Reduction ratio.* Most microform readers in common use in media centres can accommodate materials with a 16-30x reduction. A reduction ratio outside this range should be noted using the following terms:
    Low reduction—up to an inclusive of 15x"

p. 55: bibliographic details of original (Cited in #9A)

CHOICE OF ACCESS POINTS

AACR 2

21.1B2. "Enter a work emanating from one or more corporate bodies under the heading for the appropriate corporate body if it falls into one or more of the following categories:

...

    *f) cartographic materials emanating from a corporate body other than a body that is merely responsible for the publication or distribution of the materials.

**"In case of doubt about whether a work falls into one or more of these categories, treat it as if it did not."

**21.1B3. "When determining the main entry heading for works that emanate from one or more corporate bodies but that fall outside the categories given in 21.1B2, treat them as if no corporate body were involved."

**21.1C. "Enter a work under its title when:

...

3) it emanates from a corporate body but does not fall into one or more of the categories given in 21.1B2 and is not of personal authorship."

NBM 2

p. 18: entry of reproduction same as original (Cited in #9A)

The reader would consult AACR 2.

Comment

In the original AACR 2, this work would have been entered under title unless, under a broad interpretation of 21.1B2c, the map were to be regarded as representing the collective thought and effort of the Canadian Hydrographic Service. See the discussion of choice of access points in example #4B in the chapter on cartographic materials.

FORM OF HEADING

AACR 2

24.17. "Enter a body created or controlled by a government under its own name ... unless it belongs to one or more of the types listed in 24.18."

NBM 2

Outside the scope of this code. The reader would consult AACR 2.

---

*Addition of category 'f' appears in AACR 2 revisions.

**This rule was considered but not applied.

9E   BRAHMS WALTZES

DESCRIPTION OF ITEM

Components: 1 16mm microfilm reproduction of a music score; black and white, in cardboard container.

The original score has 13 numbered pages. This work was originally composed for one piano, four hands.

Frame 1 of film reel:

J. BRAHMS
WALTZES FOR 2 PIANOS AND 4 HANDS
Film 32

Frame 2:

Filmed by the Jamaica Music Study Guild
1965   Jamaica, New York

Frame 3 (reproduction of original):

Schirmer's Library of Musical Classics
Vol. 1530
JOHANNES BRAHMS
Op. 39
Waltzes
Two Pianos, Four-Hands
Edited by Edwin Hughes

G. Schirmer, Inc.
New York
Copyright, 1929, by G. Schirmer, Inc.

CATALOG RECORD

Brahms, Johannes, 1833-1897.
[Waltzes, piano, 4 hands, op. 39; arr.]
Waltzes, two pianos, four-hands, op. 39 [microform] / Johannes Brahms ; edited by Edwin Hughes. — Jamaica, N.Y. : Filmed by the Jamaica Music Study Guild, 1965.
1 microfilm reel : chiefly music ; 16 mm.
Film #32.
Microreproduction of score edited by Edwin Hughes. New York : G. Schirmer, c1929. 13 p. (Schirmer's library of musical classics ; v. 1530)

I. Hughes, Edwin.

Option: GMD could follow uniform title.

LC VERSION

Brahms, Johannes, 1833-1897.
  [Waltzes, piano, 4 hands, op. 39; arr.]
  Waltzes, two pianos, four-hands, op. 39 [microform] / Johannes Brahms ; edited by Edwin Hughes. — New York : G. Schirmer, c1929.
  1 score (13 p.). — (Schirmer's library of musical classics ; vol. 1530)
  Microfilm. Jamaica, N.Y. : Jamaica Music Study Guild, 1965. 1 microfilm reel ; 16 mm.

  I. Hughes, Edwin.

SCOPE / CATEGORIZATION

AACR 2

0.24: cardinal principle

1.11A: describe reproduction

11.0A: chapter covers microfilms (Cited in #9A)

(Chapter on music):
5.0A. "The rules in this chapter cover the description of published music.... For microform reproductions of music, see chapter 11."

NBM 2

p. 54: "microforms" chapter; includes microfilms (Cited in #9A)

Comment

The starting point for description will be the microfilm; however, the cataloger will need to make extensive use of many of the rules for music scores, and for the construction of uniform titles.

SOURCES OF INFORMATION

AACR 2

11.0B1: title frame at beginning of item (Cited in #9A, amplified by #9B)

NBM 2

p. 54: title frame (Cited in #9A, amplified by #9B)

TITLE PROPER

AACR 2

11.1B1: as in 1.1B

1.1B1: transcribed exactly except for punctuation, capitalization (Cited in #9A)

(Chapter on music):
*5.1B1. "If a title consists of the name(s) of one or more types of composition and one or more of the following statements—medium of performance, key, date of composition, and/or number—record those elements as the title proper."

NBM 2

p. 18: exactly from chief source except for capitalization, punctuation (Cited in #9A)

GENERAL MATERIAL DESIGNATION

AACR 2

11.1C1: follows title proper

1.1C1: North American list

11.1A1: square brackets

A.4G: lowercase

p. 567: definition of microform (Cited in #9A)

(Chapter on uniform titles):
**25.5E. "*Optionally*, if general material designations are used ..., add the designation at the end of the uniform title."

NBM 2

p. 9: North American list

p. 18: lowercase, singular, square brackets; follows the title proper

---

*Altered rule appearing in AACR 2 revisions.
**Option not applied in this example.

NBM 2 (cont'd)

p. 54: microform (Cited in #9A)

p. 18; Rule continues:
"An exception to the placement and bracketing of the general material designation is made for items which are catalogued with a uniform title. *The cataloguer has the option of placing a general material designation after the uniform title, capitalized and separated from the uniform title by a period and one space (.). If the uniform title is enclosed in square brackets, the general material designation is included in these brackets."

PUBLICATION, DISTRIBUTION, ETC., AREA

AACR 2

1.11C: describe reproduction

11.4C1: as in 1.4C

1.4C1: place of publication in form on item

1.4C3: add name of state

11.4D1: name of publisher

1.4D3: "Do not omit from the phrase naming a publisher, distributor, etc.:
a) words or phrases indicating the function (other than solely publishing) performed by the person or body ..."

11.4F1: as in 1.4F

1.4F1: date of first edition (Cited in #9A)

NBM 2

pp. 19, 20: name of place as given on item; add state; name of publisher in shortest form; publication date (Cited in #9A)

PHYSICAL DESCRIPTION AREA — EXTENT OF ITEM

AACR 2

1.11D: describe reproduction

---

*Option not applied in this example.

11.5B1: microfilm—add *reel* (Cited in #9A, amplified by #9B)

p. 567: definition of microfilm (Cited in #9B)

NBM 2

p. 54: microfilm—add *reel* (Cited in #9A, amplified by #9B)

p. 109: definition of microfilm (Cited in #9B)

PHYSICAL DESCRIPTION AREA—OTHER PHYSICAL DETAILS

AACR 2

11.5C1: indicate if negative

11.5C2: illustrations as in 1.5C

1.5C1: physical data as in following chapters

2.5C1: illustrations

2.5C2: indicate illustrations of particular types—music (Cited in #9A)

2.5C6. "If the publication consists wholly or predominantly of illustrations, ... [and if] those illustrations are all of one type (see 2.5C2), use *all [name of type]* or *chiefly [name of type]*."

NBM 2

p. 54: indicate if negative; list illustrations (Cited in #9A)

Comment

Once again the rules for description of "other physical details" are inadequate. It did not appear appropriate to use rule 5.5C from the chapter on music for this item. "Other physical details" in the context of the chapter on music refers to enhancements (such as portraits) to the music scores, and would thus be appropriate only if the principal character of the item has already been suggested by the specific material designation *score*. In contrast, the specific material designation in this example indicates the *physical* form of the material. Thus, the *intellectual* character of the content must presumably be noted, as in the Baynes Sound example in #9D, in the "other physical details" area.

PHYSICAL DESCRIPTION AREA—DIMENSIONS

AACR 2

11.5D1: as in following rules (Cited in #9A)

AACR 2 (cont'd)

11.5D4: diameter not given if reel is three inches; give width (Cited in #9B)

NBM 2

p. 54: diameter not given if reel is three inches; give width (Cited in #9B)

NOTE AREA

AACR 2

11.7B19: numbers

1.7A4, 11.7B22: notes relating to original (Cited in #9A)

NBM 2

p. 22: numbers (Cited in #9A)

p. 55: bibliographic details of original (Cited in #9A)

CHOICE OF ACCESS POINTS

AACR 2

21.1A1. "… composers of music are the authors of the works they create …"

21.4A: entry under personal author (Cited in #9B)

NBM 2

p. 18: entry of reproduction same as original (Cited in #9A)

p. 18: entry under personal author (Cited in #9B)

UNIFORM TITLE

AACR 2

(Chapter on uniform titles):

25.1. "Uniform titles provide the means for bringing together all the catalogue entries for a work when various manifestations (e.g., editions, translations) of it have appeared under various titles."

25.27B. "If the title … consists solely of the name of one type of composition, use the accepted English form of name if there are cognate forms in English, French, German, and Italian, or if the same name is used in all these languages. Give the name in the plural ... unless the composer wrote only one work of the type."

25.36B. "For a collection containing works of one type, use the name of that type. Add a statement of medium unless the medium is obvious or unless the works are for various media."

25.29A1. "Add a statement of the medium of performance[10] if the title consists solely of the name of a type, or the names of two or more types, of composition."

Footnote:
"10. A statement of the medium of performance is a concise statement of the instrumental or vocal medium of performance, or both, for which a musical work was originally intended."

25.29D1. "Use English terms whenever possible [for individual instruments]."

25.29D2. "For keyboard instruments use:
   piano (*for one instrument, two hands*)
   piano, 4 hands
   pianos (2) (*for two instruments, 4 hands*)"

25.31A1. "If the title consists solely of the name(s) of type(s) of composition, add as many of the following identifying elements as can readily be ascertained. Add following the statement of medium of performance and in the order given:
   ...
   b) opus number or thematic index number
   ...
Precede each element by a comma."

25.31A3. "**Opus numbers.** Include the opus number, if any, and any number within the opus, if any."

25.31B2. "**Arrangements.** If a work described as an arrangement, etc., is entered under the heading for the original composer ..., use the uniform title for the original work and add, preceded by a semicolon, *arr.*"

"Add *arr.* also to the uniform title for a transcription by the composer."

NBM 2

p. 80 (Chapter on sound recordings):
"A uniform title is necessary to bring together various versions, editions, and arrangements of a work ..."

"Uniform titles are formulated according to the rules outlined in the *Anglo-American Cataloguing Rules*, 2nd edition, chapter 25."

NOTES

1.   Library of Congress, Processing Services, *Cataloging Service Bulletin*, no. 14 (Fall 1981), pp. 56-58.

2.   *CSB*, no. 11 (Winter), p. 26.

3.   *CSB*, no. 14 (Fall 1981), p. 17.

10

KITS

The category of kits is independent of any given medium or type of material, since this category is defined as a unit comprised of more than one type of material, with no predominant medium. Although many catalogers use the term *kit* to indicate a filmstrip and sound recording combination, any combination of media could be included in the category. In addition, the decision as to whether a combination contains a predominant medium is likely to be subjective in many instances.

AACR 2 includes rules for kits in its general chapter for description, while NBM 2 provides a separate chapter for this category. Both codes offer an option for full description of each medium within the kit. If a full description is desired, the cataloger must consult the appropriate chapter for each component type of material.

10A METRICS AND ME

DESCRIPTION OF ITEM

Components: 20 booklets	10 (blank) green cards
2 wooden folding rulers	10 (blank) red cards
10 plastic rulers	10 measuring spoons
2 cloth bags	10 thermometers
containing beans	

All of above in cardboard box, 29 x 23 x 12 centimeters (height x width x depth)

Title page of booklets:

Metrics And Me
by
Florence Taber, Ed. D.
Alonzo Hannaford, Ed. D.
    i   Interpretive
    e   Education   c1977

Container front:

Metrics And Me
Interpretive Education c1977

Container side:

i   Metrics And Me
e   Interpretive Education
     Division of Illinois Envelope Company
     400 Bryant St. Kalamazoo, Michigan 49001

The kit is designed to introduce students to the metric system.

CATALOG RECORD

Metrics and me [kit]. — Kalamazoo, Mich. : Interpretive Education, c1977.
     20 booklets, 10 measuring spoons, 10 thermometers, 10 plastic rulers, 2 bags of beans, 2 wooden rulers, 20 colored cards ; in container, 29 x 23 x 12 cm.
     Booklet by Florence Taber and Alonzo Hannaford.
     Summary: Designed to introduce students to the metric system.

     I. Taber, Florence. II. Hannaford, Alonzo. III. Interpretive Education.

SCOPE / CATEGORIZATION

AACR 2

Chapter title: "General Rules for Description"
1.10A. "This rule applies to items that are made up of two or more components, two or more of which belong to distinct material types (e.g., a sound recording and a printed text)."

1.10C. "If an item has no predominant component, follow the rules below in addition to the rules in this chapter and the rules in the appropriate following chapters."

NBM 2

p. 40:
Chapter title: "Kits"
"*Kit*: a set of material composed of many textual parts, or, two or more media, no one of which is identifiable as the predominant constituent of the item."

Comment

NBM 2 has a chapter specifically for kits. AACR 2 includes kits among the general rules for description, which are considered as "rules of general applicability" (rule 0.23), presumably since the category of "kit" is not limited to any one type of material. Another possibility might have been to treat kits in a manner similar to serials—that is, to assign kits to a separate chapter and consider the rules therein as rules of partial generality. Whatever one's opinion of AACR 2's categorization of kits, it is still apparent that the rules for kits in this code need to be expanded, as will be seen in subsequent parts of the discussion of this example and the ones to follow.

SOURCES OF INFORMATION

AACR 2

1.0H. "Items with several chief sources of information

...

Multipart items. Describe an item in several physical parts from the chief source of information for the first part.... If there is no discernible first part, use the part that gives the most information. Failing this, use any part or a container that is a unifying element. Show variations in the chief sources of information of subsequent parts in notes, or by incorporating the data with those derived from the first part."

NBM 2

p. 40:
"Information for the catalogue record is taken from the following sources in this order:

1. The container (Chief source of information);
2. The part which gives the most information (Chief source of information);
3. Other sources."

Comment

There is a notable absence of rules in AACR 2 for determining the chief source of information for kits. The Library of Congress has issued the following rule interpretation:

1.10. The chief source of information for kits is the item itself (including all components) together with the container and any accompanying material.
    If the chief source (cf. above) includes more than one title, select as the title proper the one that collectively describes the contents as a whole. If there is more than one such unifying title, choose the one from a unifying piece (e.g., container or manual) that identifies the contents as a whole most adequately and succinctly.[1]

The model for treating the whole item as chief source can be found in chapter 10, covering three-dimensional materials, which defines the chief source as "the object itself together with any accompanying textual material and container issued by the 'publisher' or manufacturer of the item" (Rule 10.0B1).

Note that NBM 2 prefers the container as the chief source. AECT 4 also prescribes that the title of the kit be taken from the container (p. 112).

TITLE PROPER

AACR 2

1.1A2. **"Sources of information.** Take information recorded in [the title and statement of responsibility] area from the chief source of information for the material to which the item being described belongs."

1.1B1. "Transcribe the title proper exactly as to wording, order, and spelling, but not necessarily as to punctuation and capitalization."

NBM 2

p. 18 (General rules):
"The title proper ... is copied exactly from the chief source of information. However, capitalization and punctuation follow prescribed rules."

Comment

AACR 2's rules for title transcription require that a chief source of information be determined. The lack of guidelines for determining the chief source for kits presents no problem in this example, since the same title appears on both the booklets and on the container.

GENERAL MATERIAL DESIGNATION

AACR 2

1.10C1. "If general material designations are used (see 1.1C):
...
For an item with a collective title, follow the instructions in 1.1C4."

1.1C1. "If general material designations are to be used in cataloguing, ... North American agencies [should use] terms from list 2."

1.1A1. "Enclose the general material designation in square brackets."

(Appendix A — Capitalization):
A.4G. "Lowercase the words making up a general material designation."

1.1C4. "If an item contains parts belonging to materials falling into two or more categories in the list chosen and if none of these is the predominant constituent of the item, give the designation *multimedia* or *kit* (see 1.1C1 and 1.10)."

NBM 2

p. 9 (Chapter on cataloging policy for media centers):
"The North American list of general material designations is used in this book. Those electing [to omit the general material designation or to use] the British list ... or the ISBD list may use the rules on the following pages by disregarding the general material designation or by substituting the appropriate term from the British or ISBD lists."

p. 18 (General rules):
"A general material designation is listed in lower case letters, in the singular, and in its own square brackets immediately following the title proper."

p. 40:
"The general material designation 'kit' is applied only to those media which are to be catalogued as a unit."

Comment

The Library of Congress will display the general material designation for kits.

STATEMENTS OF RESPONSIBILITY*

AACR 2

1.1A2. sources of information (Cited in *Title proper* section of this example.)

1.1F1. "Record statements of responsibility appearing prominently in the item in the form in which they appear there. If a statement of responsibility is taken from a source other than the chief source of information, enclose it in square brackets."

NBM 2

pp. 18, 19 (General rules):
"The statement(s) of responsibility is listed wherever possible in the wording and order found on the source(s) of information.... Statements of responsibility may include ... any person or corporate body which has contributed to the intellectual or artistic content. Contributors of minor importance may be listed in the notes."

---

*Rules considered but not applied.

NBM 2 (cont'd)

"There are many instances in nonbook materials where it is difficult to establish clear responsibility... When there is doubt concerning the responsibility for the artistic and/or intellectual content of the item, it is wiser to omit the statement than to construct one of dubious truth."

Comment

Here the selection of a chief source will make a difference, since only the booklets contain a statement of responsibility. However, no statement is recorded here since there is no indication that Taber and Hannaford are responsible for the unit as a whole.

PUBLICATION, DISTRIBUTION, ETC., AREA

AACR 2

1.4A2. "**Sources of information.** Record in [the publication, distribution, etc.] area information taken from the chief source of information or from any other source specified for this area in the following chapters. Enclose information supplied from any other source in square brackets."

1.4C1. "Record the place of publication, etc., in the form ... in which it appears."

*1.4C3. "Add the name of the country, state, province, etc., to the name of the place if it is considered necessary for identification, or if it is considered necessary to distinguish the place from others of the same name."

1.4D2. "Give the name of a publisher, distributor, etc., in the shortest form in which it can be understood and identified internationally."

1.4F6. "If the dates of publication, distribution, etc., are unknown, give the copyright date ... in its place."

NBM 2

pp. 19, 20 (General rules):
"List the name of the place as it appears on the item and add the name of the province, state, country, etc., if it is necessary for identification."

"List the name of the publisher, producer, distributor, etc., in the shortest form that can be identified internationally."

"If the dates of publication or distribution cannot be ascertained, list the copyright date."

---

*For LC rule interpretation, see example #4B, p. 81.

PHYSICAL DESCRIPTION AREA

AACR 2

1.10C2. "Apply whichever of the following three methods is appropriate to the item being described:

a) Give the extent of each part or group of parts belonging to each distinct class of material as the first element of the physical description (do this if no further physical description of each item is desired), ending this element with *in container*, if there is one, and following it with the dimensions of the container.

...

or b) Give separate physical descriptions for each part or group of parts ...

or c) ... give a general term as the extent ..."

Chapter on three-dimensional materials (By analogy, to give dimensions of container):
10.5D1. "If multiple dimensions are given, record them as height x width x depth ..."

NBM 2

p. 40:
"If a full description of each part is not wanted, list the number and name of each type of material in the order of their importance[35] to the item as a whole. If this cannot be determined, list the number and name of each type of material in alphabetical order.[36] Follow this with the term 'in container' and the container dimensions when appropriate."

[or] "... list a description for each type of material ..."

[or] "If the parts are difficult to name ..., such phrases as '18 various pieces' ... may be used."

p. 125 (Appendix A — Notes):
"35. 1.10C2a implies this order in the example."

"36. 'alphabetical order' drawn from ISBD(NBM), [revised chapter 12 of AACR], & NBM/1"

p. 21 (General rules):
"[Three] dimensional materials [are measured] height x width x depth."

Comment

In AACR 2, it is necessary to do a little "borrowing" to find guidelines for stating the dimensions of the container. NBM 2, on the other hand, has provided a general rule for this instance which can be applied whenever appropriate.

Of the three methods of description offered in AACR 2 and NBM 2, method "a" seems most appropriate for this example, since the individual pieces do not appear to merit detailed description, and there is a small enough number of media categories to warrant enumeration.

Note that AACR 2 does not specify the order for listing the component pieces.

NOTE AREA

AACR 2

1.7A5. "A general outline of notes is given in 1.7B. Specific applications of 1.7B are provided in other chapters in Part I."

1.7B6. **"Statements of responsibility"**

(Chapter on three-dimensional artefacts and realia — by analogy):
10.7B6. **"Statements of responsibility.** ... Give statements of responsibility not recorded in the title and statement of responsibility area."

1.7B17. **"Summary"**

(Chapter on three-dimensional artefacts and realia — by analogy):
10.7B17. **"Summary.** Give a brief objective summary of the content of an item unless another part of the description gives enough information."

NBM 2

p. 22 (General rules):
"Statements of responsibility. This may include additional information ... not listed in the title and statement of responsibility area ..."

"Summaries. *These are not necessary for media which can be readily examined or adequately described by title and/or series statement."

Comment

Since the rules for notes in AACR 2 are given only in general outline form, the reader would have to seek an appropriate chapter which is suited to the types of material comprising the kit. The chapter on three-dimensional artefacts and realia has been selected for this example.

CHOICE OF ACCESS POINTS

AACR 2

21.1C. "Enter a work under its title when:

---

*Rule considered but not applied.

... 3) it emanates from a corporate body but does not fall into one or more of the categories given in 21.1B2 and is not of personal authorship"

*21.1A1. "A personal author is the person chiefly responsible for the creation of the intellectual or artistic content of a work."

NBM 2

p. 40:
"A kit is entered under author where the author has been responsible for the creation of the kit as a whole. If each component has a different author, or if authorship of the kit as a whole cannot be established, enter under title."

Comment

In this case, there is no indication that Taber and Hannaford are responsible for anything other than the booklets. Since no one can be identified as being *chiefly* responsible for the work, entry is under title. Responsibility has to be considered in terms of the kit as a unit, since it is the kit as a whole that is being cataloged.

10B   SYLVESTER AND THE MAGIC PEBBLE

DESCRIPTION OF ITEM

Components: 1 hardcover book	2 marbles ("magic pebbles")
1 tape cassette	1 activity guide
2 hand puppets	1 poster

All of above in container.

Dimensions of container: 34½ x 46½ x 7½ centimeters (height x width x depth)

Container front:

SYLVESTER AND
THE MAGIC PEBBLE

BY WILLIAM STIEG

A CALDECOTT MEDAL WINNER

---

*Rule considered but not applied.

Container side:

> MK-2601
> Sylvester and the Magic Pebble
> SVE - Society for Visual Education, Inc.
> 1345 Diversey Parkway, Chicago, Illinois 60614
>> SINGER
>> Education Division

Container side:

> Copyright C1976 Society for Visual Education, Inc.

Activity guide, title page:

> Activity Guide
> SYLVESTER
> AND THE MAGIC PEBBLE
> Based on the book by William Stieg
> SVE — Society for Visual Education

Activity guide, page 4:

> Project Director
> Alma Gilleo
>
> Book
> by William Stieg
>
> Box wrap and poster designs
> David Povilaitis
>
> Puppet designs
> Alma Gilleo
>
> Narrator
> Stephen King

The activity guide contains no illustrations, has 24 unnumbered pages, and is 23 centimeters high. The verso of the title page gives a copyright date of 1976.

Tape cassette

Label, side one:

> Use with book: Cassette
> Sylvester and the Magic Pebble   MK2601-1YC

(Label, side one, continues on next page)

SINGER   Time
Education Division   13:15
SVE — Society for Visual Education, Inc.
(P)SVE, 1976 All rights reserved.

Label, side two:

Sounds to identify;   Cassette
New stories to complete   MK2601-1TC

                                               Time
                                               4:55

The tape cassettes are 3⅞ x 2½ inches, with a tape width of ⅛ inches. The playing speed is 1⅞, and there are two tracks.

The book contains 32 unnumbered pages, has colored illustrations, and is 31 centimeters high.

The poster is in color, is 45 x 61 centimeters (height x width), and has no title.

The two hand puppets are made of fabric and papier mâché, and are gray and blue. The labels give the name of the characters represented. Each puppet is about 28 centimeters in height.

There are two red marbles in a plastic container.

CATALOG RECORD

Version "a"

Sylvester and the magic pebble [kit] / [based on the book] by William
    Stieg. — Chicago, Ill. : Society for Visual Education, c1976.
    1 book, 1 sound cassette, 1 poster, 2 puppets, 2 marbles, 1 activity
guide ; in container, 35 x 47 x 8 cm.
    Project director, Alma Gilleo ; narrator, Stephen King.
    Intended audience: kindergarten and primary grades.
    Summary: The kit is centered around the Caldecott medal winner
book of the same name. Recordings give a reading of the story with
sound effects.
    "MK-2601"

    I. Stieg, William. Sylvester and the magic pebble. II. Society
for Visual Education.

Version "b"

Version "b" has the following differences:

>   1 book ([32] p.) : col. ill. ; 32 cm.
>   1 sound cassette (19 min.) : 1⅞ ips, 2 track, mono.
>   1 poster : col. ; 45 x 61 cm.
>   2 hand puppets : fabric and papier mâché, gray and blue ; 35 cm.
> high.
>   1 activity guide ([24] p.) ; 23 cm.
>   2 marbles : red.
>   Project director, Alma Gilleo ; narrator, Stephen King.
>   Intended audience: kindergarten and primary grades.
>   In container, 35 x 47 x 8 cm.

SCOPE / CATEGORIZATION

AACR 2

1.10A: multi-media types

1.10C: no predominant component (Cited in #10A)

NBM 2

p. 40: "kits" chapter (Cited in #10A)

SOURCES OF INFORMATION

AACR 2

1.0H: container as unifying element (Cited in #10A)

NBM 2

p. 40: container (Cited in #10A)

Comment

In this case, there is no problem in identifying a "unifying" title, in AACR 2's terms, since the title appearing on the book and on the container is appropriate to the kit as a whole, while the titles on the cassettes and activity guides apply only to those specific items.

TITLE PROPER

AACR 2

1.1A2: sources

1.1B1: transcribed exactly except for punctuation, capitalization (Cited in #10A)

NBM 2

p. 18: exactly from chief source except for capitalization, punctuation (Cited in #10A)

GENERAL MATERIAL DESIGNATION

AACR 2

1.10C1: as in 1.1C

1.1C1: North American list

1.1A1: square brackets

A.4G: lowercase

1.1C4: kit (Cited in #10A)

NBM 2

p. 9: North American list

p. 18: lowercase, singular, square brackets; follows the title proper

p. 40: kit (Cited in #10A)

STATEMENTS OF RESPONSIBILITY

AACR 2

1.1A2: sources of information

1.1F1: in form appearing on item (Cited in #10A)

1.1F8. "Add an explanatory word or short phrase to the statement of responsibility if the relationship between the title and the person(s) ... named in the statement is not clear."

NBM 2

pp. 18, 19: in wording on source (Cited in #10A)

Rule continues:
"A word or phrase may be added in square brackets in order to clarify the type of responsibility."

PUBLICATION, DISTRIBUTION, ETC., AREA

AACR 2

1.4A2: sources

1.4C1: place of publication in form on item

1.4C3: add name of state

1.4D2: name in shortest form

1.4F6: copyright date (Cited in #10A)

NBM 2

pp. 19, 20: name of place; add state; name of publisher in shortest form; copyright date (Cited in #10A)

PHYSICAL DESCRIPTION AREA

AACR 2

1.10C2: 3 options for description

10.5D1: container dimensions (Cited in #10A)

Rule also includes:
"b) Give separate physical descriptions for each part or group of parts belonging to each distinct class of material (do this if a further physical description of each item is desired). Give each physical description on a separate line."

NBM 2

p. 40: 3 options for description (Cited in #10A)

Rule also includes:
"If a full description of each part is wanted, list a description for each type of material on separate lines."

Comment

This item would lend itself either to version "a" or "b" of the options for description presented by AACR 2's 1.10C2 and NBM 2. Users would probably appreciate a full description of the component parts, although many libraries will not have the resources available for such detailed cataloging. Both versions are presented here, and the rules appropriate to version "b" follow. The Library of Congress has decided not to use method "b" in any case.

PHYSICAL DESCRIPTION AREA — VERSION "A"

AACR 2

1.10C2a: give extent of each part (Cited in #10A)

NBM 2

p. 40: number and name of each type of material (Cited in #10A)

PHYSICAL DESCRIPTION AREA — VERSION "B"

DESCRIPTION OF BOOK

AACR 2

(Chapter on books, pamphlets, and printed sheets):
2.5B7. "If the volume is printed without pagination ..., ascertain the total number of pages ... and give the number in square brackets."

2.5C1. "Describe an illustrated printed monograph as *ill.* unless the illustrations are all of one or more of the particular types mentioned in the next paragraph."

2.5C3. "Describe coloured illustrations (i.e., those in two or more colours) as such."

2.5D1. "Give the height of the volume(s) in centimetres, to the next whole centimetre up ..."

NBM 2

Books are outside the scope of this code. The reader would consult AACR 2.

DESCRIPTION OF SOUND RECORDING

AACR 2

6.5B2. "Add to the [specific material] designation the stated total playing time of the sound recording in minutes (to the next minute up) ..."

6.5C3. "**Playing speed.** ... Give the playing speed of a tape in inches per second (ips)."

*6.5C6. "**Number of tracks.** For tape ... cassettes, ... give the number of tracks, unless the number of tracks is standard for that item.[2]"

---

*Rule must be considered, to decide that no statement is given.

AACR 2 (cont'd)

Footnote: "2. The standard number of tracks for a ... cassette [is] 4."

6.5C7. "**Number of sound channels.** Give one of the following terms as appropriate: ... mono."

*6.5D5. "**Sound cassettes.** Give the dimensions of the cassette if they are other than the standard dimensions (3 ⅞ x 2½ in.) in inches, and the width of the tape if other than the standard width (⅛ in.) in fractions of an inch."

NBM 2

p. 81 (Chapter on sound recordings):
"List in parentheses after the specific material designation the total playing time stated on the item ..."

"*Other physical details*
Tapes. List playing speed in inches per second (ips).
*List number of tracks only if it is not standard for the item. List mono., stereo ..."

"*Dimensions*
Cassettes. List the dimensions in inches only if they are other than 3 ⅞ x 2½ in.
*List the width of the tape in fractions of an inch only if it is other than ⅛ in."

DESCRIPTION OF POSTER

AACR 2

(Chapter on graphic materials):
8.5C10. "**Posters.** Give an indication of the colour ..."

8.5D1. "Give for all graphic materials except filmstrips, filmslips, and stereographs the height and the width in centimetres to the next whole centimetre up."

NBM 2

p. 71 (Chapter on pictures):
"*Other physical details*
Pictures ... posters ... List b&w or col."

---

*Rule must be considered, to decide that no statement is given.

"Dimensions
Photographs ... posters ... Height x width are listed in centimetres."

DESCRIPTION OF PUPPETS

AACR 2

(Chapter on three-dimensional artefacts and realia):
10.5C1. "**Material.** When appropriate, give the material(s) of which the object is made."

10.5C2. "**Colour.** When appropriate, give the abbreviation *col.* for multi-coloured objects, or name the colour(s) of the object if it is in one or two colours ..."

10.5D1. "Give the dimensions of the object, when appropriate, in centimetres, to the next whole centimetre up. If necessary, add a word to indicate which dimension is being given."

NBM 2

p. 75 (Chapter on realia):
"Other physical details. If appropriate, list material from which the object was made, the colour ..."

"Dimensions. If appropriate, list dimensions in centimetres with a word or phrase identifying the dimension."

Comment

The physical description for each component is formulated according to the rules given in the chapter dealing with the appropriate class of material. Thus, the descriptions for the book and the activity guide are formulated according to the rules for books, the poster according to the rules for graphic materials, and the puppets and marbles according to the rules for three-dimensional materials.

If the book were the principal component, and were thus the unit to be cataloged, no specific material designation would be given unless there were more than one volume. However, in this case, the book is one of a number of different items comprising the bibliographic unit being described. Thus, in this example, the specific material designation is given (*1 book*), modified by the number of component parts, i.e., number of pages. The number of pages is enclosed in parentheses, as indicated by the examples (there seems to be no explicit rule given for this punctuation), and since the pages are not numbered and the pagination has been ascertained by the cataloger, the pagination appears in brackets. Note that the option to omit the word *sound* from the specific term *sound recording* could not be applied here, since the specific material designation will not be the same as the general material designation.

NOTE AREA

AACR 2

1.7A5: rules in general outline form

1.7B6; 10.7B6: statements of responsibility (Cited in #10A)

1.7B10. **"Physical description"**

(Chapter on three-dimensional artefacts and realia — by analogy):
10.7B10. **"Physical description.** Give important physical details that have not been included in the physical description area ..."

1.7B14. **"Audience"**

(Chapter on three-dimensional artefacts and realia — by analogy):
10.7B14. **"Audience.** Make a brief note of the intended audience for, or intellectual level of, an item if this information is stated in the item."

1.7B17; 10.7B17: summary (Cited in #10A)

1.7B19. **"Numbers borne by the item (other than those covered in 1.8)"**

(Chapter on three-dimensional artefacts and realia — by analogy):
10.7B19. **"Numbers.** Give important numbers borne by the item other than ISBNs ..."

NBM 2

p. 22: statements of responsibility (Cited in #10A)

p. 22 (General rules):
"Additional information concerning the physical description ..."

"Audience level as stated on the item is listed. *Such information may not be desirable in a public catalogue, particularly for juvenile and youth collections."

p. 22: summary (Cited in #10A)

p. 22 (General rules):
"Numbers associated with the item other than ISBNs ..."

CHOICE OF ACCESS POINTS

AACR 2

21.9. "Enter a work that is a modification of another under the heading appropriate to the new work if the modification has substantially changed the

---

*Rule considered but not applied.

nature and content of the original or if the medium of expression has been changed."

21.1C3: corporate body falls outside 21.1B2—title entry (Cited in #10A)

21.30M. "Make an added entry (analytical) under the heading for a work contained within the work being catalogued ..."

"Make such entries in the form of the heading for the person ... under which the work contained is, or would be entered. Unless the entry is under title, make the added entry in the form of a name-title heading."

NBM 2

p. 40: no author for kit as whole—title entry (Cited in #10A)

Comment

Although William Stieg is clearly the person responsible for the book which provided the idea for the kit, the kit itself is the product of collaborative responsibility of various kinds, none of which can be regarded as principal. A number of people are indicated in the activity guide as "responsible" for the kit—for example, project director, book designer, narrator. Of these creative functions, only a few could be considered as functions relating to the intellectual content of the work. Since no creative function can be associated with a predominant component, we cannot point to any principal responsibility behind the creation of the kit. In both codes, the governing principle is the same, although it is more explicitly stated in NBM 2.

10C   LISTENER'S GUIDE

DESCRIPTION OF ITEM

Components: 1 filmstrip, 35 millimeters, color, inaudible advance signals
1 tape cassette
Both of above in playback cartridge
1 text/commentary (six pages)

—————

The kit is designed to enhance the appreciation of Schumann's piano concerto by presenting an analysis of the work on the filmstrip and a performance of the work on the sound recording.

—————

Label on side of cartridge:

A Listener's Guide to
Schumann's Piano Concerto

———————————

Label on top of cartridge:

Music Appreciation Series 9
Schumann
Piano Concerto
67 frames   32 min.

———————————

Label on cassette:

Robert Schumann   CONCERTO IN A
for piano
& orchestra

Radu Lupu with the London Symphony, Previn   stereo
tr. 1 & 2
1 kHz.
pulses
track 4

courtesy of London Records   Hilary Bauer Productions
Salem, Oregon

———————————

Filmstrip:

Frame 1:	Music Appreciation Series. 7.
Frame 2:	Robert Schumann
	Concerto in A minor
	opus 54
	for Piano & Orchestra
Frame 3:	Radu Lupu
	with the London Symphony
	Conducted by Andre Previn
Frames 4-65:	Commentary and music notation
Frame 66:	Commentary by Hilary Bauer
	Copyright 1981 by H.B.
Frame 67:	END

———————————

CATALOG RECORD
Version "a"

A listener's guide to Schumann's piano concerto [kit]. — Salem,
Or. : Bauer Productions, c1981.
1 filmstrip, 1 sound cassette, 1 booklet. — (Music appreciation
series ; 9)
Title on cassette: Concerto in A for piano and orchestra.
Title on filmstrip: Concerto in A minor, opus 54, for piano
and orchestra.
London Symphony; Andre Previn, conductor; Radu Lupu,
piano.
Commentary on filmstrip by Hilary Bauer.
Inaudible advance signals.
Filmstrip and cassette enclosed in playback cartridge.
Summary: Designed to enhance the appreciation of Schumann's
piano concerto by presenting an analysis of the work accompanied by
its performance on a sound recording.

I. Bauer, Hilary. II. Previn, André. III. Lupu, Radu.
IV. Schumann, Robert, 1810-1856. Concertos, piano, orchestra, op.
54, A minor. V. London Symphony. VI. Bauer Productions.
VII. Series.

Version "b"

Version "b" has the following differences:

1 filmstrip (67 fr.) : col. ; 35 mm.
1 sound cassette (32 min.) : 1⅞ ips, stereo.
1 commentary. —
(Music appreciation series ; 7)

SCOPE / CATEGORIZATION

AACR 2

1.10A: multimedia types

1.10C: no predominant component (Cited in #10A)

NBM 2

p. 40: "kits" chapter (Cited in #10A)

Comment

This item could be treated in any of three ways, depending on one's view as to what constitutes the dominant medium: 1) as a sound recording, 2) as a filmstrip, or 3) as a kit.

While a filmstrip-cassette unit normally features the visual medium, and thus is usually cataloged as a filmstrip with accompanying sound recording, in this case it is the sound recording which forms the focal point. The musical work, as represented on the sound recording, could be considered as the focus of the commentary and the *raison d'être* for the kit. Note also that the filmstrip credits, which include the composer and the performers, are given in reference to the performance of the musical work. The filmstrip explains or enhances our appreciation of the recording, which presents the musical work in its entirety.

It could also be argued that both media contribute equally to the total work. This will be the position taken for this example. While it might also be suggested that this is a music score on a filmstrip medium, it should be noted that the musical score for Schumann's work is presented only in bits and pieces, and the filmstrip itself is more like a treatise, or written commentary, which uses parts of the musical manuscript to illustrate its points.

SOURCES OF INFORMATION

AACR 2

1.0H: container as unifying element (Cited in #10A)

NBM 2

p. 40: container (Cited in #10A)

Comment

If "the whole item" were to be treated as the chief source, there would still be three possibilities for chief source: filmstrip frame, tape cassette label, and cartridge label. AACR 2's rule 1.0H has indicated that "if there is no discernible first part, use the part that gives the most information. Failing this, use any part or a container that is a unifying element." I decided in this case that the label on the cartridge, i.e., container, provides the title that serves to unify the work as a whole, and indicates the character of the item. It is the cartridge label that suggests that the kit is not the concerto itself, but a guide to the appreciation of the concerto.

NBM 2 contains specific rules for source of information for kits, and indicates that the container is to be regarded as the chief source. In the general rules for chief source, NBM 2 gives its own interpretation of AACR 2's term *the first part* in rule 1.0H, and states that "in nonbook terms this might be the part which gives meaning to the various parts, e.g., a manual or a container which is the unifying element" (p. 17). This interpretation accords with my own application of rule 1.0H to this example, as well as with the LC interpretation discussed in example #10A.

TITLE PROPER

AACR 2

1.1A2: sources

1.1B1: transcribed exactly except for punctuation, capitalization (Cited in #10A)

NBM 2

p. 18: exactly from chief source except for capitalization, punctuation (Cited in #10A)

GENERAL MATERIAL DESIGNATION

AACR 2

1.10C1: as in 1.1C

1.1C1: North American list

1.1A1: square brackets

A.4G: lowercase

1.1C4: kit (Cited in #10A)

NBM 2

p. 9: North American list

p. 18: lowercase, singular, square brackets; follows the title proper

p. 40: kit (Cited in #10A)

STATEMENTS OF RESPONSIBILITY

AACR 2

1.1A2: sources of information

1.1F1: in form appearing on item (Cited in #10A)

NBM 2

pp. 18, 19: in wording on source (Cited in #10A)

PUBLICATION, DISTRIBUTION, ETC., AREA

AACR 2

1.4A2: sources

1.4C1: place of publication in form on item

1.4C3: add name of state

1.4D2: name in shortest form

1.4F6: copyright date (Cited in #10A)

NBM 2

pp. 19, 20: name of place; add state; name of publisher in shortest form; copyright date (Cited in #10A)

PHYSICAL DESCRIPTION AREA

AACR 2

1.10C2: 3 options for description (Cited in #10A, amplified by #10B)

NBM 2

p. 40: 3 options for description (Cited in #10A, amplified by #10B)

PHYSICAL DESCRIPTION AREA—VERSION "A"

AACR 2

1.10C2a: give extent of each part (Cited in #10A)

NBM 2

p. 40: number and name of each type of material (Cited in #10A)

PHYSICAL DESCRIPTION AREA — VERSION "B"
DESCRIPTION OF SOUND RECORDING

AACR 2

6.5B2: playing time

6.5C3: playing speed

6.5C6: number of tracks not given if standard

6.5C7: mono.

6.5D5: no dimensions if standard (Cited in #10B)

NBM 2

p. 81: playing time; speed; number of tracks if not standard; mono.; dimensions if not standard (Cited in #10B)

DESCRIPTION OF FILMSTRIP

AACR 2

(Chapter on graphic materials):
8.5B2. "Add to the [specific material] designation for a ... filmstrip ... the number of frames ..."

8.5C4. **"Filmstrips and filmslips.** *Give an indication of sound if the sound is integral.... Give an indication of the colour ..."

8.5D2. **"Filmstrips and filmslips.** Give the gauge (width) of the film in millimetres."

NBM 2

p. 30 (Chapter on filmstrips):
"Extent of item. List the number of filmstrips, ... and in parentheses the number of frames."

"Other physical details. If the sound is integral, list it. List b&w or col."

"Dimensions. Width is listed in millimetres."

---

*Rule must be considered, to decide that no statement is made.

SERIES AREA

AACR 2

1.6B1. "If an item is one of a series, record the title proper of the series as instructed in 1.1B ..."

1.6G1. "Record the numbering of the item within the series in the terms given in the item."

NBM 2

p. 21 (General rules):
"If applicable, a series statement in parentheses follows the physical description area. The series area in 3rd level cataloguing could include:

title proper of series

...

numbering within series"

p. 125 (Appendix A — Notes):
"39. ... AACR/2 gives no direction for placement of the series area when each medium is listed on a separate line. This is the authors' suggestion."

p. 44:
Example showing authors' suggestion (Sample Card 39):
" ...

1 question sheet ([4] p.) ; 22 cm. —

(The Earth & man. The Earth without man ; 4)"

Comment

NBM 2's solution to the problem of where to place the series statement appears to be a good one. It avoids the ambiguity that would result if the series immediately followed one specific medium in the listing, or if, on the other hand, the series were listed as a separate paragraph without connecting punctuation.

NOTE AREA

AACR 2

1.7A5: rules in general outline form (Cited in #10A)

1.7B4. "**Variations in title**"

(Chapter on three-dimensional artefacts and realia — by analogy):
10.7B4. "**Variations in title.** Make notes on titles borne by the item other than the title proper."

1.7B6; 10.7B6: statements of responsibility (Cited in #10A)

1.7B10; 10.7B10: physical description (Cited in #10B)

1.7B17; 10.7B17: summary (Cited in #10A)

NBM 2

p. 22 (General rules):
"Variations in title"

p. 22: statements of responsibility (Cited in #10A)

p. 22: physical description (Cited in #10B)

p. 22: summary (Cited in #10A)

Comment

No note was given for the source of title, since the whole item is being considered as the chief source.

CHOICE OF ACCESS POINT

AACR 2

21.1C3: corporate body falls outside 21.1B2 — title entry (Cited in #10A)

21.30M: analytical added entry for work contained within name-title heading (Cited in #10B)

Rule continues:
"When appropriate, substitute a uniform title (see chapter 25) for a title proper in a name-title ... heading."

*21.23A. "Enter a sound recording of one work ... under the heading appropriate to that work."

NBM 2

p. 40: no author for kit as whole — title entry (Cited in #10A)

p. 81 (Chapter on sound recordings):
"Title added entries are never made for nondistinctive uniform titles which require the name of the composer for accurate identification, e.g., Scherzo, piano, op. 20, A major."

"If the work for which an added entry is made requires a uniform title, the uniform title must be used in the added entry ..."

---

*Rule applied to added entry heading.

Comment

The person responsible for the filmstrip is Hilary Bauer; other persons, however, are responsible for the sound recording, and there is no indication of responsibility in terms of the kit as a whole. If the assumption is made that no one medium in the kit is dominant, it would seem to be implicit that we can regard neither the author of the filmstrip nor the "author" of the sound recording as responsible for the work as a whole.

An analytical added entry is made for Schumann's piano concerto, as a work contained within the work being cataloged. The added entry appears under the heading for Schumann as "author," and the title given is the uniform title that would be formulated for this work according to the rules in chapter 25.

UNIFORM TITLE

AACR 2

(Chapter on uniform titles):
25.27B. "If the title ... consists solely of the name of one type of composition, use the accepted English form of name if there are cognate forms in English, French, German, and Italian, or if the same name is used in all these languages. Give the name in the plural ... unless the composer wrote only one work of the type."

25.29A1. "Add a statement of the medium of performance if the title consists solely of the name of a type ... of composition."

25.29D1. "Use English terms whenever possible [for individual instruments]."

25.29G. "For works for one solo instrument and accompanying ensemble, use the name of the solo instrument followed by the name of the accompanying ensemble.

...

[Concertos, piano, orchestra...]"

25.31A1. "If the title consists solely of the name(s) of type(s) of composition, add as many of the following identifying elements as can readily be ascertained. Add following the statement of medium of performance and in the order given:

*a)   serial number

b)   opus number or thematic index number

c)   key.

Precede each element by a comma."

25.31A3. "**Opus numbers.** Include the opus number, if any ..."

---

*This portion of rule considered but not applied.

25.31A5. "**Key.** Include the statement of key in the uniform title for pre-twentieth century works. If the mode is major or minor, add the appropriate word."

NBM 2

p. 80 (Chapter on sound recordings):
"A uniform title is necessary to bring together various versions, editions, and arrangements of a work ..."

"Uniform titles are formulated according to the rules outlined in the *Anglo-American Cataloguing Rules*, 2nd edition, chapter 25."

NOTES

1.   Library of Congress, Processing Services, *Cataloging Service Bulletin*, no. 11 (Winter 1981), p. 12.

SELECTED
READINGS

CATALOGING CODES AND BIBLIOGRAPHIC STANDARDS

SOURCE DOCUMENTS

1. International Federation of Library Associations and Institutions. *ISBD (NBM): International Standard Bibliographic Description for Non-Book Materials.* Recommended by the Working Group on the International Standard Bibliographic Description for Non-Book Materials set up by the IFLA Committee on Cataloguing. London: IFLA International Office for UBC, 1977. 61p.

    An international standard specifying requirements for the description of monographic nonbook documents. One of several published or projected ISBDs designed to aid the international communication of bibliographic information.

2. Croghan, Antony. *A Code of Rules for, with an Exposition of Integrated Cataloguing of Non-Book Media.* London: Coburgh Publications, 1972.

    The effort of an individualist, these rules were not established by, or accepted as a standard by, an organization. Of value mainly for the many interesting ideas contained in the narrative which accompanies the rules. As much a theoretical treatise as a set of rules.

For detailed discussion of the following codes, see pages 16-64.

3. *Anglo-American Cataloging Rules, North American Text.* Chicago: American Library Association, 1967.

4. *Anglo-American Cataloguing Rules.* Second edition. Chicago: American Library Association, 1978.

5. Weihs, Jean Riddle; Lewis, Shirley; and Macdonald, Janet. *Non-book Materials: The Organization of Integrated Collections.* Preliminary edition. Ottawa: Canadian Library Association, 1970.

6. Weihs, Jean Riddle; Lewis, Shirley; and Macdonald, Janet. *Nonbook Materials: The Organization of Integrated Collections.* First edition. Ottawa: Canadian Library Association, 1973.

7. Weihs, Jean; Lewis, Shirley; and Macdonald, Janet. *Nonbook Materials: The Organization of Integrated Collections.* Second edition. Ottawa: Canadian Library Association, 1979.

8. *Anglo-American Cataloguing Rules.* Second edition. *Revisions.* Chicago: American Library Association, 1982.

9.   National Education Association. Department of Audiovisual Instruction. *Standards for Cataloging, Coding and Scheduling Educational Media*. Washington, DC: National Education Association, 1968.

10.   Tillin, Alma, and Quinly, William J. *Standards for Cataloging Nonprint Materials: An Interpretation and Practical Application*. Fourth edition. Washington, DC: Association for Educational Communications and Technology, 1976.

MANUALS AND GUIDES

1.   Olson, Nancy. *Cataloging of Audiovisual Materials*. Mankato, MN: Minnesota Scholarly Press, 1980.

Cataloging examples illustrating the application of AACR 2. Each example includes photographs of the chief sources, a complete catalog record, and discussion of rules and special problems. Section with sample worksheets illustrates basic coding and tagging.

2.   Fleischer, Eugene, and Goodman, Helen. *Cataloguing Audiovisual Materials: A Manual Based on AACR II*. New York: Neal-Schuman, 1980.

Cataloging problems include pictorial examples, main entry cards for all three levels of descriptive cataloging, and rationale for solutions.

3.   Maxwell, Margaret. *Handbook for AACR2*. Chicago: American Library Association, 1980.

Commentary and examples illustrate the application of AACR 2. Extensive coverage of nonbook materials.

4.   Wynar, Bohdan, with the assistance of Arlene Taylor Dowell and Jeanne Osborn. *Introduction to Cataloging and Classification*. Sixth edition. Littleton, CO: Libraries Unlimited, 1980.

Includes examples illustrating AACR 2, citation and discussion of rules. Extensive coverage of nonbook materials.

5.   Rogers, JoAnn V. *Nonprint Cataloging for Multimedia Collections: A Guide Based on AACR 2*. Littleton, CO: Libraries Unlimited, 1982.

6.   Horner, John. *Special Cataloguing; With Particular Reference to Music, Films, Maps, Serials and the Multi-Media Computerised Catalogue*. London: Clive Bingley, 1973.

Examines problems of special materials in general, and of specific media. Summarizes and evaluates a number of the principal cataloging codes going back to 1904. Theoretical discussion with some examples; a useful and readable commentary on some of the earlier codes.

7.   Daily, Jay E. *Organizing Nonprint Materials: A Guide for Librarians*. New York: Marcel Dekker, 1972.

Stresses aspects of administration in the organization of nonprint materials. Emphasis on community analysis. Includes sources for audiovisual materials, a classified list of subject headings, and guidelines for and example of a procedural manual. Some cataloging examples, but this is not the major emphasis of the book, and what examples there are depart from AACR 1.

8.   *Cartographic Materials: A Manual for Interpretation for AACR2*. Prepared by the Anglo-American Committee for Cartographic Materials; Hugo L. P. Stibbe, general editor. Chicago: American Library Association, 1982.

CATALOG CODES AND BIBLIOGRAPHIC CONTROL

1. Massonneau, Suzanne. "Bibliographic Control of Audiovisual Materials: Opportunities for the 1980s." *Catholic Library World* 51 (April 1980): 384-87.
   Survey of recently published and forthcoming codes and manuals for the cataloging of nonbook materials.

2. National Commission on Libraries and Information Science. *Problems in Bibliographic Access to Non-print Materials. Project Media Base: A Final Report.* Washington, DC: NCLS, 1979.
   Background and findings of a study with specific focus on the bibliographic control of audiovisual resources. Gives status of efforts to develop such control, and presents requirements for the future.

3. Ravilious, Christopher P. *A Survey of Existing Systems and Current Proposals for the Cataloguing and Description of Non-Book Materials Collected by Libraries, with Preliminary Suggestions for Their International Co-ordination.* Paris: UNESCO, 1975.
   Summary of efforts on national and international levels to achieve bibliographic control of nonbook materials. Exhaustive analysis of 23 cataloging codes of different countries. Purpose of analysis is to identify data options for the ISBD (NBM).

4. Grove, Pearce S., and Clement, Evelyn G., eds. *Bibliographic Control of Nonprint Media.* Chicago: American Library Association, 1972.
   Papers from an institute entitled Systems and Standards for the Bibliographic Control of Media. Contributors include noted nonprint media specialists. Discussions of existing and emerging standards.

5. Clack, Doris Hargrett, ed. *The Making of a Code: The Issues Underlying AACR2.* Chicago: American Library Association, 1980.
   Papers given at the International Conference on AACR 2 at Florida State University. Of interest here are Frances Hinton's paper on "Cartographic Materials, Manuscripts, Music, and Sound Recordings" and Ronald Hagler's paper on the nonbook materials in AACR 2's chapters 7 through 11.

6. Rogers, JoAnn. "Nonprint Cataloging: A Call for Standardization." *American Libraries* 10 (January 1979): 46-48.
   Findings of survey give evidence of widespread use of a variety of codes in the cataloging of nonbook media. AECT and NBM among the leading codes.

GLOSSARY OF ABBREVIATIONS

AACR
Anglo-American Cataloging Rules; North American Text. Chicago: American Library Association, 1967.

AACR 2
Anglo-American Cataloguing Rules. 2nd ed. Chicago: American Library Association, 1978.

AECT 4
Standards for Cataloging Nonprint Materials. 4th ed. Washington, DC: Association for Educational Communications and Technology, 1976.

ALACR
A.L.A. Cataloging Rules for Author and Title Entries. 2nd ed. Chicago: American Library Association, 1949.

ISBD(NBM)
International Standard Bibliographic Description for Non-Book Materials. London: IFLA International Office for UBC, 1977.

NBM/PE
Non-book Materials: The Organization of Integrated Collections. Preliminary ed. Ottawa: Canadian Library Association, 1970.

NBM 1
Nonbook Materials: The Organization of Integrated Collections. 1st ed. Ottawa: Canadian Library Association, 1973.

NBM 2
Nonbook Materials: The Organization of Integrated Collections. 2nd ed. Ottawa: Canadian Library Association, 1979.

NBMCR
Non-book Materials Cataloguing Rules. NCET Working Paper No. 11. London: National Council for Educational Technology with the Library Association, 1973.

RDC
Rules for Descriptive Cataloging in the Library of Congress. Washington, DC: The Library, 1949.

INDEX